FRANK MERRIWELL'S "FATHER"

Frank Merriwell's "Father"

AN AUTOBIOGRAPHY BY Gilbert Patten

("BURT L. STANDISH")

EDITED BY HARRIET HINSDALE
ASSISTED BY TONY LONDON   *   *   *

UNIVERSITY OF OKLAHOMA PRESS : NORMAN

When I read the book, the biography famous,
And is this then (said I) what the author
  calls a man's life?
And so will some one when I am dead and gone
  write my life?
(As if any man really knew aught of my life,
Why even I myself I often think know little
  or nothing of my real life,
Only a few hints, a few diffused faint clews
  and indirections
I seek for my own use to trace out here.)

—WALT WHITMAN, "When I Read the Book," from *Leaves of Grass*

Library of Congress Catalog Card Number: 64-13591

Copyright 1964 by the University of Oklahoma Press,
Publishing Division of the University.
Composed and printed at Norman, Oklahoma, U.S.A.,
by the University of Oklahoma Press. First Edition.

*Dedicated to Barr Patten, Maybelle Patten,
and Gilberta Patten Richmond*

PREFACE

NEW YORK PUBLISHERS Street and Smith, when preparing for celebration of their one hundredth anniversary, wrote to Mr. Tony London asking if he had any significant memorabilia on Gilbert Patten which they might use. Mr. Patten was probably their most important writer in the early days of the now highly successful firm, and Frank Merriwell their favorite son in a century of publishing.

Previously Mr. London had acquired from the Patten heirs all rights to the Frank and Dick Merriwell published stories to be produced on radio, television, comic strip, stage, screen, or any other medium except soft cover reprints. He sent Street and Smith what he had found among Gilbert Patten's papers which might interest the publishers—but there was really little new in this material.

However, at that time (1959), there were several large boxes of Gilbert Patten's old manuscripts stored in the basement of Mrs. Harvan Barr Patten's home in Vista, California, which had remained undisturbed since the author's death in 1945. Mrs. Patten was soon to move away from Vista, and she asked Mr. London if he would like to determine the value, if any, of this additional literary material. Otherwise it would soon be destroyed.

Searching through this mass of manuscripts and loose papers for the first time, Mr. London came upon a find of real significance—nothing less than Gilbert Patten's autobiography, which had been buried, as it were, for all those years since his passing!

Adding greatly to this exciting discovery was the fact that the first fifty pages of the manuscript were holographic, being in the author's own handwriting, which of course added tremendously to its worth as a collector's item. With its present publication many of the various personal oddities in spelling and "grammer" mentioned by Mr. Patten have been corrected.

In a telephone conversation with Mr. Savoie Lottinville, University of Oklahoma Press, Mr. London offered to loan the original manuscript for exhibit at The Division of Manuscripts of the University of Oklahoma Library. This offer was enthusiastically received, since Mr. Lottinville was of the opinion students and other researchers would find the manuscript of unusual import in this particular field.

However, the actual autobiography ended some years before the author's life came to a close, and it was an interesting task to follow Gilbert Patten's career for those remaining years, which brought him from New England to California, after losing his beloved wife Carol. It might be said that from then on, his zest for life slowly lessened and so did his concern with the writing which had so crowded his earlier years. This too, began to seem part of the irrevocable past. Then came the end, in 1945.

Now, some fifteen years later, tracing his activities was a question of locating Patten's letters, various magazine and newspaper articles, and tapping the memories of a few who had known him in those final decades. To begin some acknowledgment of these varied sources, first must come a tribute to that stormy petrel of American letters, Mr. George Jean Nathan. His "Suggestion for a Biography" (*American Mercury*, September, 1925) included these words: "Standish was one of America's most peculiarly eminent practitioners of the art of fiction." This accolade took on added luster, coming from such a famous figure noted for caustic wit and ruthless dramatic and literary criticism. To be praised by Nathan was to be praised indeed.

A goodly number of publications yielded items which helped to fill out the story of Patten's latter years. The *Boston Post, Newsweek, The New York Sunday Mirror, The New Yorker,* and *The New York Times,* contributed much which proved worth-

Preface

while. *Sports Illustrated* was an inevitable and useful source of color. While *The Saturday Evening Post* brought "Dime Novel Days" by Gil Patten himself, in the issues of February 28 and March 7, 1931.

James M. Cain's previous *Post* article appearing June 11, 1927, also yielded some nuggets. Like the eager prospector who digs hopefully and with constant anticipation, the researcher never fails to feel the thrill of such finds, be the nugget large or small. It becomes rather a game of fitting pieces together into the meaningful pattern of a man's existence. *Reader's Digest*, too, contributed some useful bits for filling in the picture.

Acknowledgment is also due the University of Maine *Bulletin* dated May, 1934, which contained a study of "Gilbert Patten and his Frank Merriwell Saga," by John Levi Cutler (M.A., University of Maine, 1933). The well-known columnist Louis Sobol in his "The Voice of Broadway" (*New York Journal*, November 21, 1921) did a short biographical sketch based on an interview with Patten. O. O. McIntyre and others of that New York group made mention of him as part of the literary scene.

Perhaps the richest in source material was that modest but unique publication, *The Dime Novel Round-up*. Mr. Edward T. LeBlanc, its editor and also an avid collector of dime and nickel novels, was unfailingly cooperative. While of course *The House of Beadle and Adams,* the three-volume study of *The Dime and Nickel Novels,* by Albert Johannsen shed much light on Gilbert Patten's era in American literary history.

Personal encouragement by Mr. Irving Wallace, the noted author and Mr. Edward Levy, devoted collector of Merriwelliana, was both friendly and timely, as was the aid of Mr. J. P. Guinon, a resident of Little Rock, Arkansas, and dime novel authority and collector. To all these mentioned and others as well, thanks are extended.

The surviving members of Gilbert Patten's family are his granddaughter, Gilberta Patten Richmond, and Mrs. Harvan Barr Patten, widow of his only son. They have been more than ordinarily helpful in giving their personal recollections of

"Grandy" during those final years spent with the family in Vista, there in the lush avocado region of Southern California.

It is in a letter written by Gilberta that we have such a warm and affectionate account of her grandfather's last days. It is surely good to know this was a season of peaceful relinquishment unmarred by pain or regret—a fitting end for a gentle and friendly man who in his time brought so much to so many of his fellows of every age, creed, color, and station in life.

Harriet Hinsdale
Tony London

BEVERLY HILLS, CALIFORNIA
JUNE 8, 1964

INTRODUCTION

A BOOK I SHOULD LIKE TO READ—and doubtless there are thousands of ex-youngsters of the 1880's and early '90's who have the same feeling about it as I have—would be a biography, or better still an autobiography, if he is still living, of the man known as Burt Standish, author of the famous Frank Merriwell literature. Who was this Standish; whence came he; what was his history?

For week after week and year after year, he poured forth in gaudy-covered brochures the trials and conquests, the adventures and amours, the deeds of derring-do and hair's-breadth escapes of the eminent and well-remembered François, hero and idol of perhaps half the kids of the Republic in the years when Cleveland, Harrison and McKinley held the throne. I doubt, in all seriousness, if there was an American writer of twenty-five and thirty years ago who was so widely known and so widely read by the boys of the time.

His readers numbered millions, and included all sorts of young men, rich and poor. For one who read Mark Twain's *Huckleberry Finn* or *Tom Sawyer*, there were ten thousand who read Standish's *Frank Merriwell's Dilemma, or the Rescue of Inza*, and *Frank Merriwell at Yale, or the Winning Last Quarter-Mile*.

For one who read Thomas Nelson Page's *Small Boys in Big Boots*, or Judge Shute or Archibald Clavering Gunter—or even, for that matter, Horatio Alger, Oliver Optic or Edward S. Ellis—there were five hundred who weekly followed with avidity the exploits of Standish's magnificent Franz. The little candy and cigar stores of that day, the chief distributing centers of the Standish opera, had longer lines of small boys with nickels in their hands every Friday than Barnum's or Forepaugh's circus could ever boast.

The exact number of Standish works on the illustrious Merriwell, I don't know; but my guess is that it ran well over 15,000. Merriwell was one of the most profitable publishing ventures, I'm told, that the country has ever known, and Street and Smith, his impresarios, made a fortune out of him.

Standish, unlike many of the so-called dime novel writers of his era, was a highly moral fellow; he never wrote a suggestive line; his tales always pointed a Sunday School moral; and hence the papas and mamas of the Republic did not curtail his sales by threatening their little Emil with a good licking if they ever caught him reading "such stuff" again. So as Diamond Dick and Frank Reade and Nick Carter and Old Cap Collier lost in favor with the comptrollers of the family treasury, the favor of Standish and his Merriwell grew and the coins flowed into his pocket from hundreds of thousands of boys from the Atlantic to the Pacific.

Surely, such a fellow is just as deserving of a biography as the department store owners, safety-razor manufacturers and ham actors whose lives currently line the library shelves. His influence on American young men was vastly greater than any of these, and the man himself, together with his story, is surely of considerable more interest. Standish was one of America's most peculiarly eminent practitioners of the art of fiction. His curious song deserves to be sung.[1]

This was the opinion of George Jean Nathan, that distinguished and usually caustic literary pundit, and his words have the ring of sincerity when he says that "Burt L. Standish" was "one of America's most peculiarly eminent practitioners of the art of fiction. His curious song deserves to be sung."

Yet I must confess that the name "Burt L. Standish" until recently meant nothing to me, nor, I am reluctant to admit, did that of Gilbert Patten. But Frank Merriwell? Of course. That is a name which has become a living part of our language, like Tom Sawyer or Huck Finn. To "pull a Merriwell" needs no explanation, except perhaps to a foreigner just learning some of the phrases which color the American idiom. Calling a boy a "regular

---

[1] George Jean Nathan, "Suggestion for a Biography." *The American Mercury*, Vol. VI, No. 21 (September, 1925), 109.

Introduction

Frank Merriwell" immediately brings up the picture of an honest, healthy straight-shooter and star athlete, always on the side of truth and honor, outwitting scalawags and tricksters, often with some clever tricks of his own, naturally.

So far so good. But who was this "Burt L. Standish" who, they said, created Frank Merriwell, 'way back when? Thus came the discovery that he was in reality Gilbert Patten, "King of the Dime Novelists," who held the record for single-handed marathon story writing. Unlike Balzac, Dumas, and other astonishingly prolific authors, Patten was a one-man fiction factory, without assistants or sub-writers.

At first in longhand, then pounding a brute of an early typewriter, finally dictating to a typist, he walked up and down the room as, over a period of some seventeen years, he turned out an almost unbelievable torrent of words. It leaves one astounded at the man's staying power, fertility of imagination, and devotion to a set of characters which in time grew so varied and numerous that a catalogue was needed to keep them in line!

The statistics of this unmatched accomplishment are really staggering, and difficult to grasp. As a matter of comparison: the American Bible Society's figures state that from 1816 to 1959, there were published in this country 47,295,151 Bibles, and of Testaments and other Biblical supplements, 545,214,000. These are impressive figures covering a period of 143 years. Yet in the short span of less than 20 years, it has been estimated by the publishers, that of the Merriwell books alone, about 500,000,000 were printed, not to mention the hundreds of other tales Patten wrote under so many different pen names; he himself finally lost track of them.

This, then, is his autobiography—Gilbert Patten, or "Burt L. Standish," the man who "fathered" Frank Merriwell—a character who was thought by countless youthful readers for more than two decades to be not a fictional person, but a living, breathing American boy!

Born in 1896, Frank appeared each week well into the early 1900's, and the author later estimated that at least 200,000 copies were sold every seven days until the final ending of the series. And afterward, the Merriwell books were being constantly reissued in hard-cover editions by the astute publishers. "Burt L. Standish" and his creations, Frank and Dick Merriwell, were part of one of the most exciting and significant eras in United States annals—from just before the Civil War into the new twentieth century.

Those were the colorful years of the dime novel. Generations of kids would hide the garish little yellowbacks inside their bigger schoolbooks as they "studied" under the eyes of Teacher, with the innocent faces of freckled cherubs. The books were traded from boy to boy and to the girls, too, and literally read to tatters—behind barns, in dusty haylofts, attics, and chicken coops, even in Chic Sales!

Whatever detractors might say, Dime and Half-Dime Novels were a peculiarly American phenomenon, not pallid copies of English tales laid in haunted castles or on the Spanish Main. For the first time, those who could afford only a dime or nickel for a book learned about trappers, scouts, Indian guides, mighty rivers, magnificent mountains, and buffalo-darkened plains. They read highly colored tales of their own country, whose western wilderness had seemed as remote, almost, as Asia or Africa—blatantly melodramatic stories to be sure, and crudely told, but in their day they served an important purpose.

The flood of dime novels which began inundating the country in 1860 was later to carry to its crest a writer yet unborn. Gilbert Patten was destined to become the best-known writer of them all, and last surviving "King" of this unique fiction domain. He was born in Corinna, Maine, October 25, 1866, five years and four months after the first dime novel appeared.

Thirty years later saw the advent of Frank Merriwell, the most popular and widely admired hero of any. But first, Frank's future creator had to grow up, which he did, very fast and tall. And when Gilbert Patten, or William George, to mention the given name he never liked and soon changed, reached the ripe age of ten or eleven, he was an avid dime novel addict!

Introduction

By this time they were dubbed "Libraries," and many had become what Irvin Cobb called "Nickul Liburies." No doubt in Corinna, Maine, schoolboys were reading yarns from the "Little Chief Library," "Old Sleuth Library," "Boys of New York Library," "Old Cap Collier," "Horatio Alger, Jr.," and many others. Girls read them too, of course.

The tone and output gradually changed from frontier adventure and "winning of the West" to more urban locales. This inevitably followed the swing in American life from post–Civil War pioneering to the more sophisticated existence of a mushrooming industrial age. Tales of city slickers and Bowery boys, the wildest of melodramatic fiction were being issued. Parents, teachers, and many preachers began to crack down on such highly seasoned fare for impressionable youth.

Meanwhile, in the village of Corinna there was growing up that weedy young boy named Patten, who, like most other lads, read in secret every one of those mother-banned yellowbacks he could lay his hands on! The boy was, in fact, leading a life of imagination far different from the commonplace existence of his small home town. In grammar school the future "King of the Dime Noveleers" was a lackadaisical scholar, studying only those subjects which interested him, and naturally he didn't get along any too well with teachers. A feud developed with one of them and came to physical violence. But let Gilbert Patten describe the incident from the vantage point of a letter written in 1934.

> I disliked Hosea Rackliff quite a bit after he struck me with a closed book and knocked me headlong over a table. He, I'm sure, thought me a damned fool. I always wanted to give him a good licking, but by the time I might have done so, he was—in my eyes—a pitiful old man of perhaps thirty-five or forty. As he was a farmer and hard as nails, I have no doubt he could have thrashed me any time up until he was forty-five or more. But I didn't think so after reaching twenty-one myself—until very lately.[2]

It was not until later that he discovered the joys of fine literature. Dime novels were still his meat. By the time he was thirteen

[2] Letter to John Levi Cutler, March 1, 1934.

or fourteen, the young malcontent even began to try his hand at writing one of the adventure yarns he loved to read, which set him apart from other small town youths; for how many of them tried, however awkwardly, to put down their thoughts on paper?

This, too, had to be kept secret from a pious mother, who was determined her only son should be a preacher, and from his carpenter father, who believed "Willie" ought to learn how to earn a practical living with the strong hands and back his Maker had given him. The boy's whole nature resisted these parental pressures, and perhaps the urge and strength to rebel may have come from ancestors farther back than those who brought him into being.

To this gangling New England lad, daydreams were more real than reality, and he always pictured himself in the role of those fictional heroes about which he read and wrote so secretly. He himself came from adventurous Scotch-Irish stock, the first of them landing in the New World colonies in 1692. William Clark Patten, Gilbert's father, was born in 1824 and grew to be a huge man, six feet, four inches tall and weighing well over two hundred pounds. After a few years of schooling he became a woodsman and river driver, which, next to farming and fishing, was the chief outdoor occupation that flourished in heavily timbered Maine.

This powerful, somewhat primitive lumberjack was called "Bill," a real he-man name his son thought, and one he longed to have. But no, he was called "Willie," no doubt at first by his doting, gentle-natured little mother. She came of pioneer stock also, her father having been a captain in the War of 1812. When he died, his widow, Betsey Simpson, received a government pension, which made her financially independent in a modest way for the remainder of her long life.

At about the time Gilbert was born, this maternal grandparent came to live with the Pattens, whom she was able to aid in establishing a home in Corinna at a time they badly needed help, because of the bread-winner's ill health. So into the world came

Introduction

their son who, through Grandma Simpson, had a direct connection with a hero of the War of 1812. A generation farther back, another ancestor was a soldier of the Revolutionary War, while through his father, Willie might be said to have had contact with Abraham Lincoln!

This encounter with the future Great Emancipator in Decatur, Illinois, during a political rally, was a highlight in Bill's otherwise humdrum life. Down the years he loved to tell the story to the neighbors and his young son, whose daydreams must have been brightened by this nearness to one of his country's immortals. Many years later Gilbert Patten did not fail to relate the incident about Abraham Lincoln, which as a child he had heard from his father.

But a change had come over Bill Patten. When in 1851 he married Cordelia, Betty Simpson's only daughter, he quit the hard, adventurous life of the northern forests to become a townsman and take up carpentering for a livelihood. A daughter named Zelma was born to them in 1856, and it was ten years after her birth that Cordelia Patten had another child. This time it was a son, whom they christened William George. Zelma died very young, so her brother had no recollection of an older sister. To all intents and purposes, he was an only child, the focus of his parents' lives and the more important to them because, in all probability, they would have no further additions to the family.

When he arrived in 1866, Cordelia was forty years old and her husband was forty-two. By the age standards of their generation, they were considered middle-aged, and most married persons in their forties were grandparents. While trying to envision the boyhood of Gilbert Patten and the influences which shaped his nature, it is significant that he was born of older parents, undoubtedly more "fussy" and set in their ways than the mothers and fathers of most of his playmates. Their restrictions inevitably helped build up frustrations and rebellion in a sensitive boy growing into the confused years of adolescence.

Bill, the giant logger with his backwoods adventures, had become a hard-working carpenter, a trade entirely lacking in interest for his son. Yet how difficult, if not impossible, it was for a simple, conscientious man past youthful impulses to understand this. Still, sometimes the old, untrammeled spirit must have stirred within Bill Patten, as when he was almost sixty and could not resist getting out on the millpond ice, wearing "Willie's" skates, to show the young folks how to cut fancy figures. A bad fall injured his hip so seriously that he became progressively lame and eventually was incapacitated for work. By this time, the rebellious son was doing so well at his chosen "trade" of writing that he was able to support not only his own wife and son, but the parents who had tried to turn him away from his true bent in life. Perhaps there's a bit of irony here.

Pious, God-fearing Cordelia was an ardent Adventist and most likely the influence which brought her husband into this strictly fundamentalist belief. She was a small, slender wisp of a woman with dark brown eyes, inherited by her son, and weighed little over one hundred pounds. As with many wives of her physical make-up and gentle nature, her influence was strong over the giant of a man she married. Mrs. Patten did not even call her husband "Bill," as everyone else did. To her he was "William," and "Willie" for their son naturally followed. And how he hated it!

There he was, growing up very fast physically and mentally in a tiny New England town, hedged about with fundamentalism and parental anxieties, which sadly irked fledgling wings. Having to go to church three times on Sunday—early Sunday school, plus morning and evening service—he was also constantly admonished that it was wicked to fight. He must always turn the other cheek, no matter how his school mates provoked him to anger by yells of "sissy." This creed was increasingly hard for "Willie" to believe in and live up to, but worst of all, his father called him lazy and good for nothing because he did not want to take up carpentering. All this book reading and daydreaming was nothing but a poor excuse for getting out of honest work!

What neither parent could understand was that their son "Willie," was a nonconformist at heart, and they were fostering his adolescent rejection of what they wished him to become. Preacher or carpenter?—those seemed the two alternatives for teen-age Gilbert Patten. As he himself expressed it from an adult point of view, "It seems to me that from my earliest thinking boyhood, I have always been a secret or open rebel against restraint."

An anecdote he related in later years recalled the confusion with which as a boy he had witnessed it—superstition, mysticism, or deep religious conviction? There was a large church handbell involved, of which his father was the custodian.

> One winter our home became infested with rats. So my father took the bell and went into the upper part of the house where he began ringing it loudly as he moved slowly about and moved from room to room. He descended the stairs still ringing as hard as he could and then went through all the rooms on the main floor. Still banging away with the bell, he went down into the cellar, where he rang it a long time. The rats must have fled out by the cellar drain like evil spirits, for we were not troubled by them again for many weeks.[3]

This was a strange phenomenon for an imaginative lad to try to explain to himself, since he probably knew nothing then about exorcism of evil spirits. A more serious difficulty was his growing tendency toward what might now be called a "split personality," caused largely by his parents' attitude toward youthful "scrapping," a normal activity for most healthy youngsters. He later wrote:

> Both of them lectured me almost daily on the shamefulness of fighting, which had increased my own natural aversion to brawls, and converted me into a shrinking lad with a sense of inferiority.

So this shy, retiring boy, too tall for his age and with a definite inferiority complex, became more and more a secret reader of what in his home were called sinful books—those dreadful dime novels! This was a perilous business, with the ever-present risk of detection and punishment. But to him, escape into the realm of wild adventure was worth the risk.

[3] Letter to John Levi Cutler, March 7, 1934.

A boy lay reading in bed in a big, unfinished chamber of an old house in Corinna, Maine. He was reading by the yellow light of a kerosene lamp that stood on a wooden chair beside the bed. The lamp had been placed in that low position so that its light, shining through an uncurtained window a few feet away, would not fall upon the gable end of a lurching barn at the rear of the house, where it could have been seen by the boy's father and mother, who occupied a bedroom on the first floor. The greater part of the chamber was in shadow and darkness. The position of the lamp compelled the boy to lie close to the edge of the bed and the light to fall on the fine print that covered the pages. Entranced, spellbound, the young reader followed the swift course of the sanguine tale. . . .

There were sounds in the shadow-haunted chamber, the faint rasping of an unoiled door hinge, the soft fluff of a stockinged foot, the creak of a loose floor board. Holding a candle and shading it with one hand, the boy's nightgowned mother stood in the doorway.

"Willie," she whispered. "What are you doing, Willie—reading at this hour? It's midnight and after. You'll ruin your eyes. If your father ever caught you! What's this?"

She had advanced quickly to the bed and taken the little book out of the boy's hand. One glance at its cover was enough.

"A Dime Novel!" There was reproof and sorrow in her voice and on her face. "Where did you get it? Such dreadful stuff! It'll be the ruination of the boys of this country. . . ."

She carried away the little book she had caught him reading. As she took away the kerosene lamp also, he could not fish a companion book from under his pillow, where it lay hidden, and go on with his forbidden pleasure after her departure. He was compelled to resign himself to sleep and dreams.[4]

This was the boy, these were the well-meaning parents and the little town upon which Gilbert looked again in recollection more than half a century later, when he and the entire world had moved completely away from the Victorian era of his childhood.

There is a refreshing quality about the early memories of Gilbert Patten, an unspoiled simplicity of outlook as he remembers

---

[4] Gilbert Patten, "Dime Novel Days," *Saturday Evening Post*, Vol. CCIII, No. 35 (February 28, 1931), 6.

Introduction

back to more primitive days. The nostalgic charm of those old times lost, never to return, breathes through the chapters devoted to youth in a backwoods town. They picture boys as they were pretty much everywhere in these United States, whether on the banks of the Mississippi or the Old Bog in a small New England stream.

As the world moves so rapidly into the Space Age, it may well look back with considerable longing upon an era so close in time —yet so distant actually from present-day life. Gilbert Patten's seventy-nine years spanned this gap, and you will see with what clarity, humor, and understanding he made that autobiographical journey backward through the decades.

Harriet Hinsdale

CONTENTS

Preface   vii

Introduction   xi

Part One

1. Reckless Boy, *3*
2. Saved by a Miracle, *7*
3. The Liar, *9*
4. About the Pattens, *15*
5. Signs in the Sky, *21*
6. Reading and Writing, *28*
7. Forbidden Fruit, *34*
8. The Dawn of Wonders, *46*
9. The Worm Turns, *53*
10. Bad Business, *61*
11. I Learn a Lesson, *67*
12. The World Is Mine, *75*
13. Forging Ahead, *80*
14. The Prodigal's Return, *86*
15. I Step Out Again, *92*
16. The Wrong Track, *97*
17. Doomsday Passes, *103*
18. The Owl Hoots and Dies, *109*
19. Escape, *115*

Part Two

20. Stop-overs on the Way, *121*
21. Ninety-eight William Street, *127*
22. The New York That Was, *131*
23. All Around the Town, *136*
24. The Lure of Broadway, *143*
25. The Bottom and the Rebound, *149*
26. I Crash the Gate, *156*
27. Youth and Laughter, *164*
28. Mr. Smith's Letter, *171*
29. So Came Frank Merriwell, *176*
30. Parting and Tragedy, *181*
31. False Moves, *188*
32. After Many Moons, *194*
33. In Denver, *202*
34. Shifting Winds, *209*
35. After the Ball, *213*
36. Danger, *216*

FRANK MERRIWELL'S "FATHER"

PART THREE

37. I Become a Gambler, *223*
38. While Building a House, *229*
39. Frank Merriwell's Brother, *235*
40. As I Remember, *241*
41. The Birth of a Magazine, *248*
42. Merriwell and the Movies, *252*
43. More Shifting Winds, *256*
44. The Crack-up and Afterwards, *263*
45. Carol, *270*
46. Fate or Folly, *274*
47. The Enchanted Hour, *279*
48. Camp by the Singing Waterfall, *283*

Finale   *290*

Appendix
    Frank Merriwell to the Rescue   *223*

Index   *326*

ILLUSTRATIONS

between pages 166–67

Gilbert Patten

Colonel Prentiss Ingraham

Patten in his "Poe" Period

Pencil Sketch of Patten

Major Gordon Lillie (Pawnee Bill) and Mrs. Lillie

Patten at Work

Patten and his Home, "Overocks"

Patten and his Wife, Carol

Part One

1 · RECKLESS BOY

I LOOKED OUT OF THE WINDOW, seeking a way to escape. On more than one night I had cautiously raised that window, propped it up with a long stick, and descended to the ground by way of the old rail fence at the far lower corner of the sloping roof. But now it was day, early morning not long after we had breakfasted by lamplight, following which my father had harnessed up our old white horse and driven away in the rattletrap wagon to his work as a carpenter.

The double swinging doors of the sagging barn—kept from tumbling down by three fence poles which served as props—were standing wide open.

Our hens, marshaled by the big red rooster, were busily gobbling up the feed my mother had recently scattered for them in front of the open barn doors. And now I could hear my mother washing the breakfast dishes at the sink in the combined kitchen and dining room downstairs; therefore she would be facing the window over the sink and could look out at the barn and see the hens.

"Can't get out this way," I told myself. "She'd see me crawling along the edge of the shed roof sure as shooting, darn it!"

But I had to get out; I just had to!

There was a thin layer of snow on the ground, left there by the short storm two days ago, and ice had been forming around the edges of the ponds before that storm. Since then there had been two bitter cold nights, and I was sure the ponds were now fully frozen over. For in two days it would be Thanksgiving and we were already sure of skating on Thanksgiving Day, sometimes it was a little earlier.

Now I wanted to be one of the first to skate on the Old Bog above the upper dam—the first, if possible. With this in mind, I'd brought my skates, hidden under my jacket, up into the old open back-chamber where I slept, and had them there now.

Strangely, though I was not a courageous boy, was in fact somewhat timid, I had won the reputation of being reckless or foolish, and neighbors had warned my parents that something unfortunate would happen to me unless I were guarded more closely. Herself a timid, worrying woman, my mother had become frightened for my safety and this had led to restrictions which were irksome to me and seemed very unjust.

Always I was confined by command to the close vicinity of my home, while other boys that I knew were permitted much more freedom, and, being of a rebellious nature, I had taken to running away in the face of scoldings and whippings. Indeed, punishment made me more rebellious and more determined to go to any extreme to obtain the freedom I considered rightly my due.

Of course, I could now steal quietly down the front stairs, slip out by the front door, and scuttle off down the main street into the village, there to skate with other boys on the middle pond; but what I wished to do was to be the first one to skate on the Old Bog, which was always treacherous and dangerous except in midwinter when the ice was thick and solid.

I had been called " 'fraid cat" and "skeery" by those other fellows, which had driven me to do many dangerous things with my heart in my mouth, just to "show 'em."

Now, peering forth from the one window of the old open chamber, I was struck by a thought. "I know how to do it," I muttered. "I can dodge her while she's standing at the sink."

With the heel straps buckled together, my skates were slung round my neck and suspended, one on either side, before me. I was wearing heavy woolen pants, cut down and made over by my mother from an old pair of my father's, and a warm woolen jacket. On my feet were long-legged boots, into which my trousers were tucked. My cap, with earmuffs, was a fuzzy thing of imitation fur. A red woolen scarf was around my neck and heavy red mittens protected my hands. I was prepared for cold weather, and surely this morning, when the water in my washbasin had been covered by ice half an inch thick, was cold enough.

Carefully avoiding the stair treads that squeaked, I made my way down into the front hall, opened the door slowly and cautiously, and closed it behind me when I'd slipped out.

Then, with the thin spread of snow crunching a little under my feet, I stole round to the west side of the house and, crouching low, passed under two windows through which I could have been seen by my mother had I walked erect. Then I followed along the rail fence that was the dividing line between our small lot and Ben More's mowing field.

The crisp morning air nipped and stung, but it was good. My breath smoked. The sun was up and snow crystals sparkled like gems. I laughed over the way I had slipped out undetected by my mother. I felt great.

Climbing over the fence, I passed out through Ben More's dooryard to Academy Street and then climbed another fence to cross Sumner Titcomb's field, which sloped down toward the upper dam and the stump-filled lower end of the Old Bog.

There it lay before me, the Old Bog, and, as I'd felt sure, it was frozen over from shore to shore. Nowhere on its surface could I see a skater. I hurried, my blood leaping with eagerness.

Above the stumps and worthless logs frozen into the lower end of the bog, I sat down on an icebound log and prepared to strap on my skates, the steel runners of which were set in wooden foot-supports. I had bored gimlet-holes in the heels of my boots into which I twisted the heel-screw of the skates before pulling the straps tight over toes and insteps and buckling them. Then I stood up and slid cautiously out upon the white snow-ice near the shore.

It was solid, solid and safe. I was the first to skate on the Old Bog; I had beaten them all. Gosh, this was living!

Up and down a strip of ice near the shore I sped, my skates ringing in the crisp air. I whooped for joy. I would do some bragging this year, telling them how I had got ahead of everybody. What if I did get a whipping by my father? I could yell and take it, couldn't I?

Little by little I ventured further out from shore. The ice was still safe under me, but there were more stumps and old gnarled logs further up the shore, restricting me to a comparatively short skating stretch. But over on the east shore the ice was clear of deadwood as far northward as I could see, and northward there were woods on both shores.

Up there I had hunted and shot partridges with my dad's old percussion-cap, single-shot, muzzle-loading gun. Cooked one of them once, in a coal-and-ashes lined hole in the ground and eaten the half-roasted flesh with other boy hunters. We were western hunters and trappers such as I'd begun to read about in dime novels, and it was grand.

Now I felt a desire to skate away up there toward the dark evergreen woods at the head of the Old Bog, but between me and the other shore stretched a winding streak of black ice that marked a channel along which a moving current had kept the water open until last night. It looked all right at a distance, and I still thought it looked safe enough when I had moved out to inspect it.

"Oh, it's no more'n twenty foot or so wide, and I can scoot over it so fast it won't have time to break," I told myself.

So I moved back toward shore to get a good start and was off as fast as I could go, headed for that strip of black ice. The moment I struck it I felt my skates cutting through and knew water was spurting up behind me at every stroke. But I could not stop. To do so, or to slacken my speed even for a moment, would mean to go through at once. And I didn't have time to stop, anyhow. Suddenly I went down, the ice having given way under me.

2 · SAVED BY A MIRACLE

SHARP AS THE STAB OF A KEEN BLADE was the shock of my plunge into that ice-cold water. I grabbed at the jagged edge of broken ice and did not go wholly under, even though the ice broke in the clutch of my mittened hands. Fortunately, summer days of swimming in the "deep hole" just below the Upper Dam now served me well, for otherwise I would have gone down and been sucked under the ice by the sluggish current that moved in that tortuous channel.

Kicking froglike with my legs, I managed to turn about and face back toward the nearer shore that I had left. Then, with a surge, I flung the upper part of my body out upon the ice. Instantly it broke beneath my weight and let me back in again.

Of course I was frightened, but this was not the first time I had broken through the ice while skating, and always on previous occasions I had been able to get out safely. But this was different; previously I had been nearer shore, and I could touch bottom and stand up where there was no danger of sinking and drowning.

Now I could find no supporting bottom under my feet. Nor were there other boys near to assist me. I was alone, with no human being in sight, without even a human habitation to be seen. This time I must save myself by my own efforts or perish.

Again I flung myself as far out as possible upon the thin black ice, and again it broke. This time I went under entirely and, gasping, drew icy water into my lungs. I came up choking and coughing—and still more frightened. Also, the great coldness of the water was piercing me through and swiftly robbing me of strength, causing me to realize that I could not long continue the struggle. I must escape quickly, I thought, or not at all. Panic clutched me.

Once more I lunged forth upon the ice, but not so far as previously. It did not break, but it buckled, allowing water to flow up around me—and slowly, very slowly but surely, I slipped back in until I lay with only my arms extended upon the unbroken ice.

My strength was nearly gone. It did not seem that I could make another attempt to save myself, and something seemed to tell me that this was the end, that I was surely going to die. I did not want to die. Death was frightful and life was lovely beyond any previous conception. For the first time I seemed to realize fully how wonderful it is to live in this wonderful world—to live and laugh and whistle and sing.

"I won't die!" I vowed. "I won't!"

Summoning all my remaining strength, I made a last despairing effort and surged out again upon the ice. I lay there, gasping weakly, but slipping back slowly, very slowly. Slipping! Slipping!

And even though the thin ice had buckled without breaking, it seemed to make no difference; for, no matter how slowly I slipped, I would eventually be back in again up to my chin, and I knew there would be no strength left in me to make still another effort to save myself. Useless had been my vow not to die; there was no escaping the doom my folly had brought upon me.

With that horrible thought in my mind, I took a last look at the wintry world around me. Bleak and bare and cold it was— but beautiful! I had never known a scene so lonely and desolate could be so beautiful.

I prayed then, something I had not thought to do before. But I made no foolish promise to be forever good if I were saved. Apparently there was no answer to my prayer.

Moments passed. Then I suddenly realized that I had ceased to slip back off the ice. For still more moments I lay there, my mittened hands extended at arm's length before me; waiting for what?

Finally something seemed to tell me to make another effort. Of course, what told me was my desire to escape and live a while longer in the fair world I had come to appreciate more fully in the dreadful moments when I seemed sure to leave it forever.

Now I made no desperate lunge; gently and carefully I sought to pull myself out to safety. To my surprise, the effort did not cause me to slip back in again. Something seemed to have taken hold of my hands to aid me!

Slowly but surely I pulled myself out still further upon the unbreaking ice. And when I had drawn myself out so far that there was no danger of slipping back in again, that something released my hands and I crawled away, on hands and knees toward the shore.

What had saved me? This I know, and it is true. While I lay there with my mittened hands extended upon the ice beyond where water had flowed up around me, my mittens had frozen to the dry ice, thus giving me the help I needed to pull myself out completely. Was this in answer to my prayer? However that may be, only for that assistance I believe I must have perished in the icy waters of the Old Bog.

---

3 · THE LIAR

WEAK AND BENUMBED, I sat down on the same log I'd sat upon while strapping on my skates. Knowing my wet clothes would soon freeze, I lost no time in pulling off my mittens and fumblingly unstrapping and removing my skates. Then I hoisted myself to my feet and stumblingly retraced the faint tracks I'd made across Sumner Titcomb's pasture and the mowing field beyond. I hoped no one would see me, and by the rarest of chances, no one did, not even my mother when, crouching low, I passed below the two back windows of my home and let myself in again by the front door.

Tiptoeing up the stairs, I reached the old open chamber and made haste to get my icy clothes off. There, stripped to the skin, I scrubbed my body dry with a towel. Then I dressed in some outworn and outgrown clothes and went down, apprehensively, to face my mother in the kitchen dining room, where I could warm my chilled body beside the wood-burning cookstove.

That room was like Paradise just then—warm and lovely and

sweet with the ravishing odor of the doughnuts Mother was frying.

"Oh, yum, yum!" said I, grabbing one of the golden brown doughnuts and sticking my teeth into it. "I knew I smelled something good."

As my Grandmother Simpson had gone back to her bedroom off the kitchen to take her daily morning nap, I settled into her rocking chair close to the stove and handy by the pan of doughnuts on the table at which we ate our meals.

I was all set to make a bluff, having figured out the story I would tell my mother if she became suspicious and inquisitive. It would never do to tell her the full truth, for she was a thin, frail woman and a habitual worrier. A neurasthenic person and so small that she could stand under the outstretched arm of my strapping father, who towered almost four inches above six feet, she was forever apprehensive of harm, particularly to me.

Nevertheless, buoyed up by religious fervor, she was cheerful at times when not given to alarm and foreboding. From her I inherited a slightly gloomy and mystical temperament that was, fortunately, outbalanced by the optimistic nature received from my father.

Young as I then was, I had come to realize the danger of yielding to the timidity and apprehensions which often beset me, and I was striving to conquer them by rash and venturesome acts similar to the one that today had nearly cost me my life. And, of course, it was my mother, far more than my husky 235-pound father, who was responsible for the severe restrictions imposed upon me—restrictions against which I had begun to rebel in action as well as thought.

Now Mother glanced at me sharply, suspiciously. "Why, your hair's all wet," she said "What have you been up to, Willie?"

"Oh, don't call me Willie," I protested. "You know I don't like it, Mom."

"But it's your name," she said. "William George Patten, and it's a good name."

"Well, anyhow, I'd rather be called Bill, as my dad's called.

The Liar

Bill—that's a real he-man name. Willie's a sissy—gee, Mom, these doughnuts are splendiferous." I got another.

She looked at me again, sharply, suspiciously. "You're full of syrup this morning, Willie. What *have* you been up to? How did you get your hair so wet?"

"Aw, the darn old curly stuff," I complained. "Can't comb the kinks out of it so they'll stay out, no matter how much I wet it."

"But it's pretty hair," said she. "Any girl in town'd swap her hair for it."

"Well, they can have it, an' welcome. I wish I had straight hair, like other fellers have. They poke fun at my hair and it makes me darn mad."

"Don't say darn, Willie. 'Tain't nice."

"Nice! Nice—huh, who wants to be nice? Nice fellers are saps. They make me sick."

She shook her head. "You're queer. You seem to be getting queerer every day, Willie."

I choked over my second doughnut. "There you go some more with that darn old name! Willie! Willie! Maybe I *am* queer, but I'm going to get rid of that old name some day. I'll dump it and call myself Bill when I'm a man."

I thought I had her really sidetracked, but I was wrong. Once more she was staring at me suspiciously, but this time it was my clothes, not my hair, she was looking at.

"For goodness sakes," she said, "what've you got them old clothes on for? You hated them, you said, and they're too small for you now, anyhow. Where are your other clothes?"

"Oh, they're upstairs," said I carelessly. "I'm saving 'em for school wear. These are all right 'round the house—part of the time, anyhow."

It didn't work.

"But you had your others on when you ate breakfast," she said. "Now look here, Willie, what—have—you—been—up—to?"

I had to give it up. "Oh, nothing much," said I. "Just went skating with the other fellers on the millpond—a little."

She stared at me reprovingly, without speaking.

"Now don't be that way, Mother," I protested. "I gotter have a *little* liberty. Other fellers do. You just can't expect to keep me tied up round this old house every minute I'm not in school. And this is Saturday, when all the boys have some fun."

She spoke deliberately: "I want you to tell me just what's happened, Willie, and I want the truth."

"Well, all right—all right. I went skating—just for a little while, Mom—down to the millpond. I knew all the other fellers'd be there—and they were, too. Their folks didn't keep 'em at home —not with the pond all froze over solid."

She nodded slowly. "If it was so solid, how did you get wet?"

I declared it was safe enough everywhere except one place near shore—an air hole. Other fellows had skated all the way across the pond, but I hadn't taken such a risk; I'd tried to be careful. I was playing tag with the other fellows when I skated right into that old air hole without noticing it. The water wasn't very deep there, but, just the same, I got soaking wet from head to heels on crawling out. That was all there was to it, not even a little bit of danger.

She wanted to believe me and did not accuse me of telling a falsehood. She sat on a chair, still looking at me and shaking her head slowly.

"Oh, Willie," she said, "I declare I don't know what we're going to do with you. I *don't* know why you won't listen and mind. If your father finds out about this he's going to be awful mad. Maybe he'll give you a whipping."

That caused the rebel in me to stir again. "Well, he hadn't better!" I cried. "I'm just about done with taking whalings from him—or anybody."

"Why, how you talk!" she exclaimed. "Your father never has given you a whaling in all your life. He's never punished you half as hard as some boys get it. Not half as hard as you've deserved. You frighten me. You're getting so you just won't mind at all, and you do such dangerous things. You're so reckless, Willie."

"Reckless!" I laughed. "Why, Mom, I'm just showing the other

The Liar

fellers I ain't a coward, that's all. They've been calling me a 'fraid cat, and I've stood it long enough. I can climb anywhere they dare to, and, by golly, I can do some things they dassent try to do. I'm a good swimmer, too—pretty nigh's good as any feller in this old town. And I can dive and stay under longer'n anybody—'cept maybe Herb Fisher or that big Sam Adams. I can—"

"Oh, I wish you couldn't!" she broke in. "Next thing you'll get to fighting, and you know what'll happen then. Your father's warned you."

Now my father had won a reputation in his younger days, when he had been a logger and a Penobscot River driver. Never quarrelsome, he still had been a man it was unwise to insult or bulldoze. When unable to avoid trouble with self-respect, he had met it vigorously, as more than one swaggering bully had learned to his complete discomfiture; and throughout the logging camps and up and down the river had gone the word, "Let Bill Patten alone or you'll get your head broke."

However, in later years, having experienced religion, Father had become an extreme pacifist. Seeking to keep me out of brawls with other boys, he had even threatened to give me a thrashing any time he found out I had been fighting. And thus far, perhaps because of my inherited timidity or a feeling that I was no match for boys of my own age, I had heeded this warning, not a little to my own suffering and humiliation.

For back there in those far-gone days any boy who failed to stand up for his rights and self-respect by using his fists and strength was held in contempt by all lads who knew him, and was set upon and knocked around by fellows who took sadistic delight in beating and torturing the timid or those weaker than themselves.

"But you don't understand, Mother," I protested; "any feller just has to fight sometimes. When they find out he won't, ev'ry Tom, Dick, and Harry runs all over him and knocks him around; I guess I know."

Again she tried to reason with me, as she had many times before. Fighting was abhorrent to her; only brutal creatures fought, and they could be subdued by kindness. The way to treat an enemy who had smitten you on one cheek was to turn the other cheek also. She was sure such meekness would fill him with shame.

"But I've tried it," I cried, "and it just won't work with some fellers. They sock you all the harder and laugh at you. Even my own father had to fight when he was younger; I know, for I've heard him say so. That was how he kept bullies and toughs from pickin' on him, and it's the only way to stop 'em. I'm getting good and sick of being pummeled around and laughed at. I've just got to stand up'n fight some time, and, by golly, I'm going to do it even if Dad does give me a whaling ev'ry time I get into a scrap."

She made a gesture of despair. "No," she said, "I don't know what we're going to do with you. You're getting completely out of hand. Other folks know it. There's Ed Folsom—he warned me. He saw you walking the railing of the bridge when the flood came last spring, and he said you'd be drowned or killed 'less we took care of you better."

"Bah!" I barked. "That old tattletale! He better look out for his own boys and quit pokin' his long nose into other folk's business."

She threw up her hands. "I'll give up!" she cried. "I can't do a thing. Go get your wet clothes and fetch 'em down here. I'll dry them out in front of the fire, and I hope your father don't come home and catch me doing it."

Then I knew, much to my relief, that she would not voluntarily tell him of my disobedience. Neither of my parents ever lied, but sometimes they refrained from telling each other things unless compelled to by necessity.

I was the liar in the family, but some of my falsehoods did not seem like lies to me. Many were born of daydreams that seemed quite as real as actual happenings. Bidden or not, such dreams came to me often in reveries which let me escape into a magic land of fanciful excitement and adventure.

Some were dark and tragic dreams; some were bright and beautiful. And—this I declare is true—not a few of those fanciful imaginings seemed so much like actual occurrences that I practically accepted them as having really taken place.

So I was always the chief actor in those imaginary events. I now regard them as compensating efforts of an ego that found real life offering practically no opportunities for heroic deeds.

---

4 · ABOUT THE PATTENS

IN MY BOYHOOD my emotions for my husky father were a strange mixture of admiration and distaste. Being too young to analyze my reactions then, I was more than a little puzzled by such conflicting feelings, which caused me no little secret shame.

Nevertheless, I came in time to understand them and to know that our poverty—we were almost what then was called "dirt poor"—had very little to do with the matter. Indeed, I became proud of the fact that Father was a thoroughly honest man who nevered lowered himself to accumulate "worldly goods" by the despicable methods employed by several of the well-to-do citizens of our community.

Though frequently in debt, he always paid his bills eventually, and his credit remained sound throughout his life. Likewise, I came in time to perceive that Father's religion was the real cause of his improvidence. He was an Adventist who sincerely believed the second coming of Christ was near, and he was doing his best to follow the teachings of Jesus, who had said it was easier to pass through the Needle's Eye than for a rich man to enter the Kingdom of Heaven. No one then seemed to know that the Needle's Eye was a gate in the walls of Jerusalem instead of the eye of a needle.

The former belief that character never changes has been shown to be a fallacy. Character, like everything else in this world, is constantly changing; in fact, nothing known to science is static and unchangeable. And religion often brings about the most surprising changes in human beings, this being the cause that altered my father from an independent but nonaggressive person to an extreme pacifist who believed in, and sought to practice, the turning of the other cheek.

At his stern behest, I had vainly sought to do likewise, only to discover that it brought upon me the contempt of my young associates and even more ruffianly treatment by the natural bullies among them. This, combined with what I regarded as unfair restrictions by my parents, eventually turned me to rebellion and made my mother distraught by my "queerness."

I admired my father for his past independence and upstanding he-manhood, but, although I loved her for her gentle and affectionate nature, I thought my mother had a very poor understanding of human beings, boys in particular. She considered me willful, stubborn, rebellious, but after the death of my sister, before I was born, Mother's parental affection finally turned wholly to me, and thenceforth I was treated like an only child.

There were other reasons for my pride in my father. Soon after he had sown his wild oats somewhat profusely, he married my mother, a daughter of Captain Simpson of Newburgh, and shortly following the birth of my sister he made his first and only strong bid for fortune by moving to Decatur, Illinois. There he acquired a degree of skill as a carpenter and builder, a trade he then followed during the rest of his life.

There also he met and, to use his own words, rubbed shoulders with Abraham Lincoln.

When urged to tell how this came about, he usually began by saying that he had once received a personal invitation from Mr. Lincoln to join him on an open-air platform, from which the future President was making a political speech. Then he would pause a moment for dramatic effect before adding that he was standing in the midst of a great crowd of listeners when the speaker abruptly paused in his discourse and leveled a long finger in Father's direction.

About the Pattens

"There," said Lincoln, "is a man as tall as I am. Come up here, sir, and let's measure."

Now Father was really modest, and I can well imagine his surprise and embarrassment at being thus abruptly made to feel conspicuous. I can vision him hanging back a little and grinning awkwardly as he was pushed forward by the hands of the laughing persons near him. But he had to go through with it, and when the riverman and the rail-splitter stood back to back on the platform it was seen that the latter was slightly taller. And maybe that clever bit of byplay won more votes for Father Abraham than the persuasive reasoning of his speech.

At any rate that seems to have been one of my father's pleasantest memories of his sojourn in Illinois. He had begun to prosper fairly well after a slow start, when he contracted malaria, of which doctors at that time knew very little.

Under that attack of the fever germ he wasted away to a mere shadow of the lusty, healthy man he had been; a gaunt sallow creature of skin and bones, barely able to drag himself around and steadily growing more hopeless of recovering. With hope flickering like a spent candle, his heart turned toward home.

"Come, Cordelia," he said to my mother, "let's go back to Maine. I want to see the old place again before I die."

"All our money's gone for living and doctor's bill's," said she. "How can we get back there?"

Said he, "Our Heavenly Father will provide."

By selling almost all of their possessions except the clothes on their bodies, they obtained enough money to buy second-class railroad transportation for themselves and my little sister, and had a little left over for meals during the journey.

When they arrived back in Maine not only were they penniless, they were also homeless. But my Grandmother Betsey Simpson, widow of Captain Jason Simpson, whose death had brought her a small pension, came to the rescue. She bought the little old place in Corinna Village for their home and went there to live with them.

At that time, Corinna was a town of less than one thousand inhabitants and, if possible, its two doctors knew even less about malaria than the ones who had treated Father in Decatur. Therefore, he continued to grow still weaker until somebody told him of a medicine for malaria called Indian Collogog, or he read about it in an advertisement.

"It's no good," declared both Corinna doctors. "There is no sure cure for malaria."

Nevertheless, Father had Ed Folsom, the village druggist, procure a bottle of the patent medicine for him, and he began taking it according to the directions. Before long he appeared somewhat improved; the chills and fever that had frozen him by turns seemed to be abating. The improvement continued, and, after some time, the attacks ceased entirely. By then he was eating like a starved dog.

His color had changed from sickly yellow to normal and his bones were again being padded with healthy flesh. Once more his cleansed blood was pulsing strong through his veins. He could sleep. He could work. He could sing, and his laughter was booming again. It was a miracle. His special doctor said it was—and then blew up like a firecracker when Father told him about Indian Collogog.

"Don't be a fool, Bill Patten," he barked. "I don't care a hoot if you haven't been taking my medicine for over a week, that Collogog stuff hadn't a thing to do with your recovery. My medicine started you right and your natural vitality did the rest." And then, perhaps to wipe a grin off Father's face, he added, "But, anyhow, malaria's still in your blood and you'll have another attack sometime."

But whatever brought about the cure, that doctor was utterly mistaken. My father lived nearly fifty years thereafter and was never again troubled by the slightest symptom of malaria.

William Patten had all the Maine Yankee's disregard for ancestry and pomp, but this was not true of my cousin Franklin Patten. With great difficulty and patience, Cousin Frank traced our ancestry back into Scotland up to the time of Hector Patten's marriage with Lady Margot Ingraham, widow of Sir Penrod Ingraham, who had fled from England to Scotland to escape the religious persecutions of Bloody Mary.

In the veins of the children of Hector Patten and Lady Margot mingled Scotch and English blood, but whether it was further mixed by Irish blood after their descendants migrated to Dilbo— or maybe it was Bildo—near Dublin in Northern Ireland, there was no evidence.

However, in 1727, young Hector Patten the Latter, with his wife Pauline and their three sons, migrated to Boston, Massachusetts, and they and their descendants soon scattered along the coast northward into the near interior.

They became shipbuilders, woodsmen, and farmers, and a later descendant, my great-grandfather, Colonel James Patten, settled in the town of Nelson, some twelve or fourteen miles from Corinna. The wife of Colonel James was a Susan Dunning, half Scotch and half Irish, which makes it certain I have a touch of Irish in my blood.

All my forebearers in this country were extremely anti-British, and several of them fought the English and their Hessian helots during America's struggle for independence.

Even though my father believed the Abolitionists were right about slavery, his ill health and pacifist convictions prevented him from volunteering to serve in the Union Army when our war with the seceding South began.

Nevertheless, after he had fully recovered, he was drafted. Even though he was what is now called a conscientious objector, he answered the call and proceeded, with other drafted men, to journey to Augusta to report for service. But on reaching there he was informed that certain citizens of Corinna had raised money and bought a substitute for him.

They had sent him this message: "Come back home, Bill Patten; we need you here." So he returned without shame, but deeply grateful that—as he believed—the Lord had intervened to prevent his being forced to kill his fellow men and brothers.

I often heard my father speak of the hard times which followed the Civil War. In those days, and even after I was born years later, people lived much of the time on baked beans, cornmeal bread or mush, pork, and such vegetables as they could raise in their own gardens.

Only for Father's religious convictions we could have lived much better after I was born. For it is true that there was a revival of building, and Father was quite steadily employed at his trade. But he could never resist the temptation to help the needy and money simply would not stick to his open hands.

In Cordelia Simpson my father had obtained a worthy helpmate, though she was quite as improvident as he. She had stood by him staunchly when the skies were blackest and even his strong heart was faltering, and she never failed him at any time.

She worked constantly from morning lamplight until late evening, sewing, mending, spinning, and weaving, and doing a hundred and one other things. She was not, however, a good cook, and those were the days when excellent cooks abounded in Maine.

My Grandmother Simpson was too old and feeble to help Mother with the housework. I can plainly recall her now, sitting near her open bedroom door and warming her slippered feet at the open door of the cookstove. She had a Roman nose, a fine sensitive mouth, and fragile, almost transparent, hands. She was very neat, almost finicky, about her clothes. Over her thin white hair she usually wore a dark silk cap with lace edging.

When company came she also wore black lace half-mitts and a lace shawl, brought her from some foreign land by her sea-faring husband. Being a proud old lady, she loved to talk of Captain Jason's record in the War of 1812, and afterwards as master mariner on the high seas.

I don't know why I had the feeling that she was not very proud of her daughter's husband, for she always treated him with dignified respect, but perhaps that's the reason—perhaps she was too dignified and respectful in his presence. I imagine he had failed to live up to her expectations, as, unlike most of the Pattens, he had not become one of the leading citizens in his community, nor had he accumulated even a modest amount of worldly wealth.

However, if that were the reason, no hint of it ever came from her lips, and I think she never regretted the impulse that had led her to provide a home for my parents in the hour of their deepest distress.

To this day I am uncertain about her feelings for me. She was not a demonstrative person, and I do not remember that she ever showed any deep affection for me. But neither did she appear to dislike me. Of course I annoyed her at times, as I did my parents. I don't think she ever scolded me, but I can recall hearing her say to my mother one day, "Never saw a boy like Willie. All he wants to do is read or write or run away. Hates to work. Lacks ambition. Never'll set any rivers on fire when he grows up."

That meant she thought I'd never amount to much, but others had said the same—and worse. Even my own mother was discouraged about me. It does not seem possible that I held that remark against my Grandmother Simpson, even subconsciously.

Nevertheless, a strange thing happened. Even though I can remember a hundred trivial occurrences of my boyhood, I have no recollection whatever of Grandmother Betsey Simpson's death and funeral. All I can recall is that there came a time when she was no longer with us.

---

5 · SIGNS IN THE SKY

RELIGIOUS PERSONS TOOK THEIR RELIGION in heavy doses when I was a boy; but, even as today, many of them did not work at it much except on Sundays. During the rest of the week they seemed to put it aside or lock it up somewhere for safekeeping, and they could be as shrewd and unscrupulous in business affairs as any sinner. With them business was business, which meant that it was legitimate and nowise dishonorable to get the better end of a bargain by hook or by crook.

In fact, they rather prided themselves upon it when they had cunningly deceived and cheated another person, even though he were a near neighbor or close friend. In business matters they were like the poker player who announces that friendship ceases when he gets into a game.

But it was different on Sunday. Then, having taken their weekly bath on Saturday night—perhaps they felt that it washed away their little sins of the last six days—they bedecked themselves in their Sunday-go-to-meeting garments and paraded to church in family groups, there to sit solemnly through a long-winded sermon by a solemn parson or, perchance, to be peppered by hot shots from a furious pulpit-pounder who threatened them with eternal damnation and everlasting hell-fire unless they repented in sackcloth and ashes at the foot of the Cross.

Those hell-fire preachers fascinated and terrified me when I was very young. Later there came a time when they ceased to terrify me; instead, they amused me as the old-fashioned jumping-jack toys amused children. But those who preached damnation and hell for unbaptized babies made me angry and finally contemptuous, causing me to avoid listening to their sadistic fulminations.

However, I continued to go to Sunday school, for there was no public library in our little village and there was a Sunday school library from which I could get a book a week to read, and reading was one of my greatest enjoyments.

True, those books were very wishwashy and saccharine, but they were better than none, and I had not yet begun to read dime novels, which later destroyed my taste for infantile literature and led me eventually to devour the worthwhile works of great writers.

My parents were Adventists, sometimes called "Go-uppers" by scornful persons. They believed in the second coming of Christ, the resurrection of the saints from the dead, the destruction of the wicked, and the ascension of the redeemed with their Saviour into a Heavenly Kingdom.

They did not believe in a personal devil or a burning hell in which sinners would be tormented forever. In their creed, the wages of sin was death and extinction for the sinner; only those who had been "washed in the blood of the Lamb" would receive the ineffable reward of eternal life and happiness.

It seems to me that their chief folly lay in a conviction that their "enlightened" leaders were able, with the aid of the Scriptures, to foretell with considerable accuracy the time of the Saviour's second coming. And that was what those supposedly inspired leaders attempted to do more than once, as I can remember.

In demonstrating the method by which they had reached their conclusions, they displayed huge canvas charts on which appeared many fantastic figures drawn from descriptive passages to be found in the Book of Revelations and the records of the Prophet Daniel.

Those charts fascinated me. On them I beheld crudely colored pictures of angels with trumpets, wildly galloping horses with fierce-looking riders, ferocious dragons, huge and horrible serpents, savage beasts, some having more than one head and many horns, a woman in scarlet, and vials from which wrath and destruction were pouring upon a flaming world of terrified sinners.

And how convincingly for simple minds could those preachers demonstrate, with their charts and certain passages from the Bible, that they had figured out the time that would elapse between the Saviour's crucifixion and His second coming!

What if I could not follow and understand their line of reasoning? Others did—older people who shouted, "Glory hallelujah!" and "Come, Lord Jesus, come quickly!"

Now I didn't want the world to come to an end and I just couldn't love a God who would destroy it and all the people in it who were unbelievers and therefore wicked sinners. That meant that practically all my playmates would be destroyed, which was horrible to think of—sickening.

Young as I was, it aroused me to resentment and antagonism. I brooded over it. And finally I told myself that a God who would destroy human beings, His own children, just because they were mistaken in their honest beliefs could not be a just God.

"He is a bad God and I'll have nothing to do with Him," I said aloud—and waited for the thunderbolt. None came, and presently I stopped shivering and felt rather proud of myself.

Thus I cast my lot, secretly, with the sinners; but I was very careful not to let my parents suspect it, knowing how greatly they would be shocked and distressed. Especially my mother, who not only was determined that I should be a good boy but entertained the hope that I would become an Adventist preacher "if time continued."

Had Mother not embraced Adventism, I believe she might have become a spiritualist. She thought she was psychic, though I doubt if she ever heard that word. She believed in dreams and omens and did seem to possess a strange ability vaguely to foretell coming events of a calamitous nature which concerned her immediate family.

She maintained that she had been forewarned in a dream of my sister's death, and nothing very serious ever happened to me while Mother lived that she did not seem to feel it impending.

The Adventists sincerely believed it was easier for a camel to pass through the eye of a needle than for a rich man to enter the Kingdom of Heaven, and a part of their creed was "Sell what thou hast and give to the poor." But most of them never had much to sell for that purpose without unduly depriving themselves.

Unfaltering in their faith that they soon would be endowed with an abundance of heavenly treasures, they could see no reason to strive for perishable earthly treasures. Sustained by that faith, Father was satisfied to live frugally, even scantily, from day to day while waiting for the great event that was never to occur in all the years of his long life.

In spite of the fact that I was a rebellious little sinner, I could not avoid hearing much about signs and portents which would proclaim the end of the world as near at hand. Not only did such talk cause me to look for signs, it gave me many a dream from which I awoke gasping and shivering.

I remember telling myself more than once that I had com-

Signs in the Sky

mitted "the unpardonable sin" by defying God, and I actually seemed to find a sort of morbid satisfaction in the thought. I seemed to feel that I was different from the common run of sinners; not worse, but superior.

Then came a year when, during the latter part of a summer that had been marked by freakish weather, the skies became gory red at sunrise and sunset. Futhermore, the atmosphere was tinted faintly golden pink during the mid-hours of the day and the sun seemed to swim in a faintly scintillating haze. In cloudy weather the air felt heavy and oppressive.

Of course this unusual condition was accepted by some of the Adventists as foreshadowing the swift approach of the destruction of the world by fire. They did not appear to be alarmed on their own account, but they admitted that they were filled with sorrow for sinners, many of whom were friends and neighbors.

I think some of those sinners acted as if they were at least a little uneasy and apprehensive, even though they did not admit it. As for myself, I confess that I was quite unhappy, and my relief was great when the skies eventually resumed their normal appearance.

In the course of time, we heard that there had been violent volcanic eruptions in some far-away region. I think they were said to have occurred in Alaska. Presumably the fine volcanic ashes had been swept over a portion of Maine by air currents, there to linger a while and reflect ruddily the rays of the sun. Anyhow, correct or not, that was accepted as an explanation of the phenomenon.

Then something else happened.

Shortly before daybreak one chilly autumn morning, Father came upstairs and shook me awake. "Get up, son," he said. "I want to show you something you've never seen before."

He had lighted the kerosene lamp that stood on a chair beside the head of my bed and it threw his shadow, huge and grotesque, upon the whitewashed wall and ceiling. His voice sounded ominous. Startled, I sat up.

"Wh-what is it, Father?" I gasped.

"You'll see what it is," he replied. "Put some clothes on and hurry downstairs." Then he left me.

At that moment I didn't want to see something I'd never seen before. I wanted to crawl down into my warm nest again and cover my head with the bedclothes.

Father's black and distorted shadow had made me think of the ugly dragons I'd seen on the charts of the preachers. But I knew I'd catch it if I didn't obey; so, with my teeth chattering like hail on a tin roof, I jumped out of bed and into my trousers, yanked on my shoes, and hustled down to the kitchen.

Mother was up and dressed and Father was waiting. He led us out behind the house by way of the back door and pointed to something low in the southwestern sky. "There it is," he said.

Well, it sure was something worth seeing; it was the strangest, the most awe-inspiring thing I'd ever seen. Maybe my memory is playing me false, but that thing, as I remember it, seemed to be a fiery ball as big as the head of our rainspout water barrel.

Something that looked like a glowing tail almost as long as the rainspout streamed away from the fiery ball flaring out widely and thinly toward its end. I stared at it, my heart in my mouth. Here at last, I thought, was a genuine sign in the heavens.

Then Father explained that the thing was a comet, and I think he told us the name of the man who had discovered it—also the number of years since it had last been visible to the naked eye. He had obtained this information from the *Old Farmer's Almanac*, which he faithfully scanned year after year.

For him, that comet bore no portentous significance. It was simply an unusual sight—something one should not fail to see even though he had to get out before daylight on a frosty morning to behold it. When I realized how he regarded it, I was greatly relieved.

Already had Sundays become long and dreary days. On that day of the week, I was almost completely deprived of freedom of action. Sometimes I was compelled to attend church in the forenoon, afternoon, and evening. That was too much of a good thing to be a good thing for me. I hated it.

Signs in the Sky

When there were no afternoon services I was restricted to the immediate vicinity of my home, where I could hear our next-door neighbor, the Widow Blake, playing on her old melodeon and singing "Rock of Ages," "Nearer My God to Thee," and similar all-too-familiar hymns. It was just about the limit. Those Sunday afternoons would have been doleful enough without the added torture of listening to Laddie Blake's caterwauling to the accompaniment of a moaning melodeon in sad need of tuning.

There was no Sunday baseball in those days, no movies on any day, no radio to bring entertainment and cheer from the throbbing far-away world, no automobiles flying over the highways, not much of anything to do but sit around and take it.

On the Sabbath those who came to church from a distance made the journey in horse-drawn vehicles, and after church hours were over, the brown dirt roads soon became practically deserted. And in autumn, when all the birds had departed, time seemed to hang dead still in the dead and silent air.

I was too closely guarded on Sundays to succeed in running away. I tried it once or twice only to be called back or to feel my father's heavy hand on my jacket collar and my ears properly boxed and ringing.

Nevertheless, I cherished a growing desire to escape, to get away, not only from my home but from Corinna—to flee far beyond the distant hills of Dixmont, lying low and white against the southern sky in winter, blue as turquoise in other seasons.

Those hills! True, they were pretty hills, but for me they were like prison bars behind which I was locked away from the great world of action, life, and wonders which I had heard older people tell and of which I had read a little.

Would I ever live long enough to find a way to break through those white or blue bars and escape into that wonderful world? Would I on some happy day, like the birds in autumn, fly over those hills and away into the beckoning mystical land beyond?

I waited—impatiently.

6 · READING AND WRITING

DURING THAT PERIOD of what I considered undue restraint I found reading not only a time killer but a delightful diversion that could make me forget my unhappy condition. Thus I found a habit that has given me both pleasure and benefit throughout my life. But the amount of reading matter in my home was limited, and some of it, like the *Herald of Life,* a religious publication for Adventists, just didn't click with me.

Having chosen the crooked path that leads to destruction, I shied away from needless reminders of my woeful plight. However, there came a time when, having read every other book in the house, some of them repeatedly, I turned to the Bible.

To my surprise, I found therein—particularly in the Old Testament—not a few interesting stories, although it seemed to me that they were too briefly and badly told. Fortunately, I was still too young to look for the kind of interesting passages that real "bad" boys usually find in the Bible.

Among the few books in my home the one that provided me with the most satisfaction was a ponderous Harper's *History of the Civil War in America.* It was profusely illustrated with woodcuts, many of them covering a full page and depicting battles between the Northern and Southern forces.

There were also cuts of Lincoln, Jefferson Davis, Grant, Robert E. Lee, and all the well-known officers of both armies. I scanned those pictures until I could close my eyes, anywhere and at any time, and visualize them almost as clearly and in as much detail as when gazing upon them in the book.

The narrative text and the pictures inspired me to attempt to write some little war stories, most of which never got beyond a page or two before I found myself stuck and unable to go on. I could start easily enough but I couldn't seem to follow through. I hid those attempts in an old trunk in the open chamber and destroyed them after a while, my ardor for that sort of thing having oozed away.

Reading and Writing

I have no illusions about those early efforts to write; I was no youthful prodigy. I've never imagined myself as more than a lucky guy who has succeeded in "getting by" while doing the kind of work he could sweat and groan over with enjoyment.

Then there was a book about the Mormons, a part of which was pretty heavy going for me, but the chapter about the Danites and the Mountain Meadows massacre was thrilling and horrifying enough. From the book as a whole, I got the impression that Mormons were bloodthirsty creatures. This notion clung with the tenacity of all deep youthful impressions, but was finally corrected in later life when I came in contact with Mormons in the flesh and found them essentially no different from other civilized human beings.

Sheer desperation finally drove me to read *The Prince of the House of David*, which I'd heard my father say was regarded by many persons as a divinely inspired work. It was composed of letters reputedly written by a Damascus Jewess and telling of the appearance of Jesus in the Holy Land and subsequent events leading up to and including His Crucifixion.

In fact those letters had been composed by Dr. J. H. Ingraham, the real author of the book. And in time I was to learn to my amusement that he was also the author of dime novels published by Beadle and Adams. I remember the titles of two of them, *Lafitte, the Pirate of the Gulf* and *Captain Kidd, the Pirate of Hell Gate*.

But by no stretch of my youthful imagination did I conceive that some day I was to meet Colonel Prentiss Ingraham, son of Dr. Ingraham and also a writer of dime novels, as well as reputedly the participant in seven wars. Colonel Ingraham was very proud of his father's literary productions and was not at all ashamed of his own dime-novel record.

My hunger for reading increased as it was fed, and I soon became a borrowing and begging nuisance. Naturally, few persons were eager to loan their books to a mere kid, and I got flat turndowns. These rebuffs led me to commit one of my first crimes.

One day, while playing with another boy in the attic of his home, I found a tattered, coverless book in a box containing some old magazines and miscellaneous rubbish. One good look at that shabby volume gave me a kick. It was illustrated by the most bloodcurdling woodcuts of strife and carnage on the high seas and its title was *The Pirate's Own Book*. Boy, here was a real treasure!

When I arrived home that day I was surprised to find that that book had somehow got inside my buttoned-up jacket and was still there. Of course, being so shot to pieces, it wasn't worth anything to speak of, and probably the people who owned it had intended to throw it away with the rest of the rubbish in that old box. Well, as long as I'd forgotten to ask if I could take it, I might as well say nothing about it. I could carry it back some day after I'd read it. I could—but I never did.

That purloined book proved to be pretty strong meat for a boy of my tender years. Not only were the pictures fascinating, many were repulsive in their gory brutality. And the text was equally fascinating and shocking.

I'd never dreamed that human beings could become as degraded and bestial as some of the notorious pirates whose life histories were recorded on those tattered pages. But to my satisfaction every one of those bloody wretches eventually met his just deserts, many of them on the gallows.

That book had a permanent effect on me. It gave me a distaste for sea stories, particularly those which dealt with piracy. It's true that I did read an occasional yarn of that type in later years, but only one of them ever rang the bell for me. *Treasure Island* was a bull's-eye.

At school I managed to advance in step with classmates around my own age, though there were reasons why it should have been otherwise. While it's true that some studies—history and geography, for instance—were so easy that I seemed to commit my lessons by merely glancing them over, there were others—like grammar and algebra—that were stumbling blocks over which I bluffed my way somehow.

I'm positive I never was a teacher's pet, yet more than one of my teachers must have been either negligent with me or incompetent themselves. About one there was no doubt; he certainly knew less than many of the scholars he had been engaged to instruct. He obtained his job by a pull and lost it by a push; four or five of the older fellows threw him out of the schoolhouse. It was the talk of the town for a while.

Among those older lads there were a few whom I admired or envied and longed to emulate. Certain of them seemed to have a secret that piqued my curiosity. More than once I'd seen some one of them slyly slipping something into the hand of another, who quickly tucked the object into an inner pocket. Here was mystery for my fancy to play with, and it did a lot of playing before one of those fellows unintentionally betrayed their secret to me.

Though several years older than I, Frank Nutter apparently had taken a liking to me. I thought him tops in his crowd. One day I screwed up my courage to ask him to loan me something to read. He hesitated a moment before taking a little paper-covered book out of the inside pocket of his coat and handing it to me.

"It's a dime novel," said he, "so don't let your folks see it and don't tell anybody I let you have it. They'd say I was trying to ruin you."

A dime novel!

I'd heard my elders denounce them. I'd heard a parson say they were depraving the youth of the country. My parents had pronounced them "terrible"; they had warned me never to look into one of the dreadful monsters. And suddenly I knew that those forbidden books were what I'd seen my older schoolmates surreptitiously sending on their travels from one reader to another.

Now here I was with one of them in my possession. I could read it on the sly, as Frank Nutter and those other older fellows were doing. What a thrill!

"Gosh, Frank!" said I, breathing fast. "I won't tell a soul. You bet I won't! I'll be careful."

I felt as if I'd been admitted to membership in a secret band of conspirators. It was a grand feeling.

I slept in our open chamber that night, but before I slept I heard the old clock in the kitchen below strike the hour of two. I had just finished *Marlo the Gipsy* and blown out the kerosene lamp that stood on the chair beside my bed. And I was an extremely disappointed youngster, for I hadn't found anything terrible or even remotely shocking in my first dime novel. Compared to *The Pirate's Own Book,* it was the tamest sort of sentimental Sunday school literature.

That story was a reprint of an English tale about a boy who had been stolen by Gipsies and raised to think himself one of them. He turned out to be the son of a rich and titled father, who recovered him from the kidnapers after years of searching—only to lose him again when Marlo ran away at the first opportunity to rejoin the Gipsies. But when he finally overtook them, alas, it was too late! Already Zara, his little Gipsy sweetheart, had died of a broken heart caused by their separation. So Marlo drowned himself.

Not only was the story utterly unlike what I had expected, the ending harrowed my feelings and made me sore. I'm sure my manners were bad when I returned the book to Frank Nutter.

"Is this" I asked, "what they call blood-and-thunder stuff?"

He looked surprised. "Oh," said he, "if that's what you want, I'll see what I can do for you."

He had a lot of those books tucked away and they became a reservoir of joy for me. Among them all, I don't remember another like *Marlo the Gipsy,* which probably was used as a stopgap by the publishers. At that time I was too young to observe the publisher's imprint, but I was doing so before long. This happened, I think, because Frank Nutter had said he liked the novels of Beadle and Adams better than those of other publishers.

Today I believe the early dime novels bearing the imprint of that house were distinctly superior to those that came from the presses of rival concerns. However that may be, I quickly became

Reading and Writing

a Beadle fan with a list of favorite authors headed by Oll Coomes, whose Indian stories were replete with thrilling situations, clever stratagems, surprising twists, and extravagant but clean and inoffensive humor. No story by Coomes that I can recall depended for interest upon shocking effects or gory details, and he had considerable skill in character delineation.

This kind of reading spurred my imagination to such a degree that soon I was writing stories more feverishly than ever. While I'll admit that I read more dime novel yarns than was good for me, I deny that they depraved me to the slightest degree.

To the contrary, I believe they gave me a clean code of morals and a high standard of ethics. For the original dime novels were distinctly moral and ethical—yes, even prudish. What I can't deny is that the great amount of reading and writing that I was doing interfered with my school work.

One of my great difficulties was to obtain paper on which to write my stories. My parents were too poor to give me money to spend for that purpose. So I began to meet the late afternoon train, which sometimes brought passengers into town who stopped at Homer Jones' hotel. Such persons almost always had hand luggage that I begged to carry, and sometimes I caught a customer.

For the service I usually received a two-cent piece, as it was only a short walk. One swell gave me a nickel. Only one. But with two cents I could buy a sheet of brown wrapping paper large enough to be cut up into smaller sheets on which, by covering both sides, quite a lot of words could be written.

Naturally the time came when I wrote a story in imitation of the dime novel tales I'd been reading. It was an Indian story, located vaguely somewhere in the West, and it was longer than anything I'd previously done. It may have contained as many as 3,000 words. The title was alliterative and contained the hero's name, and I divided it into several chapters, all with sensational captions, which is practically all I can remember about it, except that I thought rather well of it when it was finished.

I thought so well of it that I longed to show it to somebody instead of hiding it away as I had been doing with previous efforts. And of course Frank Nutter was the one I showed it to, after pledging him never to say a word about it to a living soul.

He read it from beginning to end while I waited, anxiously watching his face. I'm sure the thing must have been a scream, but he didn't laugh at it. Had he done so I might have been cured of my writing craze then and there. I was holding my breath when he reached the end and looked up at me as if a little surprised.

"Say, this is pretty good, Will," he said. "I don't believe I could do as well. If you keep on you'll get to be a real author some day."

I walked on air when I went home again with that story in my pocket and those words echoing in my mind. Frank Nutter was nobody's fool. He was smart. He was smarter than any other fellow in the town. When he said a thing he knew what he was talking about. Now maybe I would get to be a real author some day.

The seed of a dream had been planted.

7 · FORBIDDEN FRUIT

I CAN REMEMBER when there was no meat market in Corinna. Country butchers came along at intervals, peddling beef and pork from carts. Like my father, many villagers raised pigs to slaughter for their own consumption. Usually they were butchered after cold weather came on in November so that they could be frozen and kept in that condition while being used as required. I doubt if I ever tasted roasted beef in the first fifteen years of my life. Sometimes mother bought cheap cuts of beef for stewing or to use in the mince-meat she put up in glass jars until it was baked in pies. And pies at our house were coincidental with visitors to dine.

There was likewise, at that time, no fruit store in the town.

Native apples and purple damson plums—the latter then grew plentifully in Maine—might be bought in season from the grocers who happened to have a supply, but no imported fruit was handled regularly by any merchant.

The first time I ever saw pineapple was on a Fouth of July when the town was putting on a celebration. By hustling and some hard work I had earned thirty-six cents which were all mine to spend on that day, but they had slipped away so fast that I was down to my last dime when I came face to face with a great temptation.

On a temporary stand in front of his store, Ed Folsom was offering for sale slices of peeled and sugar-smeared pineapple.

Five cents would get me one of those sweet, juicy, cool-looking slices, and the sight of them made my mouth water like a boiling spring. I was drooling when I tore myself away. But I had saved my dime only to spend it all shortly thereafter for a bunch of firecrackers, and long years went by before I knew what pineapple tasted like.

Before long I was tempted again—and fell. This happened one day when I'd met the afternoon train and some stingy arrivals who hung onto their hand luggage and two-cent pieces.

Had one of them loosened up and let me carry his grip, he would have saved me from taking another step on the well-trodden downward path. I hadn't quite finished telling myself what I thought of the last one, who pushed me aside, when I saw something that made me forget my annoyance.

The locomotive was shifting a freight car over onto the siding, and the train crew was busy. At the moment, no one else happened to be on the station platform. Before me was the car that carried both express and baggage, which had been left on the main line with other cars bound through to Oxton, eight miles beyond. The big side-door was wide open and there was nobody in the car.

But there were some burlap-covered baskets in there, one of them having a broken slat from which protruded the blushing cheek of a rosy golden peach.

Never before had I seen a real peach, but I knew this was one because I had seen pictures of them. It was as big, almost, as my two fists and much more beautiful than the pictures. I swallowed several times, fast, and prepared to act.

I glanced cautiously around. Nobody was watching me. I moved fast. I scrambled up into the car and ripped the broken slat of that basket still wider open. Out popped that gorgeous peach right into my hand. I didn't stop to examine it there. I put it under my jacket and got out quick.

When the stream was low, one could get down onto the big rocks under the railroad bridge below the mid-town crossing. That was where I went. Securely hidden, I brought forth my plunder and admired it.

My eyes hadn't deceived me; it really was beautiful, and it smelled more delectable than my mother's fresh-fried doughnuts. I didn't dally over it; I took a big bite. It was delicious.

Never before had I tasted anything half as delicious as that stolen peach. I gobbled it in ecstasy, the sweet juice dripping from my chin. Never since have I tasted anything half as delicious.

Not until I devoured it all but the clean brown stone did I realize what had happened. Then it came to me that I had made myself a criminal beyond retreat. The peach was irretrievably gone. It was in my stomach and could not be returned to its rightful owner.

Moreover, I didn't know and had no way of finding out who the rightful owner was. Therefore even though I were to take *The Pirate's Own Book* back to the people who owned it, I would still be none the less a thief.

I had been told hundreds of times that the first false step was always followed by another. I had been warned that by just such small false steps to begin with, many a poor wretch had started on the road to prison and the gallows.

Well, maybe I was on my way; but oddly enough, when I thought of that beautiful peach and how absolutely luscious it had been, I was sorry I hadn't taken a little more time, while I was about it, and hooked at least one more. I'd often heard the saying that one might as well be hanged for stealing an old sheep as for stealing a lamb.

Although I was an introvert, I was still too young to perceive the reasons for many of my mental attitudes and my likes and dislikes. But I did know that the boys who were called good by my elders often were lackadaisical prigs with neither the courage nor the inclination to do the things that might get them into trouble. And some were downright sneaks and tattlers who spied on other boys and carried tales to their parents or to school teachers.

On the other hand, many so-called bad boys were merely boisterous, high-spirited, fun-loving fellows who indulged in rough-and-tumble horseplay and practical jokes—just natural, healthy boys who were neither bullies nor sneaks.

They were the kind I admired and longed to associate with, but they had called me a "goody-goody" because thus far I had heeded my father's warning about fighting, which made me seem to lack the spirit to stand up for my own rights. I wondered what they would think of me now if they knew what I had done. I wasn't quite sure of the answer.

One evening, to my surprise, I was invited to join some of those so-called bad boys who were smoking two-cent cheroots out behind Sam Morse's store. Still more to my surprise, I was offered a comfortable seat on a empty box and given a cheroot.

Up to that time I had never smoked anything stronger than rattan "cigars," made by cutting up the ribs of castoff umbrellas. But now, not only puzzled but flattered by the attention I was receiving, I didn't back away from that tobacco cheroot. This was my opportunity to get in right with some high steppers, and I didn't propose to muff it.

I got along swimmingly for a while; didn't choke, didn't cough —much. I knew they were watching me. I saw some of them grinning behind their hands and winking at one another.

Somebody asked me how I liked my cheroot and I said it was

"bully." I didn't like it much, but I wasn't going to let them know. I pretended to enjoy every puff. I was showing those fellows I was no softie.

Next thing, I'd have to take up chewing tobacco. That would be the finishing touch. I felt like laughing. I took the cheroot out of my mouth, tipped my head back and blew a whiff of smoke upward. I almost fell off the box. Something had made me slightly dizzy.

I looked at my cheroot and found I hadn't smoked quite half of it.

"What's the matter, Willie?" asked one of the grinning gang.

"Not a thing," said I, putting the cheroot back between my teeth and taking a good long drag at it.

That *was* the finishing touch.

The pit of my stomach squirmed and I began to feel queer all over. I tried not to show it, but in less than another minute I was convinced that I was going to be a very sick child.

I said I had to be going. They sought to detain me and urged me to go on smoking.

I dropped the cheroot, reeled to my feet, clasped my hands over my uneasy stomach, and fled from their midst and the sound of their hilarity.

Somehow I avoided my mother's sharp eyes and got up to my bed in the open chamber. But I hadn't shed more than half my clothes before I was compelled to lie down and hold fast to the bed while it whirled and reared and bucked like a wild bronco. Then my stomach started bucking also, and I didn't give a rap if the bed threw me off and broke my fool neck.

Mother found what was left of me there in the morning, limp and weak but still breathing. She was shocked by the sight of me—and the floor beside the bed. She wondered what I had eaten that had made me so ill.

I admitted that I couldn't think of anything. She kept me in bed and doctored me up while I tried to figure out some way to get even with the smarties who had made a sap of me.

Not being able to conceive a plan for retaliation, I decided to show those fellows that I could smoke as well as anybody. No matter how tough the going might be, I was going to learn to smoke. But to do so I must have money to buy cheroots or smoking tobacco, and I didn't have a copper to my name.

So as soon as I could, I started searching for any kind of a paying job and finally found one that almost broke my back. I sawed and split a cord of hard and knotty wood, for which labor I received twenty-five cents. It took me three days with my father's bucksaw and ax, and I was sore and lame for a week.

And then when I tried to buy cheroots from Sam Morse, he wouldn't sell me any. "You're too young," he said.

But there was another boy, whose father kept a store and sold tobacco and cigars, who got them for me. I paid him, but I doubt if the money ever reached his father's till.

I had to do my smoking secretly when I could find an opportunity, and it was quite a while before I was able to smoke a whole cheroot without gagging. However, I worked up to that point by degrees and spent much more than twenty-five cents before I arrived there.

Eventually the evening came when I joined the gang behind Sam Morse's store with a lighted cheroot in my mouth and kept on smoking it until the stub was too short to hold without burning my fingers.

Nevertheless, even that did not win me full fellowship with the gang. They had been surprised and impressed, but they failed to loosen up with me. I was still Willie Patten, and somehow that meant that I was still an outsider. I had to do more than smoke a cheroot to get past the barrier, but what?

I was still wondering about that, when there came a Sunday on which I made a getaway from home without being detected and called back. I did this by going up the hill away from the village. But unfortunately I ran into two boys who were coming out of the home of Amos Dunn, a farmer who lived in a white house at the top of the hill.

Old Amos and his family were away, and Bert Kilson, who was living there then, had taken Tommy Wood into the cellar to treat him to some of the farmer's hard cider, which was "fortified" with alcohol.

Now they fell on my neck with whoops of joy, and back into the cellar they went, taking me with them. I didn't get what they were trying to do until I found myself with a brimming tumblerful of old Amos' liquid chain-lightning in my hand. I'd really begun to think they were crazy.

"It'll make hair grow on your chest, Willie," said Bert. "We've had three glasses apiece and we're feeling great."

It was terrible, but I forced myself to swallow it. Before I could get my breath the glass was filled again and coming my way. I balked. I tried to beg off. Tommy Wood got me by the neck again. He was much older and stronger than I, and I knew he could handle me with one hand tied behind him.

"Down it," he said, "or we'll hold you and pour it down your throat."

I downed it—and it downed me. I'm sure I didn't drink a third glass. Sometime later I found my self lying alone, beside a pond and watching the world spin with the movements of a dying top.

At times the ground tipped until I had to clutch the grass with both hands and hold fast to keep from falling off into the sky below me. It was exciting, even terrifying. I was much more upset than I'd been after smoking my first cheroot. Let's let it go at that and skip further details of what happened there.

I didn't know what had become of Bert Kilson and Tommy Wood, and I didn't care. I wanted to get home, even though I expected to catch a birching by my father. I was sure it would make him quite angry to see his carefully guarded son come reeling home as drunk as a boiled owl.

But I was in luck. He didn't see me. Company had arrived while I was away, and an impromptu prayer meeting was taking place. I sneaked in and crept upstairs while they were singing a hymn.

I didn't have to pretend I had a bad headache when mother found me stretched on my bed after the company left.

Forbidden Fruit

"Why, Willie," she said, "why didn't you call me instead of lying up here and suffering all this time?"

They hadn't even missed me!

That discovery helped my headache as much as Mother's ministrations with cold compresses and the camphor bottle.

I'm sure Bert Kilson and Tommy Wood became worried after they sobered up and remembered what had happened. I'm sure they expected me to tell that they had got me drunk, which would have meant trouble for them. But now I believed that only "good boys" were tattletales and squealers, and I kept my mouth buttoned up just to prove that I didn't belong in that class.

Whether Bert and Tommy talked about it to others or not, I suspected they had when I saw that at last I was getting somewhere with the fellows I'd tried in vain to cultivate.

When some of them began to tell me about their escapades I listened enviously. For they were having fun on nights while I was cooped up in the house. Eventually they were talking quite freely before me, and one day I heard them planning to get together that night to raid an apple orchard.

"Say, fellers, why can't I get in on that?" I ventured.

"You?" said the leader, amused. "Why, Willie, you can't get out of the house after nine o'clock."

"Yes I can, too," I declared. "I know how to get out and get back again without my folks ever suspecting it."

"Oh, you do?" said he. "All right then, we'll be looking for you over by the old mill around half-past nine."

"I'll be Johnny-on-the-spot, Mister," said I.

Well, I had made the grade at last. Now I was one of the gang. I felt big. I went home walking on air.

I didn't have to be sent to bed that night. Up in the old open chamber, I opened my window and propped it up with the stick. I didn't undress. I took off my shoes and tied them together with the long laces.

Then I blew out the lamp to wait impatiently for my parents to turn in at their habitual time around nine o'clock. And they hadn't been sleeping long before I was climbing cautiously out through the window on to the hip-roof of our well-shed at the back of the house.

On hands and knees, I crept along to the end of the shed near the barn before descending to the lower corner and letting myself down on to the rail fence that came to an end there. Then I put on my shoes, which had been suspended from my neck by the tied-together laces, and was on my way, feeling like a character in a dime novel, to meet my brave comrades at the rendezvous.

Already most of the village houses were dark, with only a window gleaming yellowly here and there. The night was very still. There was no moon, but the sky was peppered with polished stars. The snappy air made me want to kick up my heels and caper.

Silent and grim, the abandoned mill that soon would be torn down stood at the eastern end of the dam in the heart of the village. It always seemed to be listening, regretful for past days of activity, to the steady sound of the waste-water that flowed over the middle apron of the dam. As I approached the mill, a softly whistled signal came to my ears. I answered guardedly.

I smelled burning tobacco before I saw a huddle of dark figures sitting on the ground near the aged building. There were six of them, whispering and giggling. Their cheroots glowed like fireflies on a warm night in early summer.

They slapped me on the back and confessed that they hadn't thought I would show up. They called me Bill instead of Willie, which was an improvement I had long desired.

One of them cut a cheroot in two with his pocket knife, gave me half of it, and let me light it from the one he was smoking. They were all right. Bad boys, me eye! They were swell. Nothing mean or stingy about them. This was living!

Presently one of them said: "Hadn't we better tell Bill where we are going? Maybe he's gun-shy."

"Gun-shy?" said I. "What do you mean?"

"We've decided on Libby Scones' orchard, and old Lib says he'll shoot anybody he catches stealing his apples this year."

I choked a little over my cheroot. Libby Scones was nobody to fool with when his dander was up. He owned a fine orchard, and some years his best trees had been stripped of fruit. Trespass notices threatening prosecution had been ignored. Now he had taken pains to let folks know that he'd loaded his gun with a charge of rock-salt with which he intended to riddle the hide of any thief, man or boy, detected on his land.

I forced a laugh. "Aw, Lib's an old windbag," said I. "He's a big bluff. He'd never dare to really shoot somebody."

They didn't agree with me. They said he was a bad egg when he got good and mad—wouldn't stop at anything. After a while I could see that they were fascinated by the possibility of being shot at by Libby Scones. It had enhanced the allure of his apples. Even better fruit to be found elsewhere would not have kept them out of Libby's orchard that night, and pretty soon I caught the fever myself.

Here was real excitement and adventure—and real danger, the principal incentive for all true adventurers.

Scarcely a light was gleaming anywhere in the village when we set forth on our way over the hill to gather apples or rock-salt. There were houses along the road, including my own house. We stepped softly and kept our voices down to whispers.

In sight of Libby Scones' farm buildings, but still a long distance away, we stopped to look them over by the light of the stars. The windows were dark, and the place seemed as silent as a graveyard.

Nevertheless, I had a feeling that somewhere in the shadows around those buildings a man with a gun was waiting for us, and I wondered how it felt to be shot with rock-salt.

"Let's keep as far away from the house as we can," whispered our leader. "After we're in the orchard we'll scatter and hunt for the best trees, but don't shake the apples off. That would make a noise that might be heard in the house. It'll be every feller for himself till we get together right here again. Come on."

I had been given two short pieces of stout cord to tie around the bottoms of my trouser legs so that they, as well as my pockets, could be stuffed full of apples. Soon after we were in the orchard,

I found a place where the ground beneath a tree was thickly covered with fallen apples which, though tart, were not bad, and I didn't search any further. I was nervous as a witch and wanted to get out of there as soon as possible.

It didn't take me long to load up, and I was leaving when something happened to make my hair stand and send my heart leaping up into my throat.

Somebody dropped down out of a tree I was passing, and he had something long and slim, like a gun, in his hand.

I hit the high spots as fast as I could, which, because of my apple-clogged running gear, was not nearly as fast as I wished to travel. I expected, any moment, to hear the report of a gun and feel rock-salt tearing through my flesh.

Lumbering along, I came to a fence and rolled over the top rail into a field beyond the orchard. Glancing backward, I thought I saw a dark figure in pursuit.

So away over that field I galloped, stiff-legged and panting. Once or twice I came near falling but managed to keep my feet under me and keep on going. I was pretty near winded when I came to a grove of trees and ventured to look behind me again.

This time I saw nobody coming, whereupon I made all possible haste, with trembling and fumbling hands, to untie the cords at the bottoms of my trouser legs and let the encumbering apples roll out.

I had escaped alive and unscratched, but I was still panic-stricken. As soon as I could get my breath somewhat, I plunged into the concealing darkness of the grove and pushed my way through it, tripping over roots and getting my face lashed and scratched with branches.

Beyond the grove was a highway, but I kept straight on across it, fearing to encounter somebody who might recognize me. I crossed other fields and skirted other groves. To my right I saw, now and then, a house, far away. A dog barked at me from one of them. And finally, surprised and wondering how I'd got there, I found myself down at the western end of the half-ruined upper dam at the foot of the Old Bog.

When I was fully satisfied that it was the upper dam I had reached, I sat down and rested. From there I could have cut back at an angle across Sumner Titcomb's land, which would have been the shortest way home, but I was still afraid of meeting somebody who would recognize me. So once more I did a foolish thing that might have cost me my life.

I crossed the dam in order to go round through the village, which would bring me home in a direction opposite to the course I would have followed had I returned over the shortest route from Libby Scones' orchard.

It was not difficult to get halfway across the dam, but near the middle was a space of several feet where only some slimy planks, set on end, rose above the surface of the water.

Undressed to swim in the "deep hole" below the dam, I had walked those slippery plank ends several times by day, and now, wearing my shoes, I did it again by the light of the stars. I might have been seriously injured, perhaps stunned and drowned, had a single misstep caused me to fall on those plank-ends.

Not until I had crawled back over the roof of our well-shed and was in the old open chamber again, did I realize that I had thought of my own safety only.

But I had heard no gunshot behind me while in flight, as I surely would have, had a gun been fired, and that, I told myself, indicated that my companions had made a safe getaway. Nevertheless, I slept badly that night when I slept at all.

Three of the gang were waiting for me outside the schoolhouse the following morning. "What became of you last night?" they wanted to know.

I told them how I had outrun Libby Scones when he dropped down out of the tree in which he had been hidden. I said he had chased me all the way across the field beyond the orchard. Further than that, I said I had tried to lead him on so that the rest of them could get away while he was pursuing me.

My story amused them. They shouted with laughter when I finished. One of them laughed until he choked.

"Why, Willie," he said when he could get his breath, "that

wasn't old Lib Scones. That was me. I had a long stick that I'd been knocking apples off with. And I never chased you at all."

I was Willie again!

8 · THE DAWN OF WONDERS

EVEN THOUGH MANY MEMORIES of my boyhood in Corinna are extremely vivid, that entire period of my life seems fantastically unreal and dreamlike.

Wood-burning stoves were then in nearly universal use for cooking and heating. Railroad locomotives burned wood too, and the stoves which heated the cars sometimes roasted passengers alive in train wrecks.

Homes were lighted by kerosene lamps or candles. Very poor people often used "slut candles"; such a candle was a shallow open dish containing animal fat in which burned the end of a saturated wick or woolen rag. They furnished a wretched, fluttering light, smoked horribly, and were sickeningly noisome.

Some persons in our village who had been "up to Boston" and seen gaslights still thought kerosene lamps more convenient and better for interior lighting. In time there was talk about a new kind of light produced by electricity, but how light could be obtained without a flame no one could seem to understand.

The current opinion of the best local minds was that Tom Edison, the inventor, never would get anywhere with such a crazy scheme.

Well, many of the country's leading newspapers ridiculed Edison at first, and some of them were reluctant to admit that he had succeeded for quite a while after electricity was being gradually adopted for illuminating purposes.

The telegraph was still a great wonder and I, like several other boys in town, became ambitious to learn telegraphy. We were

The Dawn of Wonders

inspired by the advertisement of a small pocket gadget of metal with which clicking sounds similar to those made by a telegraph key could be produced.

"Become a telegraph operator and earn big pay," said the advertisement, and all of us looked forward hopefully to the time when we would be earning big pay.

So we raked up dimes by hook or crook or good hard work and sent away for those pocket telegraph keys, a copy of the Morse code, and full instructions for learning telegraphy.

Only one of us became a telegraph operator in later life, and he certainly earned all the pay he received for running a small-town railway office, where telegraphy was a minor part of his job.

One day two strangers appeared in our town and exhibited a device for oral communication between distant points. The contrivance consisted of two drum-shaped cups about the size of a waterglass, with thin sheepskin heads drawn tightly over one end of each cup, and an extremely long and slender connecting cord attached to the sheepskin heads. When a small crowd had assembled to witness a free show, the strangers proceeded to give a demonstration with this simple contraption.

One of them took his stand on the main street in front of Sam Elder's store and the other walked away over the bridge and finally halted after he had nearly reached the railroad crossing. They were then separated by a distance too great for them to hear and understand each other without shouting.

Each man had one of the cups in his hand, and they carefully backed away until the connecting cord was lifted off the ground and drawn fairly taut.

"Now, gentlemen," said the man in front of the store, "please come nearer and stand close behind me where you can all understand what I say. I'm going to talk to my friend over yonder, and I think you'll be surprised by what you hear and behold."

Then, placing the open end of the cup close to his mouth, he spoke into it in such a low voice that I, not more than ten feet away, could barely understand his muffled words.

He said, "Raise your right hand, Jim."

Holding the cup to his ear, Jim raised his right hand.

"Now your left hand," was the next request.

Up went Jim's left hand.

"Now lift your hat."

Jim lifted his hat.

"You see, gentlemen," said the one who was giving the orders, "my voice travels over the connecting line and my words are distinctly understood by my friend over yonder. Unlike the telegraph, this simple but wonderful little invention can be used by anybody. Even by a child old enough to talk."

Somebody snickered and one citizen spoke up promptly. "Go on with your guff," he said. "It's a trick. That feller over there knows what you're going to ask him to do. We ain't no suckers, Mister."

The stranger smiled. "So you think it's a trick, do you? Well, as long as you're so smart, I'll let you tell me what to ask him to do. Speak up, Smarty, but keep your voice down so he can't hear you."

Accepting the challenge, the distrustful citizen suggested that Jim should raise his right foot, then his left, and then both feet at the same time.

Having complied with the first two requests, Jim came toward us until much of the cord rested on the ground and then he jumped into the air and thumbed his nose in our direction. The laugh was on our skeptical townsman.

Nevertheless, the strangers did no business in Corinna. Nobody loosened up and gave them an order for one of their "wonderful little inventions."

But not long afterwards Will Stevens, a local boy about my age, put together a similar device and installed it for communication between his father's hardware store and their near-by home. To summon a listener at the other end of the line, one rapped on the side of the cup with his fingernail. Like spoken words, the sound was transmitted by vibration.

Sometimes the thing worked and sometimes it didn't, because of weather conditions which caused the connecting cord alternatingly to stretch and relax. It was soon abandoned. However, to Will Stevens goes the honor of installing the first telephone in Corinna.

One evening my father took me to an exhibition of Edison's new electric light and his talking machine, which was given in a hall owned by Sam Fowles, where I later learned to waltz and dance the square dances of that period. The admission charge was a dime, and the hall was packed.

A long man wearing a long black coat appeared on the platform at the end of the hall and delivered a long lecture about Thomas Edison and his inventions.

He predicted that inventors like Edison eventually would produce devices of such a marvelous nature that the whole course of human life would be tremendously altered by them.

The electric light, he said, was "the first gleam in the dawn of wonders." I thought that phrase was good, and it stuck in my mind.

Two hinged cabinets stood on a table at the lecturer's elbow. Announcing that he would show the electric light first, he opened the front of one of the cabinets, exposing a glass bulb against a background of black velvet. After fiddling around mysteriously for a short while, he addressed the audience again.

"I am now going to turn on the electric current," said he, "and you will see the light gleaming within this small bulb. But I must caution you not to look at it too long or steadily. It may injure your eyes if you do."

Presently something within the bulb began to glow, but the light that came from it was disappointingly feeble.

"Aw, shucks!" muttered my father. "That wouldn't hurt a baby's eyes."

The talking machine was even more disappointing. Requested to be very quiet and listen closely, every person in the hall seemed to be holding his breath when the man started a cylinder revolving within the other case, which he had opened also.

We heard a scratching sound and a faint tinny voice, not at all like a human voice, which said: "This, ladies and gentlemen, is the Phonograph invented by Thomas A. Edison." There was more but I've forgotten the rest of it.

I felt cheated. With the dime Father had spent to get me into the hall I could have bought enough brown paper to write a dozen stories on—and some poetry to boot. By that I mean the kind of "poetry" I was then writing.

Probably my first attempts to express myself in verse were inspired by the poetry in the school readers then in use. In particular I remember "The Burial of Sir John Moore" and the stirring line, "To heartbeat and drumbeat a soldier passes by."

Among other poems were William Cullen Bryant's "Thanatopsis" and Poe's "The Bells," which were sometimes used as declamations by older scholars. These led me, later, to study metrical writing and to become familiar with the works of many famous poets then in vogue.

The poetic urge came upon me at a time when I had begun to take a sentimental interest in girls. Hitherto they had held small attraction for me as associates, and sometimes they had annoyed me.

I had tolerated them as playmates only when necessity compelled, but now I was growing up and changing with the passing years. Although I still read dime novels, I was beginning to take an interest in more romantic and fluffy fiction.

A strange restlessness was coming over me, bringing with it a disturbing sense of shame. Sometimes it caused me to be grossly rude with the girls who attracted me most, pulling their hair or pushing them around by bumping against them as if by accident or awkwardness.

There was one exception, however; I never was rude to Addie Hutchings. I was slightly younger than Addie, but she was the girl of my dreams—literally it seemed. Imagine how dashed I was when I accidentally discovered that Addie and Frank Nutter, my best friend, were secret sweethearts.

They were practically engaged but were not letting it be known because of the difference in their ages. Addie, was still so very young that it would seem ridiculous, and Frank was not anxious to be called a cradle-snatcher.

I didn't let either of them know how I felt toward Addie. I hid my secret sorrow in my heart, fully expecting to carry it with me to my grave. Nor did I let them suspect that I was wise to what was going on, for I didn't want them to think I had spied on them. But, needing a confidant, Frank eventually let me in on their secret, and I became the bearer of little notes and oral messages between them.

I dramatized the situation, becoming the noble hero who had made a mighty sacrifice for a beloved pal.

By nature I was easily moved to merriment, but now I gloomed around with a long face and behaved so queerly that my mother was alarmed and attempted to doctor me up with some kind of herb brew that was bitter as gall. One dose of that cured me—when I was around home.

Then I decided to be a hermit and took to the woods; but I always came back when I was hungry, and I slept under the paternal roof at night.

Two or three times I managed to slip away with Father's ancient muzzle-loading shotgun, with which I mercilessly slaughtered the harmless wild creatures—the birds and squirrels that I would not have harmed had not cruel fate robbed me of the woman I loved and turned me into an unfeeling brute. It was pretty silly, but I enjoyed it.

But before school opened in September I was fed up on the hermit stuff. Play acting without an audience wasn't so good. I decided on another role for myself; I would become a devil among the little ladies, a dashing Lothario, a regular Don Juan.

That was the kind of chap Bert Day was, big and handsome and a killer with the fair sex. I would be like Bert, that was what I'd do. Nothing stopped him. If anything got in his way he just laughed and kept right on going ahead.

So I spruced up as much as I could, assumed a devil-may-care air and really made myself feel like a different person. I actually winked at some of the girls right in school on the first day of the term, being careful, however, not to let the teacher catch me at it. When one of them made a face at me I grinned back at her. That was the way to carry it off, I'd been allowing myself to be squelched too easily.

At noon intermission the next day I got back early to the schoolhouse and found another boy and two girls there ahead of me. The boy, whom I will call Dick, which wasn't his name, was older than I but much smaller.

He was a snappy little chap and quite a blade with the girls. I had reason to know he was surprisingly strong and a clever wrestler, for in scuffles he had put me on my back more than once.

He was romping and laughing with the girls when I came in, and, without seeing me, one of them ran right into my arms.

I gave her a smack on the mouth before she could get away. Mad? Well, she spat in my face. I wiped it off with my sleeve and started after her.

Dick grabbed me. "What do you think you're doing, Rolling Thunder?" said he, hanging on to my arm.

Now Rolling Thunder was a derisive nickname that I'd been tagged with because of my dime-novel reading and story-writing habits. It had annoyed me, and now it made me very hot under the collar.

"Mind your own business, Peanut!" said I, giving him a snap and thrust that broke his hold and sent him staggering.

He tripped against the teacher's raised platform and fell upon it. Up he bounced like a jumping-jack and slapped my face. Then we went to it.

He stood on the platform and I on the floor, which brought our eyes about on a level. He hit me on the chin with his fists, and I poked him in the stomach and slapped him right and left with both hands.

I never saw anybody look more astonished and bewildered than he did. I was fighting mad—and fighting. It was so unexpected and incredible that he quit in less than half a minute. He backed away, staring at me in amazement.

The Worm Turns

"Come on," I said. "I haven't got started yet."

But he was all through, and I had won my first fight. It hadn't been much of a fight, but others were to follow that wouldn't be so easy.

---

9 · THE WORM TURNS

NOT ONLY HAD THAT EASY VICTORY OVER DICK surprised me, it had revealed something in my nature of which I'd previously been wholly unaware. When I became fighting mad, timidity had vanished and left me cold and calculating.

After giving him that first blow in the pit of his stomach, I had deliberately but furiously slapped him so dizzy that he had quit without hurting me at all. I had refrained from trying to beat him up because I bore him no real animosity; but thinking about it later, I told myself it would be different with other fellows.

The discovery that I could fight without fear gave me a feeling of self-respect which I had failed to acquire through all my show-off efforts to impress other boys. I was elated.

Lick or get licked, henceforth I would resist if imposed upon. And I had some scores to settle with fellows who had found sadistic pleasure in hurting me mentally and physically. To my regret, one of them who had used a horsewhip to make me dance no longer lived in Corinna.

Wisely, I began at the bottom with the intention of working up. Tim Shaw—nicknamed "Dim" by the village boys—was the first on the list. I chose my time, and we fought it out one night after school.

In a clinch, he threw me, but I turned him and got on top. He got one of my fingers between his teeth and tried to chew it off. I choked him black in the face. I held him down and pommelled him, buttoning up one of his eyes.

"I give up!" he cried. "Stop, Willie! Stop! I beg!"

"All right," said I. "But next time I'll give you a pair of black eyes and a bloody nose."

There was no next time. Dim had his fill.

There had been several witnesses, and they spread the story. Impossible though it seemed, Willie Patten had started a fight with Tim Shaw and given him a licking. When Jack Butters heard about it he girded up his loins, so to speak, and started on the warpath. He found me in a store one evening.

"Come outside, you long-legged bluff," said he, "and I'll grease the ground with you."

Several boys were waiting to see the fun when I followed him out into the street. I was taller than Jack, but he was a little older and weighed much more than I did. I knew I'd have to work fast to get the best of him, and I didn't lose a jiffy when he said he was ready.

We grappled and I backheeled him. He went down and I went with him. As we were falling I drew up one knee, which I drove into the pit of his stomach when he hit the ground.

On my feet and looking down at Jack shortly thereafter, I became frightened. Holding both hands to his midriff, he was writhing in the dirt and making horrible sounds as he gasped for breath. I thought he was going to die. It was quite some time before he was able to stand on his feet, with assistance. Then he wanted to know why I had done such a dirty trick.

"Listen, Jackie," said I. "Don't ever bother me again, for if you do I'll break your back."

He never bothered me again.

Revenge long deferred was doubly sweet, but this was too easy. I began to swell up and feel like a fighting cock before I'd even been in a real scrap.

Nor was I disillusioned when I put on the boxing gloves with Al Haskell and he cuffed me around with ease; for he was several years my elder, and I hadn't expected to hold my own with him. I wanted to learn something about boxing, and he gave me two or three little lessons which came in handy later.

The Worm Turns

I held a special grudge against the Hall boys, for they had handed me another nickname more to my distaste than Rolling Thunder.

People had wondered how their father, a poor man, had obtained the money to pay for repairing and painting his house, and some persons had openly expressed disbelief of the story that Mr. Hall and one of his older sons had been held up and robbed of a considerable sum in cash received as payment for a herd of cattle that Hall had collected to sell on commission.

The story may have been true, but I expressed my doubts, and "Tinker" Hall, the youngest boy, had given me a fancy drubbing. After that the Hall boys had called me "Bullbeef," and others were taking it up. I intended to square my account with "Tinker" but hadn't worked up to him yet.

Just before dark one evening, as I was walking down the railroad from the station, Clarence Draper called to me from the Buxton road, a short distance away.

"Come over here, Bull," he cried.

I went over. He was a strapping lad, fully my height and at least twenty pounds heavier. Sitting on an empty dry-goods box in front of a store, he grinned at me as I came up. Without a word, I swung on him with my open hand and knocked him off the box. He scrambled to his feet, holding a hand to his smarting cheek.

"What did you do that for?" he gasped.

"If you ever call me Bull again I'll knock your head off your shoulders," I told him.

He politely called me William forever after.

It was too easy. It wasn't good for me. I didn't have to play-act, I really felt like the cock o' the walk. Having so long been possessed by an inferiority complex and fought against it with rebellious resentment, I was now like a prisoner set free from a dungeon.

I walked with a strut and felt really too big for my britches. Never in my life have I felt that way that something hasn't happened, sooner or later, to deflate my ego.

"Tinker" Hall came near doing it. Unlike the others, he was

no push-over; he was a hard nut to crack. Quick as a cat on his feet, he could use his fists pretty well also. We had it, hammer and tongs, three or four times, and it was lucky for me that I'd learned a little about boxing from Al Haskell.

I succeeded in making it a draw, but "Tinker" left some marks on me that forced me to confess the truth to my parents. Mother was distressed, but, to my surprise, Father said I was now old enough and big enough to take care of myself. All the past summer he had been loosening the reins on me somewhat.

Maybe I never would have gained the ascendancy over "Tinker" if he hadn't been a trifle yellow. I never did whip him, but presently he began to avoid me, and I soon decided that he, too, was all through.

There was now only one more lad with whom I felt that I must settle the score. Others I would have enjoyed thrashing were out of my class. In spite of my puffed up condition, I knew better than to make a complete ass of myself by tackling older fellows who could lick the pants off me.

But I simply couldn't skip Bob Hayden and face my reflection in a mirror with a sense of vindicated honor. He was the son of a widow who had recently come to Corinna to live, and for some reason he had disliked me on sight and thereafter made my life as miserable as he could.

My hatred for him was intensified because I could conceive of nothing done by me to make him my enemy. I wondered if he was another quick quitter and really hoped he was not.

He wasn't. He seemed to delight in a scrap and not know how to quit. We fought time after time until we were separated. We hammered each other black-and-blue and bleeding, and neither of us ever thought of fighting fairly. Anything went—any dirty trick we could think of, and once I even tried to kill him.

We were struggling on the ground when I got hold of a rock bigger than my fist and attempted to brain him with it. I really meant to crack his skull if I could. He jerked his head aside, and I missed with my first blow. He broke free before I could strike again, and we both scrambled to our feet.

The Worm Turns

I still had the rock, and I imagine there was a murderous look in my eyes. Anyhow he turned and started to run. I threw the rock at him. It hit him between the shoulders a little below the base of his neck and knocked him down. I leaped on him, and we were rolling in the dirt again when some men pulled us apart.

The next time we met we flew at each other again. There was no end to our feud in sight when, not in the slightest to my regret, Mrs. Hayden moved away from Corinna, taking her son with her. I professed to be sorry but I really felt like celebrating. I never saw Bob Hayden again.

Frank Nutter gave me a warning. "Don't get a swelled head, Will," he said. "You didn't lick Hayden and you can't lick the whole world. No matter how good a fellow is, some day he's bound to meet a better man."

I didn't really need it much, for I'd had enough of fighting. By nature I'm peaceful and unaggressive. It takes more than a little pushing around to make me belligerent, but when I find myself crowded into a corner, my blood pressure rises and I move out suddenly. I have a strong distaste for quarrelsome persons and am contemptuous of braggarts and bullies.

My boyhood experiences made me naturally sympathetic with the under dog, but time has taught me that the under dog frequently becomes more vicious and bloodthirsty than the other, if he gets on top.

Bob Hayden is the only person I ever tried—or wanted—to kill. I've ceased to hold grudges or harbor hatred, which poisons the soul. If I have enemies, I ignore them. I fear I've become a rather colorless individual.

Frank Nutter's warning was heeded. Realizing that he had disapproved of my cocky air, I tried to refrain from bumptiousness and play acting thereafter. And the following fall and winter days were far happier than any I had hitherto known.

For now I found myself on a different plane with my fellows, the girls as well as the boys. At last I really was on the inside with them. I belonged.

No more was I hailed by other boys with derisive cries of "Hey,

Willie, how's the weather up there?" or "Throw me down a chew of tobacco, Bull," or "Say, Spindle-shanks, when did you wind up the moon last?"

Now it was, "Come on, Bill, let's play ball," or "Let's go skating," or something I was only too glad to do. And the very girls who had been offish or disdainful now were friendly, some of them plainly making an effort to be agreeable.

When skating came there were joyous evenings on the ice of the village pond, usually with a bonfire to light up the scene and get warm by. The crisp, clear air was filled with shouts and laughter and the ringing sound of skate-irons.

Frequently boys and girls skated in pairs, side by side. Usually they held hands in such a manner that their arms were crossed in front of them, and they stroked in unison as they glided hither and thither through the weaving throng.

One evening Fannie Fisher, years older than I and strictly class in Corinna, asked me to skate with her. I never would have had the nerve to ask her. Afterwards, it was a trifle hard to keep from strutting just a little.

Presently heavy snowfalls buried the ice too deep for clearing and put an end to our skating. So when the roads were ploughed out and well trodden down, we took to sledding down the hill past my home and into the middle of the village. This was risky sport in the daytime, but on nights when the main street was practically free from teams and a bright moon rode in the sky, there was little danger of an accident.

The greatest thrills came from coasting that hill on a horse-sled loaded with boys and girls. The horse-sled was always guided by a strong older boy, lying "bellybunt" on a handsled between the thills of the horse-sled, to which he held fast with both hands. A slight thaw followed by sharp weather made the course fast, and we would be speeding like an express train when the bottom of the hill was reached.

For the first time, I was invited that winter to many parties given by boys and girls in their homes. It was customary for a visiting boy to bring a girl with him, but the only girl I would have enjoyed escorting was Addie Hutchings.

That being out of the question, I arrived alone until it became embarrassing to appear that way. Finally I braced up and invited Jeanie Hamilton to accompany me. She was a big girl, red-cheeked and handsome in a way, but not at all my type. I liked them small and cuddly.

As there were not enough chairs for everybody that evening, Jeanie sat on my lap. She was in the heavyweight class and seemed to get heavier rapidly. Some of the other fellows were holding girls on their laps and plainly enjoying it, but my spindly legs were not built for the load they were carrying. They began to ache and grow numb.

I gritted my teeth and tried to hold out until the party got under way, but lacked the staying power. When I couldn't take it any longer, I tried to make a joke by suggesting that she take my chair and let me stand up a while—if I could stand.

Everybody laughed, but Jeanie turned still redder. For the rest of the evening she didn't know I was on earth. It was easy for me to put my foot in my mouth when I tried to be funny.

Later we played such games as Who's Got the Button?, Spin the Cover, The Needle's Eye, and Post Office. To play The Needle's Eye, we held hands and formed a circle around the room.

Then we walked slowly beneath the clasped hands of a boy and girl who stood on chairs, one outside the line and one inside. As the human circle moved along, everybody sang:

> *The needle's eye it doth comply,*
> *It carries the thread so true,*
> *It hath caught many a smiling lass,*
> *And now, alas, it hath caught you.*

The boy and girl on the chairs took turns in selecting somebody about whose neck they would lower their hands, and there was merriment and kidding when the one chosen tried to avoid being captured.

When the capture was made, the line ceased to move, but the singing continued until a climax was reached at which the couple on the chairs kissed above the head of the captive, who then took the place of the one whose turn it was to descend and rejoin the line.

Of the girls present Addie Hutchings was the one most frequently caught by the Needle's Eye. Practically every fellow in the room seemed to have his eye on her, and she clearly reveled in her popularity.

Some of the girls failed to hide their jealousy, and one boy was miffed; for not once did she try to catch *me* when it came her turn to make a choice.

Also I observed with resentment that Bert Day was her favorite. He would be, the big skate! Well, I would show her that she didn't cut much ice with me! I let her trot right along by when I got a chance to make a selection.

We played Post Office after that and I was surprised when the postmistress announced, "There's a letter for Mr. William Patten."

Mr. William Patten, not Willie! And I knew Addie Hutchings was in the room that represented the Post Office. There was a general titter of laughter, and I felt my face burn as I stood up.

The shaded kerosene lamp in the Post Office was turned down just enough to make even a homely girl look attractive in the dimmed light, but Addie needed no such device.

When the door closed behind me I stopped and looked at Addie, who was waiting for me in the middle of the room. She laughed softly. Her chin always took on a bewitching little twist when she laughed.

"Come and get your letter, William," she said.

Now I would show her where she got off. I said: "Addie, you're a flirt. I don't want any letter from you."

She came to me swiftly. "Don't be a silly," she said.

She put her arms around my neck and kissed me.
Long ago! Long ago! Boys and girls together.

---

10 · BAD BUSINESS

MY GREATEST ANNOYANCE that winter was caused by the efforts of certain Adventist visitors in our home to convert me. I was now successfully dodging mid-week prayer meetings and attending church no more than once on Sunday, and those zealous devotees plainly felt it their duty to bring me into the fold before I was lost beyond redemption.

"Brother" Bragg was the greatest nuisance of them all. I never knew, or have forgotten, his given name, and I have no recollection of a "Sister" Bragg. He came often to our house, where now, my father having found unusually steady employment during the past summer, our table was well supplied with creature comforts.

He was fat, greasy, and lazy, and he could eat more and pray longer and louder than any white man I've ever known. Apparently he thought my parents very remiss concerning my spiritual welfare. He never failed to corner me and ask me the same question:

"Now, Willie," he would say, "have you been washed in the blood of the Lamb?"

It sickened me. It make me think of a cosset lamb of mine that had mysteriously disappeared. I was a little shaver at the time and, greatly distressed, I had searched everywhere for my lost lamb and cried myself to sleep nights because I couldn't find it. One day my searching took me as far away as the lane on the hill that ran from our street to the Southfield road.

There the door of a building sometimes used for slaughtering purposes stood open, and I stopped to peer inside.

I saw two men in long bloodstained whitish coats calmly watching the dying struggles of some lambs that were held down by a framework about their necks. Streams of blood were gushing from the slit throats of the poor creatures, and suddenly I knew what had happened to my pet lamb.

Horrified and choking, I fled, and, no matter how hungry I might be, many years passed before the odor of cooked lamb meat did not nauseate me.

At last, having endured Brother Bragg's unwelcome solicitude to the limit, I revolted when he pestered me again with the same hateful question.

"No," I answered, "I haven't been washed in blood. I use soap and water. And I wish you'd mind your own business and let me alone."

It was crude and insolent, but I couldn't help it. It set him back on his heels, and I made my escape before he could get his breath again.

My father hauled me over the coals for my sauciness, but softened a little when I explained why I had been unable to take it from Brother Bragg any longer.

I think my parents had begun to perceive the bad effect of trying to force piety upon me and were not exactly pleased by the attempts of others to convert me. And now, for fear of being misunderstood, I wish to say that I've never been an atheist; I've always believed in a Creative Force which men call God.

Father loved a fast horse and kept one, usually, that would run away at the slightest provocation—or none at all. I rode many of them bareback and have never yet sat in a saddle. I was thrown off several times, and one of his spirited nags kicked me on the head and left me senseless on the ground—left also a dent in my skull above my left ear that I still can find with my fingers. Some persons have wondered what ails me, and maybe that is the answer.

I sometimes drove those horses harnessed to our old buggy. One of them, named Whitie, gave me and two of my friends a fast ride one day late in June, following my first gay winter.

Bad Business

The first circus of the season was billed for Buxton, and I wanted to see the "grand parade." I invited two fellows to go with me, and we jogged into Buxton somewhat late, behind that cantankerous horse, as the parade was making its way along the hilly main street of the town. The sidewalks were packed with spectators, all togged out in their Sunday duds.

On an open vehicle at the head of the procession the circus band, garbed in beautiful bright red uniforms, were blasting away. The air shuddered with the electrifying sounds of horns, the wailing of reed instruments, the booming of a big bass drum, and the clashing of cymbals.

Suddenly Whitie began to throw fits. He yearned to turn right round and go back toward Corinna. I fought him so hard that he rose up on his hind legs and tried to sit down in my lap. Then I gave him the whip—plenty.

Directly after that, we became a side attraction for the parade. Really, for we were on our way down the hill that the parade was climbing. I can't imagine how the buggy kept right side up when we turned a corner to get on to that street, nor how we missed the lion's cage for which we were headed.

Men shouted. Women and children screamed. I hung on to the reins, with every lunge of the galloping horse threatening to jerk my head off. I was having the time of my life, but I wasn't laughing any.

One man started out from the sidewalk, like a hero, with the apparent intention of trying to stop the horse, but he changed his mind and dodged back again. One of my companions started to jump out, but the other one held him, probably keeping him from breaking his bones or being killed.

We had entered Buxton by the main-traveled road from Corinna, but presently we left the village by a back road and were on our way home again. I hadn't seen more than a superficial glimpse of the parade, but that was quite enough under the circumstances. Anyhow, had I wished to I could not have stopped Whitie and turned him back. So I let him run, and I think we set a record to date for a fast trip between the two villages.

When I arrived back home, after dropping my two friends, Father's willful steed was in a fine lather and still nervous. Having checked him at the entrance to our barn, I jumped out to open the swinging doors.

Before I could get back into the buggy, Whitie stood up on his hind legs once more and lunged ahead. Starting to swing to again, one of the doors hit the hub of a rear wheel. There was a crash. A piece flew off the door and the rear axle of the old buggy was sprung a little.

I was looking the damage over when Father arrived, in his shirtsleeves. When he saw what had happened his face hardened, and his religion didn't prevent him from becoming very angry. Closing the barn doors, he took the whip out of the buggy socket.

"Take off your jacket," said he.

Now I do not think I'd ever uttered a real cuss-word up to that moment, but something flamed in me then and I swore like a pirate.

"If you hit me with that whip," I told him with embellishments, "I'll kill you!"

I knew I didn't really mean it, but I didn't mean to take a horsewhipping if I could stop him.

Mother came on the run. She was white as a ghost.

"Don't you strike that boy, William!" she cried.

Father looked at her in silence for a few moments before he turned and put the whip back into its socket in the buggy. He never lifted his hand to me again.

I was tired of empty pockets. I wanted money to jingle in them; money to buy things with—cheroots, fishing tackle, a new knife, peanuts, candy, spruce gum to chew, money to spend on treats for the girls, too. Other fellows had it and I decided to get it. I found a job at haying time for thirty-five cents a day.

The work wasn't hard, mainly raking up scatterings behind the hayrack, treading down hay in the mows and doing any odd job I was asked to do; but the hours, from crack o'day until dark, were long.

The smell of new-mown hay was delightful, and I loved the

taste of ginger beer kept cool in a jug tucked under a haycock in the field. And the work made me bear-hungry at mealtime. I ate with the hired men and stowed away my share of the food.

At night I was too tired to do any reading in bed. Though naturally a light sleeper, I became dead to the world when my head hit the pillow, and it was torture to crawl out of the sheets before daylight in the morning.

Haying over, I wondered what I could do next to bring in the dough. Then I saw an advertisement of a Magic Key Ring that retailed for a dime. I spent almost my last penny to buy a flock of those key rings at wholesale. They came in time for me to take them to Buxton on the day when another circus would exhibit there.

On business bent, I didn't mind being too late to see the parade that day. Arriving at the circus grounds with a bag containing my merchandise, I looked around for a place to pursue the plan I had formed in my mind. I found an empty box and took possession of the rear-garden plot of a house quite near the show tents. Apparently the owner of the land was away, for I was not ordered off for trespassing.

I had strung about half of my lot of nickle-plated key rings together in a chain, and now I looped the chain around my neck like a dangling necklace, following which I mounted the box.

The rest of the key rings were in the open bag, which was suspended from my shoulder by a leather strap. Lifting up my voice, I began a spiel that I had rehearsed in advance.

"Come hither, ladies and gents," I shouted. "Come hither and behold the latest marvelous invention of the day, the wonderful little Magic Key Ring, onto which you may easily slip your precious keys but from which no person unacquainted with the secret method can remove them.

"Here before your wondering eyes I will give a demonstration more surprising than anything you will see in the side shows of this circus. I will show you how you, with perfect ease and deftness, can manipulate this invaluable Magic Key Ring, which may be purchased from me—and from me only—at the ridiculously low price of ten cents each.

"Come hither. Come hither and gather before me, as I am about to perform the trick that will astound you. Come hither, everybody. Come hither. Come hither."

I thought it was pretty clever, and it was clever enough to work. Men, women, and children, they deserted the yapping sideshow barkers and swarmed over my way.

They were ready to bite, and I proceeded to bait my hook. I did the trick quickly in full view of them, snapping a key on and off a ring. Then, urging them to watch me closely, I did it very slowly.

After that I let several of them try it, and not one could do it. Then I began to sell the rings from my bag, each with printed directions for operating it. Had I remained unmolested, I think I would have sold out my stock in short order.

But I was molested very soon. I had been too busy to notice them coming, but suddenly five or six hard-looking coatless men in laboring clothes were pushing through the crowd. They were, I saw at a glance, quite angry. A big gorilla with huge and hairy bare arms shook his fist at me and bellowed, "Shut up and get out of here on the jump or we'll take you to pieces! Get going, you bum!"

Well, having looked those ruffians over, I concluded that my health required that I should get going. I didn't dally about it, either.

That was the beginning and end of my career as salesman for the wonderful Magic Key Ring. There were persons from Corinna in the crowd, and my native town was chuckling over the story within twenty-four hours. I was mortified. I was so ashamed that I felt like committing suicide, and I kept under cover at home for quite a while after that.

I don't know what became of the key rings left on my hands, but it is a sure bet I never tried to sell any of them around Corinna.

Psychologically that humiliating experience did something to me. As a salesman, I was ruined. To this day I have a dread of attempting to sell anything whatever. Neither can I bargain in making a purchase, even though I know I'm being played for a sucker. When the purchasing price is named, I either take the commodity at that price or leave it.

---

11 · I LEARN A LESSON

THE ADVENTISTS HELD THEIR ANNUAL CAMP MEETINGS in a pleasant grove near Harmel Village, some eighteen miles from Corinna. My father's commodious tent was covered by a "fly" that kept it dry in rainy weather, while a small "air-tight" stove made it warm and cozy when the weather was cold.

One of my pleasant memories is of waking up in my comfortable bed in that tent on a cool dawn and listening to the sounds of persons already astir—the murmur of voices, the sharp *chock* of a woodcutter's ax, the distant intonations of supplicants at morning prayer, the soft clatter of dishes as my mother prepared breakfast, the sizzling of frying ham or bacon. And the aroma of brewing coffee was—indescribable.

Nearly all the campers occupied tents pitched in a hollow square, the center of which was occupied by a huge tent beneath which the services were held. Although I had become a skeptic, I enjoyed the congregational singing and often took part in it. But my parents had ceased to demand my regular attendance, though Mother occasionally chided me for absenting myself.

The campers, like all Adventists in those days, were poor people, though I remember none who were absolutely poverty-stricken. Like my parents, they could see no object in accumulating worldly goods in a world that was soon to come to an end.

A few of them were rather illiterate, but I remember none who appeared more ignorant than the average run of country persons in those days. And in spite of the aspersions cast upon them and gossip of irregularity at their camp meetings, I never saw anything of an immoral or objectionable nature at those gatherings. There were occasional emotional outbursts during services, but nothing resembling the wild frenzies of the Holy Rollers.

There was one preacher, Elder Aaron Brown, to whom I loved to listen. He was a well-dressed, grey-bearded man and apparently a person of no small intelligence and more than average education. But what interested me most was his habit of breaking into tumultuous laughter in the midst of expounding a serious sermon. However, while this idiosyncrasy was comical, I doubt if he was a humorous person; for it often happens that one who laughs a great deal is wholly devoid of humor.

Nevertheless, Elder Brown's abrupt transitions from seriousness to shouting laughter never failed to convulse me with merriment, and my attempts to imitate him, far from offending her, led my mother to believe that she would not be disappointed in her hope that I, myself, would become a minister of the Gospel.

The feature that made those camp meetings most attractive and pleasant for me was the presence of a considerable number of boys and girls—sons and daughters of the campers—of relatively my own age. Having begun to take special interest in girls, and having learned to dance more or less well, I was edging into romanticism and adolescent dreams of love.

One cute and apparently shy little blonde girl was especially attractive to me until I made the shocking discovery that her seeming shyness came from the fact that she was a deaf mute—the first one I had ever seen. And I was actually repulsed and horrified when, with startling abruptness, all her apparent shyness vanished and she made amorous overtures to me, actually attempting to kiss me. Thereafter I avoided her as if she were an infectious disease.

But there was another girl, Carrie Lomer, slim and gay but not very pretty, to whom I became quite attentive. Meanwhile a village boy, Horace Harmon, picked up an acquaintance with me and invited me to a Saturday night dance in the village.

"I've got a pretty sister, Will," said he, "that I think you'll like. Her name's Bessie, and she's the best looker and the best

I Learn a Lesson

dancer around here, but she don't like any of the town boys much, and you'll make a hit with her. Don't fail to come to the dance."

I promised to be Johnny-on-the-spot, but, unfortunately, I told Carrie Lomer about it and she promptly made me promise to take her to the dance. I tried to switch her off onto Clarence Draper, but succeeded only in adding him as an additional escort for Carrie.

Well, Bessie Harmon was all her brother had represented her to be—in appearance, anyhow. I was smitten *hard* the moment Horace introduced me to her. Here, I thought, was the girl of my dreams. And she could dance! Also she seemed to like me plenty. But Carrie Lomer didn't take it well; in fact, she refused to take it at all.

"You brought me here, Willie," she said, "and you're going to stick to me and take me back. I don't want any of these other fellows, 'specially Clarence Draper. I'm going to dance every dance with you after this."

I couldn't shake her quickly; three times in succession I was compelled to dance with her. And when I did break away rather rudely and hurry to Bessie, I wasn't received at all pleasantly. She regarded me with scorn.

"Go on and dance with your pasty-faced friend," she said, "and don't bother me again."

That was the end of my romance with Bessie Harmon. She turned to Clarence Draper, and he escorted her home when the dance broke up at twelve o'clock, while I walked sourly back to the campground with Carrie Lomer.

And the very next day there was a revival meeting at which Carrie became converted, after which she wouldn't play any more.

This was, probably, my briefest romance. I thought it had taught me something about "women," but I had much more to learn.

I never saw Bessie Harmon again, but I didn't miss her so much when Addie Hutchings became our camp meeting guest next year. I'm afraid that, for a day or two, I entertained disloyal thoughts for my friend Frank Nutter; and then George Elder appeared, and Addie abruptly lost interest in me, much to my dismay and wrath.

But Frank Nutter showed up the following day and caught George and Addie together. There was a scene, and I hoped that Frank would give George a black eye or two—and was disappointed when nothing of the kind happened.

I was still learning about "women."

Meanwhile I had been admitted to Corinna Union Academy as a student. I think the Academy principal, Augustus Norton—familiarly called "Gus" by many persons—winked at my poor standing in a few studies and took me in because of my aptness in others. Be that as it may, having been accepted I began to plug to keep up with my classmates. For the first time, I really did some homework.

Augustus Norton was a spectacular character. A huge man and decidedly paunchy, he was as strong as a moose, as light on his feet as a dancing master, and more than ordinarily clever with his "dukes."

He kept a set of boxing gloves in the chemical laboratory and sometimes put them on with fellows like Frank Nutter and Bert Day. Just for exercise, he said, but I think it was more to show who was running the school.

Before going to sleep nights, I still read dime novels in bed. I had found a dashing and handsome young hero who fascinated me and finally led me to attempt the writing, piecemeal, of a long western story that was to come to hand again nearly four years later and be rewritten and published.

The hero who aroused me to this activity was Deadwood Dick, a character of the Robin Hood type, who dressed in black, wore a black mask and rode a coal-black horse at the head of a band of dare-devil followers. And the locale was the Black Hills of Dakota.

I had no admiration for such common ruffians as Jesse James and the Dalton brothers and would not read fiction yarns about them, but Deadwood Dick was different. Though branded as an

I Learn a Lesson

outlaw, and with a price on his head if captured dead or alive, he was really a gallant and honorable youth, a defender of the wronged, and an ally of justice. His sweetheart was Calamity Jane, a brave and beautiful two-gun girl who wore men's clothes and could shoot like Annie Oakley.

At that time, I had not the slightest suspicion that a living Calamity Jane existed. But in later years I learned that there had been a woman so-called, a tough old harridan who not only wore men's clothes but chewed tobacco and swore like a trooper.

There also have been men who claimed to be the original Deadwood Dick. Maybe there was such a person, but I doubt if he bore much resemblance to the hero of Edward L. Wheeler's dime-novel yarns.

Before my discovery of this magnetic hero the publishers had abandoned the original format of the dime novel and changed the name by which they were designated.

Thereafter they were printed on larger sheets and called Dime and Half-dime Libraries. The Dimes contained stories relatively 75,000 words in length and the Half-dimes were somewhat less than half as long. Calling them Libraries was probably an attempt to escape from the dime-novel stigma, but the former name stuck.

Meanwhile there had been, and there continued to be, changes in our town. The quiet village was blossoming out and becoming a busy little place. The deserted mill in the middle of the village was gone and a new mill, handling lumber and building material, had been built there.

Further down the stream, Thomas Wood had constructed a dam and built a woolen factory. Elam Durrill's gristmill had fallen into desuetude, and a large brick building, containing stores, offices, and a hall for dances and shows, had been erected. Corinna had become a minor shipping point for potatoes, apples, and other farm products.

We had a baseball team of which we were very proud. The players wore uniforms, and the pitcher, who actually could throw a ball that curved, was paid ten dollars a game. The team had cleaned up all the other clubs in neighboring towns and issued a challenge to Bangor—which was never accepted.

Also we had a band that claimed to be "the best little dam' band in the state." On summer evenings it gave occasional outdoor concerts on the lot where the Stevens Memorial Building was erected later. Hatch Stevens, the hardware man, was the leader, and he sure could make his shiny cornet sing sweet and pretty.

My father suffered a serious injury early in December when I was fifteen years old. There had been no heavy snowfalls that year to bury the ice, and everybody who skated improved the opportunity nearly every evening. One night we built a big bonfire on the Wood pond and a throng of older persons came down to watch the sport.

Father had given me a new pair of skates that clamped to the heels and soles of my boots, but I really didn't like them as well as my old ones with heel-screws and straps that rendered support to my ankles. I used them that night until I reluctantly quit to go home and do some studying. Father appeared and asked me to let him have my skates.

"If I had my old creased runners," he said, "I'd get out there and show these youngsters up."

He was clamping my skates onto his boots when I left him. Mother was annoyed when I got home and told her about it.

"The idea of him skating with children at his age!" she said. "It would serve him right if he fell down and bumped his crown."

Perhaps thirty minutes later, as I was working on my lessons and Mother was knitting beside the kitchen table, the door opened very quietly and slowly and Father's head slowly appeared. Never before had I seen such a silly grin on his face.

"Now what's happened, William?" Mother cried.

He came in, bringing my skates and limping painfully, "I'm used to creased skates," said he defensively. "These new-fangled smooth runners wouldn't stay under me and I bumped my hip. It won't amount to nothing though."

I Learn a Lesson

It amounted to a great deal. He was laid up several days but persisted in doctoring his injured hip himself with some kind of liniment. And although he recovered enough to follow his trade for many years thereafter, he always walked with a limp, and sometimes his damaged hip ached steadily for days. Had he not stubbornly refused to be treated by a competent doctor immediately after his fall, he might have avoided so much inconvenience and suffering.

Some time in the following months Frank Nutter went away to Biddeford, where he obtained a job in the shops of the Pepperell Machine Company. And with his going the bottom dropped out of our town for me.

It didn't make much difference when Charlie Lewis, who had been working in the Wood mill, followed him and found employment in the same shops; for me the old town had become a lemon, anyhow. As I looked at it, a young fellow ambitious to get on in the world didn't have a show in Corinna. Well, my time would come!

The ensuing summer was long and uneventful for me. With my father I worked in haying time for Stephen Durrell, an uncle by marriage, but found few other jobs at which I could earn money. I fished and swam and played baseball occasionally on our second team. Herbert Fisher was one of our pitchers. I don't recall that he could throw a curve, but he had speed that bothered batters.

He was pitching and I was catching barehanded, close under the bat in a practice game, when a foul tip busted the index finger on my left hand and put me on the shelf for some time. That finger is still slightly deformed.

Winter came again, and another birthday anniversary was behind me. Father was buying hoop-poles and making barrel hoops in his small shop on our home lot, and I was getting along all right at the Academy, when old Whitie upset the apple-cart—literally the sleigh to which he was harnessed.

Father was alone in the sleigh when that temperamental horse started to run away, but he was thrown out on an icy spot in the road and the ankle of his lame leg was sprained. The horse cleared himself from the overturned sleigh and went galloping triumphantly away. A neighbor brought Father home, where Whitie had arrived ahead of him, much to my mother's consternation.

Father was unable to walk without crutches or a stout cane until the snow went off late in April. When he realized how badly he was injured he foresaw himself in a hole with the thousands of hoop-poles he had bought. What to do was the question. I heard him talking the dilemma over with Mother.

"I'll stay out of school and make those hoops for you, Dad," I said.

He stared at me, a mild grin creeping over his troubled face. "Why, Willie," he said, "you don't know how to shave hoops, and you just can't do it anyhow."

"Can't I?" I cried resentfully. "Well, I'll show you I can."

Mother objected. She said I wasn't strong enough. She said I was trying to get out of going to school. That got under my skin.

"Don't argue," I said. "I'm going to give notice today that I've got to leave school, and I'm beginning on that job tomorrow."

Bright and early the next morning I went to work alone, in Father's little shop, and I did not see the inside of a schoolroom until the middle of the following May.

My hands were blistered and raw and my back ached at the end of the first day. Mother doctored my hands and rubbed my back with liniment that made my skin burn. I turned a deaf ear to her efforts to dissuade me from my resolve. I was building will-power then but didn't know it.

The following day was even harder. I had to work with bandaged hands, which made me blundering and slow. I spoiled many hoops while shaving them, but stuck to it doggedly until supper time. That night, though sore and lame, I slept well enough to go at it again.

Gradually my blisters healed and became calluses, and gradually my back ceased to ache and the soreness left my muscles. Those muscles hardened somewhat, though I've never been able to build powerful muscles like my father's. Day by day I became more skillful in splitting the poles and shaving the hoops.

Sometimes Father came out to the shop on crutches to give me instructions and encouragement. Out of the softness of his heart, he told me to throw out all the crooked poles he had bought, and I threw out the worst ones. I could see that he looked at me with a new light in his eyes; respect and pride were there.

It was a hard and dreary pull, but I made the grade. And at one time I had been called the laziest boy in Corinna. Maybe I am naturally slothful, but never since that winter have I failed to work hard and steadily at any task necessary to perform. Willpower and character are more often built than inherited.

I have a few scars to remember that winter by—whitish marks, now grown faint, on my left hand where the adz cut me when it slipped out of the pole I was beginning to split. Also I have a left shoulder slightly lower than the other, caused by carrying the heavy bundles of hoops out of the shop on that shoulder. But I learned a valuable lesson in those lonely, laborious months.

The summer that followed brought with it another event. I ran away from home.

---

12 · THE WORLD IS MINE

LATE IN JULY the railroad ran a Sunday excursion to Lake Maranacook, and I was one of the excursionists. As the train pulled out of Corinna I took a good look at what I could see of the village, which I didn't expect to see again for years. Having made my plans hastily, I had been obliged to leave behind many things I would have taken had it been possible to do so without arousing the suspicion of my parents.

All I carried were an extra shirt, worn underneath my best one, and what possessions I could stuff into the pockets of the tailor-made suit—my first—which Father had paid for as a reward for my winter of labor in his shop. However, after paying for my excursion ticket, I still had a little over four dollars, money earned by working in haying time at one dollar a day, and I felt wealthy enough to face the world and win.

I had told nobody of my intention not to return on that excursion train. Deceiving my parents cost me a qualm, but I pictured their pride when I should return in the course of time, prosperous and perhaps famous. My accomplishment of the past winter had made me a great optimist.

Will Steward was taking in the excursion, and we sat together. I really can't remember much about the trip to Lake Maranacook or the hours we spent there in the midst of a throng of people. Maybe my eagerness to be on my way again prevented what would otherwise have been a great novelty from making a lasting impression. But I do remember quite clearly Will Steward's surprise when I told him I was not going back home on the returning train.

"And I'm not going back to Corinna for years," I declared. "I'm going to take a train that will get me into Biddeford. Nutter and Lewis are there, and maybe I can get a job in the machine shop where they work. Anyhow, I'll get one somewhere."

Then I urged him to go along to Biddeford with me. He could return to Corinna on Monday if he wanted to, I said. And I finally persuaded him to go, though he woefully said his father would be hopping mad.

I found out which train to take, and we were quite surprised when the conductor looked at our tickets and told us we were going the wrong way.

"You'll have to get off at the next stop," said he, and he was also surprised when he came through the car later and found us still there.

He threatened to put us off. I discussed the matter with him persuasively. I said we were practically broke but had friends in Biddeford who would loan us money to pay our fares back to Corinna. He called us a couple of young numbskulls and let us go on.

We got off at Biddeford late in the afternoon and found our way to Frank Nutter's boarding house, the address of which was known to me. Mrs. Watson, the landlady, informed us that Frank had gone over to Old Orchard Beach with some of his friends and wouldn't get back until late in the evening. Then she shut the door in our faces. Thereupon we held a consultation and decided to go over to Old Orchard ourselves, if we could get there. We were lucky in finding a train that would take us there, and hopped it.

Will Steward was beginning to worry, but I was confident we would have no trouble in picking up Nutter. Even when we reached Old Orchard in the early evening and beheld the place swarming with people, many of them excursionists, I was not much disturbed.

But after we had searched through the moving throngs for an hour or more without any luck, I began to lose some of my assurance. We were tired and hungry, and Will was blaming me for getting him into such a pickle. Then something hit me between the shoulders and almost knocked me down.

It was the good right hand of Frank Nutter. He had seen us, and there he was with Charlie Lewis and a sandy-haired chap by the name of Frank Durgin. He was grinning broadly. I felt like hugging him but shook hands with the sang froid of a man who knew his way around. They were all amused when I stated how come I was there.

"So you've run away, have you, Will?" said Frank Nutter. "Well, your old man will be coming after you with a hickory stick. He'll march you back to Corinna on the double-quick."

"If he does," said I positively, "I'll hit the high spots in getting away again. I don't propose to be found dead in that town."

I afterwards learned that my mother had begged Father to follow me and bring me home. His reply was, "That boy has made his bed, now let him lay in it till he's good and tired." It was the proper treatment for me.

Will Steward had been letting me do the talking, but now he ventured to say that he was about to perish of hunger, whereupon Frank Nutter led us into an open-face eating house where State of Maine clam chowder was a specialty. Since that evening no other kind of clam chowder has ever been for me other than a wretched imitation of the real thing. We finished on coffee and doughnuts and apple pie, with Nutter standing treat and cheering us on.

After that, every man of us—excepting Will Steward—smoking an expensive five-cent cigar, we rambled around, taking in the sights. I had never seen so many handsomely dressed people before, nor such a lot of fair maidens with come-hither in their eyes. It was very distracting but I carried myself with an insouciant air. There were shooting galleries and many amusement booths, all doing a rushing business. Everybody was spending money as if it grew on trees.

We went out onto one of the big piers and looked into a room, amazingly spacious to my eyes, where hundreds of couples were dancing to orchestra music such as I had never before heard. This was not much like the dances in the little hall of Dan Knowles, in Corinna, where I had learned to step around a bit with corn-fed country lassies. Corinna! I thought of life back there with growing distaste. No more of that for me.

Presently we went back to the beach and stretched ourselves on the clean sand, lighting up fresh cigars. The music from the big pier we had left came faintly to our ears mingled with the rushing swish and boom of white breakers rolling in from the open Atlantic Ocean. A lovely moon was riding in a cloudless sky, and the warm air held a saltish pungency new to my nostrils. Keenly alert, my senses missed nothing unfamiliar.

Many other persons were sitting or lying on the sand around us, and some couples were spooning right before my wondering eyes. Never before had I beheld such open petting, and I was both shocked and delighted. A few laughing and shouting young people were indulging a moonlight dip in the foaming breakers. This was the life for me!

An Italian violin player came along with a slender dark-haired girl, perhaps his daughter. The weird music that he drew from his violin sent chills and thrills creeping through my body. And when the dark girl sang an Italian song, with the man playing the melody, I was enraptured. My eyes became misty.

I have been called a sentimentalist. Without shame, I admit that I am sentimental.

We went back to Biddeford on the last train that would take us there, and Charlie Lewis took Will Steward in with him for the night. I shared Frank Nutter's room in his boarding house and we talked into the wee sma' hours. He sought to persuade me to go back home with Will Steward but I know he was secretly pleased by my unfaltering determination not to do so. I told him of recent happenings in Corinna and was wise, for once, in refraining from speaking of Addie Hutchings. I asked him to find me a job in the machine shops. He did not promise, nor did he refuse to make the attempt. At last we slept, and I have a vague remembrance of dreaming happy dreams.

When Will Steward went back to Corinna the next day, I sent a message to my parents by him. I asked him to tell them that I was all right and was sure of getting a job in the shops where Frank Nutter worked. Knowing I was with him, I felt, would lessen their worriment about me and maybe cause my father to abstain from coming after me.

"Well, I'll bet you'll be coming home, anyhow, within a week or two," said Will.

"If you make that kind of a bet you'll lose your money," I replied.

I saw him off at the station and spent the rest of the day looking Biddeford over. It was then a booming manufacturing town, with the Pepperell Machine Shops and the Pepperell Cotton Mills giving employment to a host of laborers. The city teemed with activity. It was, I thought, just the place for me. On the following day Frank Nutter brought me word that I was to report in person for work in the machine shops. I did so and was employed at ninety cents a day.

The world beyond the Blue Hills was mine at last!

---

13 · FORGING AHEAD

MY WORK WAS TO STRAIGHTEN CRUDE round bars of metal which were to be tool-finished for certain parts of cotton mill machinery. Using hammers adapted to the task, I pounded the crooked places out of those rough bars on a grooved anvil. Little skill but quite a lot of muscular effort was required. And the hours, from six o'clock in the morning until six at night, with a mid-day intermission of an hour, but no Saturday holidays or half-holidays, were nothing to write home about. Just try that on your anvil, Mr. Modern Workman, and see how you like it.

I don't believe I would have lasted a great while at that job if my work in Father's shop and the haying fields had not toughened me considerably. It was a great relief when I got a breathing spell on my first Sunday in Biddeford.

Mrs. Watson's house was one of fifteen conjoined boarding houses in a long, low row of brick buildings near a gate to the yards of the machine shops and directly across the street from the Pepperell Cotton Mills. The women who ran those houses obtained leases at reduced rates under an agreement to cater only to female employees of the Pepperell Mills. But a few laborers in the machine shops had obtained accommodation here and there along the row by paying slightly more than the fixed standard for the mill workers.

Frank Nutter persuaded Mrs. Watson to take me in as his roommate. Only one other man, a crabbed old bach, was living there with some twenty-odd mill girls, practically all of the latter being raucous-tongued and as coarse as gravel. I never had been in close contact with such human females before, and I saw as little of that lot as I could under the circumstances.

I paid three dollars a week for room and board, which was enough in those days, considering the small bare room and the limited tablefare. It left me two dollars and forty cents of my weekly earnings for all other expenses, which I was to find a trifle cramping. Temporarily Nutter loaned me underwear and a few other things I needed. I used his razor to scrape the fuzz off my face and make me feel like a regular he-man. To increase that feeling, and also because I could not then afford cigars, I took up pipe smoking.

As he would anywhere, Frank had made friends in Biddeford, and we got together with them frequently in leisure hours. Before shaking the dust of Corinna from his boots, he had become a "dabster" with a banjo, and he sang rather well—well enough to liven up any party. I remember only one stanza of one of his favorite songs:

> *Now there's Henry Ward Beecher, our Sunday school Teacher,*
>   *Drinks what they call Sassafras Root,*
> *But you bet, all the same, if it had it's right name,*
>   *It's the juice of the forbidden fruit.*

Then there was the chorus of "The Spanish Cavalier" on which everybody usually came in and bore down:

> *The Spanish cavalier stood in his retreat*
>   *And on his guitar played a tune, dear.*
> *The music so sweet he oft would repeat,*
>   *The blessings of my country and you, dear.*

We were young, and eleven hours of work six days a week couldn't take the starch out of us. I never heard one of those fellows whine about it, and none could be a slacker and hold his job.

The hard times following our Civil War had faded into the past and the country was on the up-grade again. The West was being opened up and a nation-wide boom was on. We read about it in the newspapers, which of course did not paint the whole picture of the land-grabbers and robber barons and the shameful treatment of the American Indian.

Optimism and assurance of a glorious free nation, where every man could get ahead according to his merits, were in the air. Starry-eyed youths of the U.S.A. were proud and patriotic, ready if needs be to fight and die for their country. I am confident there was not one of Nutter's set in Biddeford who did not feel that way.

Andrews was, I believe, the name of the supervisor under whom I worked. He was a harsh-voiced, lumpish man, cold-eyed and suspicious. His desk stood on a raised platform from which he could watch every laborer in his department.

I worked near-by, and never did I by any chance glance in his direction that his eyes did not seem to be fixed upon me, with the exception of those times when he walked around, inspecting and criticising but never expressing approval of any man's work. I soon became proficient and swift at my job but received call-downs from Andrews, like the others. He was a slave-driver.

The employees in that department were poorly paid and had no chance whatever of becoming skilled machinists if they remained there. When I found that out, as I did before long, my spirits took a tumble.

Frank Nutter and I were smoking our pipes on the high front steps of our boarding house one pleasant evening and watching the mill girls strolling up and down the block, when I heard one of the girls laugh. It was a gay, high-pitched infectious burst of merriment that struck a responsive chord within me.

"Did you hear that girl laugh then, Frank?" I asked.

"Yep," said he. "That was Annie Donlon. She's just a chicken, but Lewis has his eye on her. Here she comes with her roommate. Want to meet her?"

I did. She was fifteen years old, Irish, petite, saucy, high-spirited, and she had a mouth full of nice teeth. Her roommate was a French-Canadian girl called "Mosile" by her friends, and she could talk a blue streak. In fact both girls could talk too fast for me; their kidding had me backed against the ropes before I

Forging Ahead

could get set for the round. Nutter held up his end all right, but I couldn't get going at all, and I was much relieved when they bade us ta-ta and rambled on.

"What's the matter, Will?" Frank asked. "You didn't seem to take to them much."

"Annie isn't bad," I allowed, "But the other one's too flip."

He laughed. "You can't be choosy around here," he said. "You won't find many ladies among these mill girls."

Imagine my surprise a few days later when he told me I had made a hit with Annie.

"She asked me how my bashful friend was," said he. "She said she liked you because you didn't get fresh and talk the way other fellows do. I wouldn't be surprised if you could get ahead of Lewis with her if you braced up and played your cards right."

That was enough to put me on my mettle. I wasn't so dumb when my next opportunity came, and Annie became my girl—in a way—though Charlie Lewis gave me quite a bit of annoyance by trying to steal her off me. She amused me with her high spirits and Irish wit, but I was always conscious that she belonged in a social strata of which I was determined to steer clear.

Even in the days when my own physical incapacity and my father's admonitions against fighting had given me a sense of inferiority, I had entertained a secret belief that I was destined to rise above those schoolmates and companions who looked down on me. Maybe that was childish conceit, but a human being wholly lacking conceit, which is sometimes called self-esteem, has less than one chance in a million to make his mark in the world.

The summer slipped away. Autumn came and I was still straightening untooled metal bars, but I had made up my mind to get a better job somehow. I was barely keeping my head above water on ninety cents a day. In fact I was so completely busted when Buffalo Bill came to town in a drama called *The League of Three*, written by Colonel Prentiss Ingraham, that I couldn't dig up the price of admission.

In that play Cody was supported by Wild Bill, (James B. Hickok) and Texas Jack, (John Omohundro) real plainsmen whose names were familiar to all dime novel readers of that day. Owing Frank Nutter money I'd borrowed from him, I was ashamed to let him know I was strapped again; so I said I had a date with Annie that night, and he took in the performance with Frank Durgin and some other fellows. I cursed my pride and read myself to sleep on a mystery yarn in a weekly story paper.

My opportunity to try for a better job came one day when I was laid off because there was no work for me to do. Wearing my best clothes, I went to Mr. Gooch, supervisor of the big room where Charlie Lewis worked, and asked him for employment. I said I was from Corinna and stopping with a Biddeford friend. He wanted to know how soon I could begin working, and I said right away.

"All right," said he, "come in tomorrow morning." That looked like a jam for me, and I regretted my hasty reply.

After doing a little fast thinking, I went to Andrews and told him I had to leave. He asked why.

"My grandmother is dead, sir," said I. "The funeral———"

He cut me short, with a sneer. "You needn't tell a silly lie," said he. "I was going to let you out anyhow. I've got a man for that job."

He gave me a bill of my time and I departed, rejoicing, to collect the small amount due me at the paymaster's office.

As an unskilled laborer, my stipend under Mr. Gooch was still ninety cents a day, and my first day on the new job was disillusioning. I stood all through the long hours in a little enclosure and gave steel gadgets a hot-oil bath that greatly befouled my shop jacket and overalls before quitting time came. It was much dirtier work than I had been doing for Andrews, but I carried on with a stiff upper lip.

There was a walking boss whose name, as I remember it, was Blaisdell. He came round for a final inspection of my work shortly before six o'clock and said I had done much better at it than the last raw hand, which cheered me up. Encouragement has always spurred me to do my level best at any kind of work, no matter how difficult, and I resolved that Mr. Blaisdell should be more than satisfied by my further efforts.

To my relief, the task in that pen didn't last long and I was given some simple lathe-work to do for a few days. Then Mr. Blaisdell said he would like to see if I could learn to operate a monitor, which was a machine difficult to describe.

A small revolving wheel, something like a wheel in miniature for steering a ship, stood about breast-high on a heavy and jarless mounting, with cutting tools attached to the ends of the wheel-spokes. The wheel was turned by the hands of the operator to bring the tools to bear in shaping and finishing brass fittings about the size of a man's thumb.

The fittings were clamped to a stationary holder that rotated at high speed. Foot pressure on a floor pedal caused the wheel to move toward the whirling fittings to which the tools were applied, one after another. Some of the finer tools were very delicate and almost as brittle as glass. A tiny stream of water, containing something that smelled like soda, fell on the tools to keep them properly cooled while being used. The operator needed good eyes, steady nerves, and a light touch with his hands and pedal-foot to be successful.

At the end of an hour of instruction by Mr. Blaisdell, I had broken two or three of the more delicate cutting-tools but was rapidly getting wise to the trick of operating the monitor. He let me continue, and three days later I was sufficiently proficient to be told I could work the machine at piece rates. I made a dollar and forty-cents on the fourth day and within another week or ten days I was earning from two-forty to two-sixty daily—and rarely breaking a tool. I felt like a millionaire. The only fly in the ointment was that the fumes of the cooling liquid nauseated me slightly and made me cough.

Then Charlie Lewis slipped a bit of confidential information into my ear. He told me that none of the old hands on that floor would operate the monitor for the simple reason that several men who had worked at it for long stretches had contracted consumption. That was not pleasant to hear, for once a Corinna doctor had said that my neck, narrow at the base, was like that of his younger brother, who had died of consumption at the age of twenty.

I told Frank Nutter what Lewis had said. "I don't know anything about it," said he, "but it's my guess that Charlie is spoofing you. Maybe he's trying to scare you out of the shop so that he can have an open field with Annie Donlon."

I laughed. I hadn't thought of that. I bought some coughdrops and continued to operate the monitor when given work at it.

14 · THE PRODIGAL'S RETURN

NOW IT WAS WINTER and I had become a big-town swell with a new suit, overcoat, hat, shirts, neckties, and a pair of high shoes— protected by over-shoes in deep snow or sloppy weather—with buttons instead of laces. My first and last pair of buttoned shoes, by the way. I had also a touch of the big head, for had I not faced the world on my own and proved that in my veins ran the indomitable blood of my Scotch-Irish pioneer ancestors? My financial indebtedness to Frank Nutter had been squared, and there was money in my pockets, both the jingling and folding kind.

I could now well afford to buy a ticket to see Annie Pixley in a drama called *M'liss*. She made me laugh and cry, and the play made me think I'd like to become a playwright myself. For now I was sure I would not spend all my life at manual labor that required no creative effort. My present job, I told myself, was merely a stepping-stone on my way to a higher career and fame.

An odd thing had happened to me—something I did not like to admit, even to myself. I had become afraid. I was afraid of that machine called a monitor. Charlie Lewis had not lied when he said the old hands in the shop did not want to operate it, and it was true that several long-time workers at it had fallen ill. At least one of them had died of consumption of the lungs.

Now, without appearing to have a cold, I was troubled at times by a hacking cough that neither coughdrops nor syrups appeased much. I thought of my cousin Frank Patten and his father, both of whom had died of lung trouble, and became increasingly apprehensive about myself. But the monitor was the only machine I'd been allowed to do piece work on, and I was eager for the money I could earn on it.

Frank Nutter and I were whiling the time away in our room one blustery evening in midwinter when he ceased picking at his banjo and said abruptly, "You're on the wrong track, Will."

I looked up from the story paper I'd been reading. "What do you mean?" I wondered.

"You'll never make a machinist."

"But I don't plan to be one."

Said he, "I thought once that you might become an author. You could write pretty good stories, for your age."

"Thanks," said I. "Maybe I will become an author some day."

"You lack the education for that work," he replied. "Why, you can't even spell well."

I laughed. "That's a small part of authorship," said I knowingly.

"I didn't think you'd stick to it a month when you got a chance in the shops," said he, "but you've fooled me. You've got plenty of the stick-to-it stuff. Want me to tell you what I think you ought to do?"

"Fire away, Frank," I invited.

"Well, you ought to go back home and graduate from the Academy—maybe go to college. And you ought to keep on trying to write. I think it's something one has to learn to do, the same as a trade."

"I can learn it without going back to Corinna," said I.

"You never will the way you're going now," he declared. "When you're not working in the shop you're out skylarking around. Back home, you wouldn't have so much chance for that.

You'd find some time to practice writing. Think it over, old man."

"I have," said I stubbornly. "When I left Corinna I said I wasn't going back there for years—and I'm not."

"All right, mule," said he. "Go your own gait."

I felt that he was right, as usual, but I wouldn't admit it then. In spite of his advice and my qualms about my health, I was earning too much money to give it up easily and go back into exile behind the blue Dixmont Hills. Furthermore, my pride rebelled against that; Corinna people would laugh at me.

Annie Donlon took me to an Irish wake one night. The coffin, in which lay the body of an aged laborer, had been placed on a long table in the parlor. A small crucifix lay on the dead man's breast, and there were candles around his feet to light him through Purgatory. The room was full of his relatives and friends who were passing a bottle of liquor around and reciting all the good qualities of the departed, amid lamentation and laughter.

The air was blue with smoke; not only the men but some of the older women were puffing at pipes. Their doleful keening gave me a shivery feeling. It seemed to me that there was a faint smile on the face of the old man in the coffin, as if he heard and enjoyed all that was being said about him.

Now and then, coming from somewhere, I caught the faint sounds of a fiddle and rapidly tapping feet. Annie led me back into the kitchen, and there was the fiddler playing an endless jig tune to which two husky red-faced girls were dancing, cheered on by a throng of younger mourners. At intervals some one among the spectators would thrust a bottle into the hands of one or the other of the dancers, who would tip it to her mouth and take a long swig without missing a step. They were still going strong when Annie and I sifted out again into the cold white night.

I was looking for new experiences and that had been one.

A short while after that, my labor in the Pepperell Machine Shops came to an abrupt termination. I had been put back on to lathe-work for a while until there should be further work on the monitor.

The Prodigal's Return

"The work that's coming in will be different, Patten," said Mr. Blaisdell. "You can average about three dollars a day at it."

Three dollars a day! Now that would be real dough. I could take a short stretch at ninety cents a day with that harvest assured me.

I went to my lathe as usual the day the new work came in and waited to be called to the monitor by Mr. Blaisdell. Presently I saw Mr. Gooch conducting a young pale-faced new hand toward the monitor. Arriving there, Gooch personally began to instruct the new hand in the operation of the machine.

I couldn't believe what I was beholding. Why, that was my work! I had become, according to Mr. Blaisdell, a skillful and reliable operator of that deadly contraption that no wise man on the floor wanted to run, and, cough or no cough, I had stuck to it faithfully. Now——

I left my lathe and went in search of Mr. Blaisdell. He listened to me, a regretful expression on his face.

"The new man," said he, "is a member of Gooch's church. I can't do a thing about it, Patten."

"Well, I can," said I, hot of face and cold at the pit of my stomach. "I'm quitting right now. You've always treated me white, Mr. Blaisdell, and I won't forget it. Good-bye, sir."

Going back to my lathe, I stripped off my dungarees, rolled them up, and carried them under my arm as I marched briskly over to confront Mr. Gooch, who had returned to his desk for something.

"I'm leaving, sir," I said to him. "I'd like a bill of my time."

He looked at me coldly. "Now what's the matter with you?" he asked.

"You should know, sir," I replied. "I've become a good operator of that monitor and Mr. Blaisdell promised me the work you've just started a green hand on. That's why I'm getting out."

"And leaving a steady job at ninty cents a day?" said he.

"I can't live on ninty cents a day," said I.

He sneered. "Oh, is that so? Well, let me tell you, young fellow, you'll see the time you'll be glad to work for ninety cents a day."

Now I was calmly cold and not the least afraid of him. I think I even smiled a little, contemptuously, as I said: "Mr. Gooch, I've heard what your salary is, and sometime when I'm earning more than you are I'll drop in and tell you about it."

His face went white and then flushed almost purple. "You insolent pup!" he said. "You won't get a bill of your time. Get back to your job and work out your notice."

"I'll do nothing of the kind, sir," said I. "I'm sure you need the money more than I do and you may have it." Then I added, "And you know what you can do with it."

I went to the paymaster and asked for what was due me. To my surprise, I got it. Gooch must have made haste to send word that I was to be paid.

(As an interpolation: I made a special trip to Biddeford some years later just to tell Mr. Gooch that I had earned almost a thousand dollars more than he had in the past twelve months. To my disappointment, he was not in the machine shop. I was told that he was dead.)

I was not at all downcast over losing my job. To the contrary, I walked out of the machine shops with a light step and a feeling of relief and freedom. I hustled to buy a traveling bag and get packed up to catch an afternoon train that would let me reach Corinna that night. Frank Nutter was surprised when he came from the shops at noon and found me wearing my new suit and ready to go.

"What's the big idea?" he asked.

I told him what had happened. "Now," said I, "I'm taking your advice and going back home to finish my course at the Academy. Maybe I'll go to college, too. If I've got it in me, I'm going to write fiction for my bread and butter."

He slapped me on the back. "You're not such a fool as I thought you were," he said, laughing. "I'll miss you like the devil, Will, but you're doing the right thing and I wish you all the luck in the world."

My pal and, in a way, my mentor. He'll never read these words,

The Prodigal's Return

for he has passed into the shadows which veil the great mystery from mortal eyes.

Snow was falling in large soft flakes when I reached Corinna late in the evening. It was deep underfoot and the dwelling houses near at hand looked small and sunken on their foundations. There were lights to be seen in the little old hotel, only now and then one elsewhere. The stillness was ghastly. The old lonely feeling of being far away from the living and breathing world returned, sharp and poignant. I hurried toward home, eager to see my parents and feel the warmth of a fire and human nearness.

The house was dark. That meant, I supposed, that my father and mother were abed. But when my knocking was not answered, I concluded that they had gone out for the evening and had not yet returned. I found a window I could raise and crawled over the sill, after dropping my bag to the floor inside.

Striking a match, I found the old kerosene lamp on the kitchen table, lighted it, and looked around. Everything was the same, excepting that the room was much smaller than it had once seemed to be. Shedding my overcoat, I stirred up and replenished the fire that was still alive in the cookstove. Then I headed for the pantry.

Bread and butter and apple pies were on the shelves, and there were fresh doughnuts in an earthenware crock. How good my mother's food tasted after six months of boarding house fare! I stuffed myself, finishing by stowing away half an apple pie. Then I went down into the cellar and brought up a pitcher of cider that Father had kept sweet, as usual, by an infusion of mustard seeds. I was enjoying the cider and smoking my pipe beside the kitchen stove when I heard my parents at the door.

Panting with excitement, Mother burst in with Father limping at her heels. "I told you it was Willie!" she cried. "He's here! Alive!" She flung herself upon me, laughing and crying.

She held me off to look at me, then hugged me again. "How big!" she said, her eyes choked with admiration. "How big and strong! And handsome! Oh, it's good to see my boy again!"

Father shook hands with me, grinning. He looked me up and down wonderingly. "Why, you're quite a Jim Dandy, William," said he. "Have you robbed a bank?"

Home!

---

15 · I STEP OUT AGAIN

WYMAN B. NIPER, a tall, lank, long-legged man, was now the principal instructor at Corinna Union Academy. My own legs were long, but his walking strides took him up and down Academy Hill at speed which forced me close to running to keep up with him. He was doubtless superior in qualification and executive ability to any previously employed head of that school. He had made many changes and improvements in the curricula. Three courses, College Preparatory, Classical, and Scientific, had been introduced, all of them weighted down with Greek, Latin, English, and mathematics.

After a talk with Professor Niper, during which I not only revealed my ambition but admitted my backwardness in mathematics and grammar, I succeeded, maybe because of leniency on his part, in passing an examination test and obtaining readmission to the Academy. But still more remarkable was the fact that, with no more than a sketchy knowledge of the rules, I soon exhibited enough talent in mathematics and grammar to carry me along swimmingly.

I soon forced myself into advanced classes in both mental arithmetic and grammar. At the latter I had a way of taking a sentence to pieces and analyzing it in phrases of my own, and when opposed in argument by older classmates I usually was supported by Marie Norman, Professor Niper's capable head assistant. Maybe my intensive reading of both prose and poetry and my efforts to express myself unambiguously in writing accounted for that.

S. Alma Dexter, sister of Hugh Dexter, who later became a

successful pulp-magazine fictioneer, was the instructor in English literature and declamation. As I remember her, she was a very good-looking young lady with reddish golden hair, brown eyes, and a modulated voice that was charming. Having attempted to read Shakespeare too early in life, I had looked on his works, with the exception of some poetry, as too esoteric for my taste; but Miss Dexter made them come alive for me with interest and significance, and she inspired me further to explore the classics as opportunity offered. She was a high-bred and cultured person.

As the study of one classical language was required, I took up Latin, but today all the Latin I know may be found in the words and phrases department of English dictionaries. At that, I've met many college graduates who had once studied Latin or Greek, but had let the knowledge of it fade almost completely from their minds with the passing years.

In my spare time I turned again to the writing of stories, and now I tried more consciously and intelligently to grasp the knack of fiction construction. Not only did I read for pleasure, I sought to analyze the methods followed by authors in building their tales with emotional effects and suspense. Fortunately, while I continued now and then to peruse dime novels, I was aware of better craftsmanship by a higher class of writers; and it was this awareness that eventually led me to make characterization more important than plot in my stories. The character depiction by dime novelists was of a crude order, and many of them lacked the ability to cause the reader to *see* the characters they wrote about, who remained shadowy figures distinguishable only by their names.

The reading of Charles Dickens, to whom I was introduced by Alice Gardner, a slightly older schoolmate, gave me a slant on character delineation that I attempted to use in my own stories. Still later, the works of Robert Louis Stevenson became inspirational in the matter of dramatic situations and shock. In that respect, *Dr. Jekyll and Mr. Hyde* was in my estimation a masterpiece, with *The Master of Ballantrae* running a close second.

I had known Alice Gardner no more than casually before my runaway escapade. She was one of two daughters of Thomas

Gardner, a farmer and the proprietor at that time of a village grocery store. The Gardners lived less than a mile from the village, and their farm buildings, always spick-and-span, bespoke prosperity. The members of the family thought well of themselves, especially the older daughter, Dora, whom I considered snobbish. I've always been contemptuous of snobs, who, in spite of assumed superiority, are invariably deficient in breeding.

After returning to Corinna, I had joined the Good Templars, and it was in a social interval at one of their meetings that Alice Gardner and I fell to talking of books and authors. When she asked my opinion of Charles Dickens I was obliged to confess that I had never read any of his works.

She told me I was missing something and brought me *Nicholas Nickleby* and *Martin Chuzzlewit* when she came to school the next day. That night I met "Mr. Pecksniff," who amused me until I could keep my eyes propped open no longer and blew out the kerosene lamp beside my bed, along toward morning.

Oliver Twist followed, wherein I found "Fagin," a dirty old master thief, and "Bill Sykes," a brutal ruffian and murderer, who were to influence me in depicting low-life scoundrels in my writing. And by the time I had wept over the death of "Dora," the child wife of "David Copperfield," Dickens had become my literary god. Alice Gardner had opened the door to new mental diversions, and we were by then good friends, but it was in no respect more than friendly amity on my part.

I admired her superiority over the flipperty-jipperty run of country girls, whose interest lay in boys and gossip and the narrow affairs of their restricted lives; for we could talk a language foreign to them as well as to most of my boy associates. She could sing well and was an excellent pianist, probably the best in that small town. At her invitation, I called on her once or twice and listened to her playing. She sang for me also, "Juanita," "The Kerry Dancers," and "Douglas, Tender and True," sentimental songs of the day.

I think it was when I began escorting her home from the Good Templars' meetings that her family decided we were becoming a bit too friendly and attempted to break it up. That was a mistake on their part, for out of sheer perversity and the fun of it I became more attentive to her than before. It was a great pleasure to me to annoy her sister and her brother Lloyd, both of whom I disliked. I had never expected to find life in Corinna quite as enjoyable.

There was another girl, Nora Spratt, whom I liked in a friendly way. She was tall and thin and full of fun, and once or twice I walked with her on our way to the Academy; but when I imagined she was trying to avoid me I ceased to pay her more than passing attention. She was destined to become Mrs. Frank Nutter.

Now when it came summer again my father got around to suggesting that it was time for me to begin to think about my future.

"You'll have to learn a trade of some sort to make your living, William," he said, "and if you'll work with me I'll teach you to be a carpenter."

Although I had been expecting it, it annoyed me when it came. "Not for me, Father," I told him. "There are better trades than that. Two dollars a day are not enough for me. I knocked off two-fifty in the machine shop."

"And learned nothing that'll ever do you any good," he said. "Besides that, you contracted a cough that worried your mother to death when you first came home. What do you think you can do if you don't take up carpentering?"

"I don't think, I know what I'm going to do," I replied. "I'm going to write stories for a living."

There was pity in his eyes. "Don't be silly, son," he said. "That's no business for a man. Besides, I don't believe there's any money in it except for a few who are lucky."

"Well, you're wrong," I declared bluntly. "It pays better than carpentering."

"I doubt it," said he. "Anyhow, you have to have a pull to get started at it. They never pay any attention to writers without a reputation."

"That can't be true," I argued. "If it were so, how could anybody make a reputation in that line?"

He was exasperated now. "I've never objected to your scribbling," he said, "but the time has come when you'll have to earn money. I can't afford to let you go on without bringing in something to help run the house."

My face flushed and I felt a cold spot in the pit of my stomach. "I brought home money and some of it has gone to help run the house," said I quietly. "You won't have to support me long, sir."

Past experience with his rebellious son must have made him feel that he had gone a little too far, for he said quickly: "Oh, well, we'll get along somehow, William. I guess you've got to have time to make up your mind."

That very day I went around over town with a note-book and pencil, gathering news items of local interest, and I spent half the following night elaborating my notes and making what I wrote a breezy Corinna news-letter.

The next morning I mailed the result to R. O. Robinson, editor of *The Eastern Herald,* a weekly newspaper published in Buxton. With it I enclosed a personal letter to Mr. Robinson applying for a job in any capacity on his paper. He answered immediately, suggesting that I come to Buxton and talk it over with him.

That night I told Alice Gardner what I had done. "I'm going up there tomorrow on the train," said I, "and maybe I won't be seeing you again for quite a while."

She looked startled. Suddenly she said: "My folks have been making life miserable for me and I've been thinking I'd go away and get a job somewhere, William. Girls work in newspaper offices as typesetters. Look! Try to get a job for me on that paper, will you?"

"You?" I said. "You don't have to work and you wouldn't like it anyhow. Your folks wouldn't stand for it, either."

"You don't know them," was her reply. "They'd be sore, but they are too proud to bring me back home and set the village gossiping. You've got to get me a job up there, William Patten."

She didn't let me get away from her until I'd promised to do as she had asked me to; and when I make a promise I keep it if it's humanly possible to do so.

Not only did Mr. Robinson hire me as a local news gatherer and printer's devil, he said one of his compositors was ill and he would let Miss Gardner try her hand at the work. If she proved to be quick and capable, he would pay her living wages her second or third week on the job.

I went back home to pack up my duds and move to Buxton. My father looked a trifle crestfallen when I told him what I had done.

"Well," he said slowly, "I hope it pans out all right, but you better come back home in time to go on with your schooling. I've got a contract to build a house, and that fixes everything all right. You know your mother worries herself sick when you're away from us, William."

16 · THE WRONG TRACK

ALTHOUGH IT HAD NOT BEEN IN MY MIND when I went after that job in Buxton, it soon occurred to me that a knowledge of newspaper work and the printing business would provide me with an interesting vocation in case I should fail to make the grade as an author. While it would not be much to my fancy as fiction writing, it still would be far more agreeable than carpentry or farming. My aversion for the latter was extreme, caused possibly by my lonely boyhood and the apparently isolated life of a farmer— maybe also to some extent by the necessity that binds a farmer to one locality, and my rebellion against restrictive ties.

In the short time that I worked for R. O. Robinson I learned a little about the printing business but did practically no news gathering. And I soon began to suspect that things were not going well for him.

He had written and published an exposé of "Dr. Gerald," a brazen quack who, strange to say, was admired by hundreds of his patients, a large number of whom were women and probably hypochondriacs. Even his fluent profanity, indulged in whenever he spoke, did not seem to shock the ladies enough to do him any harm.

He was really a striking figure in his tall silk hat, Prince Albert coat, striped trousers and patent-leather boots. When drumming up trade he rode through the outlying rural sections in a glittering coach drawn by two spirited white horses. Perhaps he did perform some simple cures, for my Grandmother Simpson had done as much with herb brews and poultices, but reputable physicians asserted that he knew no more about therapeutics than a child in its cradle.

Following the publication of Mr. Robinson's exposé Gerald had begun suit for libel, naming the owners of the newspaper. Probably his action was pure bluff, and I think he would have lost had the case been brought to trial, but the owners of the paper got cold feet.

One day as I was running off some bill-heads on the jobbing press, Mr. Robinson asked me to come into his office. Wondering and a little apprehensive, I followed him.

"Sit down, Patten," he said, seating himself at his desk and waving me to a chair beside it. "How old are you?"

My surprise increasing, I answered: "Seventeen, sir. I'll be eighteen this coming October."

"That's young," he said, "but you can write pretty well, though you are a slovenly speller. You told me it's your ambition to become an author."

"That's correct, sir."

"Well now, I'm going to make you a proposition. I'm leaving this paper. Gerald has offered to drop his suit if I'm fired, and I'm getting out. The paper must have an editor right away. Think you can swing it?"

I gasped. "You—you don't mean that—that you're offering me the position of editor—do you, sir?" I stammered.

The Wrong Track

"I'm offering you a whack at it if you think you can deliver the goods," was his reply. "I've been reading proofs myself, but you'll need a proof-reader. Miss Gardner can learn to do that work. Already she sets type fast and makes scarcely any mistakes. This is a jam, for I've got a job already in Bangor, but I'll stay here three or four days to get you going. What do you say?"

Now I had thought myself ready for any emergency, but the wind was taken out of my sails by this sudden and amazing proposition. I was then—and have always been—more than a little slow in my mental reactions when abruptly confronted by the unexpected. In such a situation I am more than liable to do the wrong thing unless I take time to consider what should be done. Hasty action under pressure is dangerous for me. I have learned this through bitter experience. And Mr. Robinson's proposition was so unexpected and abrupt that I was not only bewildered but frightened. For the moment my cock-sureness vanished like whiff of smoke in a gale.

"I—I don't believe I want to try it, sir," I stammered. "It's—well, you see it isn't the kind of work I'm aiming to do, and—and I———"

"Enough said," said he. "If that's how you feel, you'd be no good at it anyhow." He stood up. "Well, I'll get somebody. Go back to your work."

When I told Miss Gardner about it that night after work, she looked at me in a way that made me feel about the size of a peanut. "Why, William Patten," she said, "you've missed the chance of a lifetime. Of course you could edit this country newspaper. It would have been a snap for you. You were crazy to turn it down."

I was already thinking so myself.

Two or three days later, a young fellow, perhaps a few months older than I, appeared and took over the editorship. He had worked a short time on a smaller rural weekly and he behaved as if there was nothing he did not know about the newspaper business.

The sight of him strutting around as I myself might have

strutted at times was more than I could take. Pretty soon he was acclaimed by other country weeklies as the youngest editor of any established newspaper in the state. That got my goat completely. I gave my notice.

I wrote Charlie Hastings, of the Cottsfield, Maine, *Advertiser,* that I was serving my notice on *The Eastern Herald,* but would like to work for him. Of course I was wise enough to state that I was green at the business. In his answer he said he had nothing to offer me but a job as printer's devil. I replied that I would be there on a certain date.

When I told Alice Gardner about it she said: "Well, I can set up type now as fast as anybody, but the other girls are getting better pay. The way for me to do that is to get a new job. I think I'll try for a job in the *Advertiser,* too."

About a week after I began to work for Charlie Hastings, she appeared in the office and was hired as a type-setter at better wages than I received at any time while employed in that establishment.

Hastings was a young man who had been set up in business by his father, at whose home I roomed and took my meals. Charlie's younger brother Harry moved up from the position of printer's devil when I came in. I didn't feel much like a swell in my lowly position, but I did my duties faithfully and learned as much about the business as speedily as I could. Sometimes I set up advertising display for the paper and occasionally I stuck the type for handbills, but mostly I did the drudgery of sweeping out, washing the ink-rollers on the big press, feeding the newspaper sheets to that old flat-bed contraption, and doing other odd jobs as required.

The Hastingses had a library in which I found a book by John Townsend Trowbridge called *Cudjo's Cave.* I read it in bed and became a Trowbridge admirer, although, strange as it may seem, I've never cared for the books of other well-known writers of juvenile literature.

George Henty's books were popular then, but I considered them abominably dull. Nor could I become interested in the sea

The Wrong Track

yarns of Kingston or Marryat. Eggleston, Ellis, and "Oliver Optic" (William T. Adams) were no good for me. I did read one of Optic's books all the way through, but never in my life could I do as much for any by Horatio Alger.

This distaste for juvenile literature was not an affectation; it was as genuine as anything could be. And let me add that I then had not the least intention of becoming a writer of juvenile literature myself. I had even dreamed of living somehow, anyhow, in a garret if needs be, and writing literary masterpieces such as I considered the works of Charles Dickens to be. While a certain amount of money to provide an existence was necessary, it was far from being my only incentive. In fact I've always held in disdain those who make the accumulation of wealth the ruling motive of their lives.

I longed to return to the Academy when the fall term began, but thinking it more to my advantage and future safety to obtain more knowledge of the printing and publishing business, I remained a while longer in Cottsfield.

Miss Gardner roomed and took her meals in the home of a family by the name of Merrithew or Merrifield. I called on her quite often evenings, and we talked of books and authors and this and that, and she played the piano and sang for me.

My memory fails to tell me how I discovered that she was entertaining another caller on evenings when I was not supposed to appear. He was Hugh Dexter, brother of S. Alma Dexter, my instructor in English literature at Corinna Academy. Nor do I recall whether I became very jealous, but I do know I was annoyed and my pride was wounded.

Going to call on Alice without being expected one evening, I saw them together through a parlor window. She was playing the piano and singing the same sentimental songs she had often sung for me. That, I think, was what annoyed me most; that and the fact that she had never spoken of him to me. I turned around and walked away swiftly. Had I been extremely jealous, I think I would have walked right into that parlor and stayed there until Mr. Dexter took his departure.

I told her about it the next day. We didn't quarrel. I said, "If you like that fellow's company better than mine you're welcome to it." She laughed and tried to kid me out of my pique.

In Cottsfield I could find neither time nor place to do much writing. However I did compose a few pieces of doggerel verse that appeared in the *Advertiser*. Nor was I allowed to do any news-gathering for the paper. More and more I regretted my loss of self-confidence when R. O. Robinson had offered the editorship of the Buxton paper. I called myself a chump for refusing.

One of my introspective moods came upon me. I reviewed all that had happened to me since the day I left Corinna on the excursion to Lake Maranacook and was alternately pleased and annoyed with myself. I felt nostalgia for Biddeford and the small bare room in Mrs. Watson's boarding house, with Frank Nutter plucking at his banjo and singing his songs. Then I heard him talking to me again as he had on that blustery evening when he advised me to quit my job and go back to Corinna.

It was as if he were present at that moment as I seemed to hear him say, "You're on the wrong track, Will." That startled me out of my reverie.

"That's it!" said I aloud. "I'm on the wrong track again."

The next day I went to Charlie Hastings, writing at his desk, and told him I wanted to leave, and why.

"How do you know you'll ever be able to make a living writing fiction?" he asked.

"I don't know it," I replied, "but I'm going to try. And I feel that I need more education."

"Well, I can get along without you," he said, "but I think you are making a mistake when you've got a chance to learn a trade. You may go when you want to."

"Today?" I exclaimed.

"Any time," said he.

"Then I'm leaving at once."

He paid me off and I left the office without a word with Alice Gardner. Maliciously and gleefully, I thought of the surprise that was coming to her. This, said I to myself, would be getting even for the way she had put it over on me with Dexter.

A week after I returned to Corinna Alice Gardner reappeared there herself.

---

17 · DOOMSDAY PASSES

MISS GARDNER WAS DEEPLY OFFENDED and haughtily distant. She ignored me coldly, and soon I began to feel that I had been anything but a gentleman. Eventually I cracked the ice a little with an apology which she accepted coolly, leaving me thinking I had behaved like a cheap-skate. Maybe that would have been the end of our friendship had she not deviated suddenly one night at a meeting of the Good Templars. Before that evening was over we were chummy again.

But now I discovered something seemingly different about her. She was absorbed in the love romances of "The Duchess" and kindred writers of languishing lollipops which she beguiled me into perusing. A specimen title of those confections is *Bread and Cheese and Kisses,* written, if I remember correctly, by B. L. Farjeon.

Apparently she had lost all interest in the works of such writers as Dickens, Thackeray, and Victor Hugo, and eventually I wondered if her former apparent admiration for the authors I desired to emulate had not been assumed to impress me at a time when I was still something of a dime novel addict.

At the Academy, I was struggling to make up for lost ground, though not giving enough time at home to my studies. Filled now with determination to earn money by writing, I began on a love story, inspired doubtless by the novels recently loaned me by Alice, as well as the short stories I'd found in some old issues of

Godey's Magazine, written by Fanny Hodgson, who, as Frances Hodgson Burnett, made fame and fortune with *Little Lord Fauntleroy.*

My story was titled "The Little Widow," and I divided it into five chapters of relatively four thousand words each. I let Alice read it when it was finished, and she pronounced it splendid. I gladly accepted her offer to copy it for me with all my misspelled words corrected. Possessing no ability to write fiction herself, her excellent penmanship, as easy to read as print, made her decidedly helpful in making what I wrote suitable for submission to an editor.

"The Little Widow" made two trips by mail, one to a magazine that rejected it, the other to the Augusta, Maine, *New Age,* which accepted it as a gift and ran it in five installments. Personally, I was disgusted with the thing, but it taught me that my talent was not of an order to concoct love romances.

"I told you, son," said Bill Patten, "that papers don't pay money for such stuff."

"Well, I'm going to write stuff they will pay for," was my reply.

In the early spring I wrote a short story, such as now would be called a short story, and sent it to the *Star Weekly,* a fiction paper published by Beadle and Adams, publishers also of Deadwood Dick dime novels.

"A Bad Man" was the title I put on my little story. It was tripe. The day that story was mailed I began another which I called "The Pride of Sandy Flat." I sent the second one to the same paper before I had received a report on the first. Then I waited with my heart in my boots.

The report that came did not lift my spirits much. A handwritten note signed by O. J. Victor, the editor for Beadle and Adams, informed me that he was returning "A Bad Man," not having found it quite good enough. But my story was not in the envelope bearing his note, nor did it arrive the following day.

So I wrote Mr. Victor a personal letter, stating that I had sent him another story before receiving his rejection of the first one submitted, and asking him as a great favor to tell me frankly if he could find any indications of fiction-writing ability in either of my attempts.

Presently—but how soon I do not remember—I received an answer that took my breath away. Mr. Victor stated that, due to an oversight, my first story had not been returned to me, and went on to say that he had read it again and decided to accept it, as my work showed promising fiction-writing talent. Furthermore, he had accepted "The Pride of Sandy Flat" and was enclosing a check for six dollars for both stories!

Trembling violently, I spread out that check, beautifully printed in green ink, and feasted my eyes upon it.

Here in my hands was the proof that I had crashed through, with that wonderful letter assuring me that I had the goods to deliver. The fact that I had expected at least ten dollars each for those stories, if anything at all, did not dampen my elation. The first step was taken on the road I had so long longed to follow.

When I exultingly showed the check to my father, he scratched his fringe of throat whiskers and shook his head. Not many checks were then seen in Corinna, where there is no bank even now, and Father had always received his earnings in cash.

"Maybe it's worthless," he said. "I don't believe anybody around here will give you money for it."

But Will Currier handed over six good dollars for that piece of paper, endorsed with the name of Harvan W. Gregg, which I had used on the stories, and again endorsed by William Patten, and Father's skepticism turned to wonderment.

"How long did it take you to write them stories?" he asked.

"Oh," I replied carelessly, "not over three days for both of them."

He whistled. "Hum! Six dollars for three days work is as much as I get."

I laughed. "That's chicken feed," said I. "I'll be pulling down ten times as much after I've been at it a while."

"Now don't get too puffed up in a hurry," he advised. "You

may never sell another one of them things. It still don't look to me like a safe and sound business."

I tried my hand at several kinds of short stories and sold them all, with a single exception, but I wrote them for the story-paper markets and never received more than five dollars each for them. Sometimes I received as little as two dollars, which the Portland *Transcript,* an odd semi-literary weekly, paid. I sold one or two pieces of verse to *Golden Days,* a somewhat high-class juvenile paper published by James Elverson in Philadelphia. But most of my poetic effusions were declined or published as gifts. Although the *Star Weekly* did not pay for poetry, Eben E. Rexford, writer of the words of "Silver Threads Among the Gold," was a steady contributor to its columns.

Rumors of my success spread quickly in my native town, but many persons were skeptical; they were unwilling to believe that "that Patten boy" could write anything for which anybody would pay in money. Why, such a thing was preposterous. A few continued to express their doubts after being told by Will Currier that he had cashed my checks.

Then "the big wind"—so-called by some persons—blew into Corinna. It came in the form of an Adventist preacher, John Nickerson, who was dubbed "John the Prophet" by somebody in the town. From Revelations and the Book of Daniel he claimed to have figured out the exact date when the world would come to an end, and it was alarmingly near at hand. A sandy-haired, vital man in his thirties, he seemed to possess magnetism and the ability to hypnotize those who listened to him.

He stood the town on end and shook it. He packed the old Union Church to overflowing, and many who came there to scoff lingered to pray for the salvation of their sinful souls. It was a strange fact that not a few of the most scornful disbelievers fell under his spell and became converts. A number of my youthful associates who had sneered at the religion of my parents were soon on their knees, begging to be spared in "Jehovah's great day of wrath."

Doomsday Passes

I attended some of those revival meetings, listened to the Prophet, studied the big chart that he had made himself, and continued to be an unregenerate disbeliever, to the dismay of my parents. They argued with me. Mother pleaded without result. Distressed by her distress, I avoided arguments and pleadings as far as possible.

"I shall keep on praying until you see the light, William," she said tearfully.

At that time I thought John Nickerson was a fakir. Later I came to the conclusion that he had hypnotized himself into believing what he preached.

When warm weather tempered the streams and ponds he began to baptise his converts. I went down to the shore of the pond, behind Asa Granlet's barn, to witness one of these baptisms. The shore was thronged with John's followers and spectators like myself.

He led his deluded recruits out waist-deep into the water, prayed shortly, uttered absolution "in the name of the Father, Son, and Holy Ghost," and tipped them over backwards beneath the surface. They came up gasping, strangling, and shouting, "Glory hallelujah!"

I didn't stay there long. I couldn't take it. I hurried to get away from that spectacle and the sound of the brothers and sisters who were singing "Shall We Gather at the River."

In that atmosphere it was impossible for me to do much writing. Maybe I was apprehensive in spite of my disbelief, but I never admitted it to anybody but myself. There were almost nightly prayer meetings in the homes of the Adventists, but I went out for the evening when there was one in our home.

All Corinna seemed tense as the day of the great event, as proclaimed by the Prophet John, drew near in the latter part of the summer. When the day dawned, bright and warm, the Adventists either remained at home, quietly but fervently praying, or assembled in small groups in the homes of their religious friends. There was no shouting or loud praying; that was all in the past for them. Now they were ready to meet their Saviour joyously but without tumult. Their grief was all for unfortunate lost souls like myself.

The day wore on. Nothing happened. Nevertheless the faithful continued to watch and pray as the sun went down and evening shadows gathered—continued as the moon rose, large and golden, in the east and seemed to shrink in size and turn silvery as it climbed the blue arch of the sky—continued as it slid silently down toward the western hills and slipped away behind them.

Morning came again. It was another day and the Prophet John was discredited.

Reporting that day in Corinna, the New York *Sun* stated that the Adventists had assembled on a high hill, there to sing and shout while waiting for the end of the world. Nothing of the kind took place. I was there, and I have here described exactly what happened. No Adventist seen by me ever made a white ascension robe or wore one. Why should they have done so when they believed they were to receive robes of light and glory such as the heavenly angels wore?

Sorrowfully, John Nickerson admitted that somehow he had made a miscalculation. Not many Adventists censured him, and not a great many of his converts deserted him from the faith, but, humbled and ashamed, he soon left Corinna to be seen there no more. He did not return to Orrington, from whence he had come, but settled in Buxton and became a boot and shoe cobbler. There was a report that he had turned atheistic.

I have heard that he once set forth from Buxton, alone and afoot, to travel from place to place and be a benefactor to his fellowmen. According to the story, he traveled no further than Cartland, some twelve or fourteen miles from Buxton, where he lifted a drunk out of a ditch and paid to have him sheltered in his, John's, own room.

In the morning the man he had befriended accused John of robbing him and had him arrested. Friends in Buxton came to John's rescue, and he went sadly back to his work on boots and shoes.

"I'm through trying to be a benefactor to humanity," he said. "Hereafter I'm going to look out for myself and let humanity go to hell."

---

18 · THE OWL HOOTS AND DIES

MY FATHER HAVING EARNED VERY LITTLE since the appearance of John Nickerson in Corinna, there was now, more than ever, a pressing reason for me to render financial assistance. This was no time for me to place anything above the demand of necessity. For the present my ambition to write masterpieces must be forgotten, and I must write anything that would bring quick returns.

I thought of the long Western story, inspired by the Deadwood Dick novels, which I had not finished before running away to Biddeford, and found it where I had stowed it away in a trunk in the open chamber.

There were approximately 16,000 words in that unfinished yarn. Reading it over again, I decided that it might pass muster as a dime novel if rewritten and about doubled in length. And so, while still attempting to keep up with my classmates at the Academy, I went to work again on that story.

To my gratification, the work went rapidly; I think I finished the thing in a little more than two weeks and shipped it immediately to Beadle and Adams. Success with short stories had restored my confidence, and I waited without anxiety for the notice of acceptance which came in due time.

For that story, 33,000 words in length, I was paid $50.00! Bearing the name of William G. Patten as author, it was soon published. I received the same price for my second novel, but after that I was raised to $75.00 for tales of that length and $150.00 for those a little more than twice as long.

One of my long stories was used as a serial in the *Star Weekly*, and Mr. Victor placed a pen name, "William West Wilder ("Wyoming Will"), upon it.

I was not guilty of that, but in time I felt that I had been guilty of an unfortunate blunder in permitting the name of William G. Patten to appear on any of that class of literature. For by so doing I had stamped myself as a dime novel writer, and in those days it was not as easy to climb out of that rut as it is for writers of today for the "pulps" to lift themselves into the "slicks." A dime novelist was then sort of a literary pariah.

Two or three of the more popular Beadle writers received $125.00 for their short novels and $250.00 for the longer ones. That was at the height of prosperity for Beadle and Adams. And once these publishers announced with great fanfare that they had paid Captain Mayne Reid, popular English novelist, $800.00 for *The Scalp Hunters*.

That kind of writing became too easy for me. I never had one of my stories written for that publishing house declined by Mr. Victor, and such a sure market was undermining for my higher ambitions. Not wishing Beadle and Adams to imagine I was not giving them my undivided interest, I used pen names on stories sold elsewhere, practically all shorts.

I dreamed less and less of higher fields of endeavor. But I still had the smell of printer's ink in my nostrils, and eventually it led me astray again. Thinking I could carry on in the double capacity of author and printer, I went off the deep end.

I bought a second-hand Washington hand-press and some fonts of type and other things needed and began to pick up some money around Corinna by doing job printing for the village merchants. At first I looked on this as something of a hobby and a change from the backbreaking labor of writing. But I was trying to do too many things at the same time, which interfered with my course at the Academy. I lacked the capacity to swing all those things at once with full success. Then a fatal Fourth of July tipped me overboard.

While the town was preparing for another Independence Day

The Owl Hoots and Dies

celebration, I got busy with a scheme to pick up a small roll of money with my printing outfit. I decided to print a one-shot local newspaper to be distributed gratis on the Fourth, my revenue to be obtained through advertising by the town's business men in its columns. Having made up a dummy, a four-page affair, I went after the advertising—and got it. The business men responded nobly, I'm sorry to say.

Alice Gardner helped me set up the type, read the proofs, did the folding and refolding necessary to enable me to print the paper a page at a time on my Washington press. By downright hard work I struck off a flock of papers and was a bit proud of the Corinna *Advertiser,* as I had named it, when the job was done.

The town swarmed with people on the Fourth and the celebration—with a procession of "horribles," a thrilling battle with "Indians," representing General Custer's battle with the Sioux on the Little Big Horn, and the popping of firecrackers and red glare of rockets in the evening—was a huge success. With the aid of two boys, I distributed the *Advertiser,* which carried the program for the day on the first page, and did not have papers enough for everybody who grabbed for them.

Came the morrow and I found Corinna urgent for me to launch a local weekly newspaper. Such a paper, the Corinna *Herald,* had made its appearance some years before and failed to survive, which should have been a warning for me. But maybe my success at writing had gone to my head. What if others had failed? Thinking myself smarter than they, I turned a willing ear to those who urged me, and made one of my usually unfortunate quick decisions.

"All right," said I, "I'll give you a newspaper if you'll promise to support me with advertising and printing jobs." They promised readily, and I was committed.

Thinking now of my conceit and lack of foresight makes me a trifle ill.

I had some money but far from enough to pay for the outfit I required, and my success in obtaining credit after making partial payments for an outfit makes me wonder. I journeyed to Boston and made my purchases in person, and perhaps I carried a front that convinced my creditors that I was reliable.

Before making that trip I had spotted a small, shabby building which I could rent cheaply, and I closed for it promptly on my return. I soon found out why a higher rental had not been asked; the place was alive with bedbugs. I destroyed them by filling every crack and cranny with quicklime, sealing the windows and doors and leaving iron pots containing burning sulphur when I went out. Never did I see a bedbug there again, but the place smelled like the devil's kitchen for quite a while.

My outfit was sufficient for such job printing as I would get, but the work of running four newspaper pages one at a time on a foot-powered Golding Jobber didn't make me shout for joy. My paper, which I named the Corinna *Owl*—a name unintentionally symbolic of the night labor I did on it—contained eight four-column pages, the four inner pages being obtained from a concern whose business was to supply country newspapers with "patent insides."

Alice became my compositor and proof-reader. She set up all the straight reading matter, assisted at times by Hallie Hollins, a girl who wished to learn type-setting. I did the type-setting for the advertising and job printing. Also I gathered the news, wrote short and—I thought—snappy editorials under the heading of Hoots and filled up space, when local doings did not provide enough news items, with some pieces imitative of Artemus Ward's so-called humor. Those pieces were ostensibly written by a neighboring farmer who signed himself Sam Plank, and I was never accused of the crime.

Humble as I sincerely am about it, I must boast a little for relief. The *Owl* not only was given notice in the columns of other papers, it was applauded, and some of its wise-cracking editorials were copied and credited.

No editor pointed the finger of derision at my little sheet, and on my exchange list were papers like the Bangor *Commercial* and Lewiston *Journal*. I lost buttons off my vest every time papers like those clipped something from the *Owl* and gave credit.

Nor did I have to take many pumpkins and potatoes as payment for subscriptions. And as another pat on the back for myself, I must add that somehow I obtained a list of over three hundred subscribers! The list was still going up slowly when my advertising and job work began to go in the opposite direction. The *Owl* had been hooting for almost six months before there came a disturbing slackening of the revenue.

By that time I had loaded up the business men of the town with bill-heads, statements, letter-heads, return envelopes and other printed matter that they did or did not need, and I was not situated to go far afield in search of work to keep things running.

The town merchants had also begun to cut down their advertising in the paper and some of them, saying they couldn't see that they were benefiting from it, had ceased to advertise at all. I talked to them; I even told them that I would have to shut up shop if they failed to stand by their promises to support me.

It did no good, and I saw the well-known handwriting on the wall. My mother must have noticed that I had gone off my feed and was beginning to wear the happy face of an undertaker, for one day she said:

"I don't see how you could buy all that printing stuff with the money you had when you started, William. I hope you didn't run in debt for it."

"Credit" said I, "is what makes the mare go. It's what greases the wheels of commerce."

"Dear me!" said she. "You must mean you did run in debt. How much do you owe?"

"Oh, not much more than five hundred dollars," I replied as insouciantly as my state of mind would let me.

I had never seen my mother faint, and she didn't then. But she seemed to turn a trifle green, and it was some moments before she could get her breath.

"Oh, my gracious!" she gasped. "That's awful, Willie! Why,

your father never went a hundred dollars in debt in his life."

"Well, will you tell me what good it's done him?" said I. "Now don't fret, Mother, I'll pay the piper."

How I was going to do it, I had not the least conception. I was shedding weight and sleeping about as soundly as a cat at a mouse's hole. What to do? If I did get to sleep, that question kept jerking me wide-awake again. It pursued me night and day. I called myself unprintable names. As I was still under voting age, the burden of my debts would fall on my father unless I could find some way to keep from crashing.

The *Owl* had cut into the circulation of the Buxton and Cottsfield papers in Corinna. Getting an idea at last, and still not feeling very hopeful that it would work, I wrote a letter to Charlie Hastings saying that I was getting tired of being a publisher, as it promised to ruin my plan of becoming an author. There was no hint in my letter about the decline of my business. I asked him if he would be interested in buying me out, and added that I would like to know quickly before offering to sell to the Buxton paper. His answer came quickly enough.

It said, "I'll be over to see you tomorrow."

He brought a man with him, and they made an inventory of my printing property and looked my books over. Then Charlie made me an offer, with the understanding that he would fill out my paid-up subscriptions with the Cottsfield *Advertiser*. I pretended to think it over a bit before deciding, but I didn't attempt to dicker. What he had offered would enable me to square all my debts and have some money left over.

I breathed once more and slept well. I got out a final issue of the *Owl* containing a valedictory thanking my supporters handsomely and without a touch of blame or bitterness. In fact my relief had wiped out my bitterness and I was feeling like a man released from the shackles of slavery.

"Now," said I to Alice, "I'm going to graduate from the Academy and take a course at Colby College."

What was it Bobby Burns said about "the best laid plans o'mice and men?"

19 · ESCAPE

IF I HAVE GIVEN THE IMPRESSION that I am charged with dynamic energy, I have been misleading. For, like many writers I have known, I am naturally lazy and prone to avoid hard work when possible. But my pride causes me to bestir myself apparently, to refute anyone who accuses me of slothfulness, and I had been called the laziest boy in Corinna. Necessity also drives me to exert myself, and I had faced necessity. Sometimes habits are formed by will-power, and will-power, like muscular power, increases with exercise. By compelling myself to work when I dreaded it, I not only overcame the dread but formed the habit of working.

Those who know nothing about it nearly always think a writer's vocation is easy, but it often is the most exhausting labor. When a writer's phrases seem to flow like a purling brook, it is a safe bet that he has sweat blood laboring over them.

Moreover, writing can be the most tyrannical of masters, driving one not only when he is at his desk but at all other times, even in his sleeping dreams. Everything he experiences—everything he sees, hears, smells, or thinks—can become so correlated to his work that he never finds an hour of freedom from it.

Being naturally lazy, it is probable I would have become a shoddy playboy and spendthrift had I been born with a silver spoon in my mouth. I've never scorned money for what it can buy. I've scorned only those who choose it for their master and become its slave. How often we hear it said that money is power! But power has destroyed the finer instincts of many men who have possessed it in abundance, especially those who have not earned it themselves.

Having escaped from the cage the *Owl* had hooted me into, I relaxed and let my natural slothfulness get a stranglehold upon me. At first I told myself I would take it easy for a little while, but I continued to take it easy as the summer days slipped away. I was promising myself each day that tomorrow I would settle down to writing, but failing to do so when tomorrow came today.

Early in September a strange weariness came upon me gradually. Strength seemed seeping out of my body, and I dragged myself around, becoming still more tired day by day. Then one night I keeled over on my bed while trying to undress. My mother got my clothes off and called a doctor.

"Typhoid," said he. "He has been walking around with it for some time."

I grew worse rapidly and soon could not help myself at all; could not turn my body over, even, without assistance. And when anybody assisted me their hands hurt so much that I cried out weakly. The ringing of the bell at the Academy, from which I had planned to graduate but never would, beat upon my ears with violence that drove me distracted. Father told them about that, and I wept when only one light stroke of the bell sounded thereafter at the usual times.

Then I became delirious. In those attacks I worked like a beaten slave. Once it seems that, using a dull saw, I was compelled to saw into stovewood lengths old gravel-impregnated railroad ties. And as soon as I had finished with one of them a fiendish man with a pickax would dig another out of the ground for me to continue working upon.

Following that I had to pull up by the roots the three big trees in our front yard. When I came out of those spells I was reeking with perspiration, and the bedding around me was as wet and cold as if it had been immersed in ice-water.

There were other delirious phantasms that I did not remember at all. Why my mother told me about them, I can't conceive. Once she said I had complained that a hideous old woman of the town had got into my bed and tried to push me out. After that I was so sore and lame that it hurt me to breathe.

I woke up one day and saw that Mother had been crying. Though I couldn't speak above a whisper, I attracted her attention somehow. She came to my bedside and leaned over me, hiding her feelings as well as she could.

"Has the doctor been here?" I whispered.

She nodded, biting her lip to prevent it from quivering.

"What did he tell you?" I asked. "Did he say I am going to die?"

I saw tears well into her eyes as she forced herself to speak. "You had been dreaming again," she said, "and you said the undertaker had measured you for your coffin."

Of course she did not tell me then that the doctor had said there was no chance for me to recover.

"Listen, Mother," I whispered. "I'm not going to die. I *won't* die, Mother. Nothing can make me die."

I was not in the slightest afraid I would die. I was sure I wouldn't. And I have always believed my complete lack of fear, together with an unbroken determination to live, saved me.

Alice Gardner came to the house and sat beside my bed far into the night.

I was sleeping when she left, and I was better the next morning. The turning point had arrived and passed and soon there were indications that I was on the mend. As he admitted to my parents, the doctor himself was amazed. Once more, as had happened when death seemed to have me in its grasp on the Old Bog, I had wrested myself free with a latent burst of will-power.

How good, how gloriously grand it was when I could get up again and was able to walk out a little way in the open air!

The world was a thousand times more beautiful than it had ever been. To breathe and feel and think again without pain was an indescribable joy. Sweet it was to sleep again without pain and dream pleasant dreams. I could laugh once more. And who has ever loved life and laughter more than I?

Alice's folks were furious because she had spent part of that night beside the bed from which it was thought I would never rise again. They told her she had disgraced herself and her family. She let me know about that when I was well recovered and trying to write stories again.

I had some old-fashioned notions about honor. We were married in my home on October 25, the anniversary of my birthday.

In the following springtime, with jingling and folding money again in my pockets, we departed together and escaped beyond the blue Dixmont Hills into the world from which I would never return to dwell again in Corinna.

Part Two

20 · STOP-OVERS ON THE WAY

Now I was on my way to New York, the great metropolis then often denounced as a hotbed of sin and iniquity and a modern Babylon, by revivalist preachers, few—if any—of whom had ever been there themselves. But there would be stop-overs along the way. The first was Camden, on the coast of Maine, a thriving town that was entering upon a business boom.

Situated at the head of one of the snug harbors of Penobscot Bay and at the feet of lofty wooded hills, the village and its surroundings were destined to become the resort of wealthy part-time residents who would build their summer homes there. Already it was attracting throngs of transient vacationists who filled its hotels and boarding houses from the middle of June until the early days of September.

Having sold their home in Corinna, my parents traveled to Camden with Alice and me, where we leased a comfortable brick house, known as the Ogier Homestead, on the crest of Chestnut Hill. The place commanded, then, a broad view of the bay, the village, and the hills and mountains in the background. I considered Camden ideal and inspiring for an author, artist, musician, or poet, and it did inspire Edna St. Vincent Millay, then a Camden schoolgirl, to write "Renascence," her first poem to be acclaimed a work of genius.

Although handicapped by his lameness, my father found employment in Camden at higher wages than he had previously received. I bought a Remington typewriter, spent three days practicing the "finger exercises" prescribed in a little book that came with it, and then wrote an 80,000-word Dime Library yarn on the machine in three weeks!

I wish I could cuff a typewriter as fast and accurately now. For that story brought me a letter from Mr. Victor asking me to mail him a few spare pages of my typewritten work, as he would like to send them to one of his authors as a specimen of what machine written copy should be.

In those days any very well-dressed person was called a dude, and I soon became one. Although my clothes were not highly expensive, they were of carefully chosen material and built by the best tailor I could find thereabouts. Likewise the rest of my wearing apparel, hats, shirts, neckties, hose, and shoes, was of the better quality. I doted on Ascot and simple bow ties, but never wore a Byronic flowing bow, thank heavens!

My curly black hair was worn a trifle long but never allowed to get out of bounds and encroach on the rightful domain of my standing collar. While I was disposed to appear different from the *hoi-polloi*, I would have resented being called a sissy at the drop of a word. Furthermore, I always have got along much more cheek by jowl with decent roughnecks than with softies.

I became friendly with a set of Camden young men who were all square shooters and more-or-less expert poker players. And poker is a game I have continued to play ever since Will Greenwood and George Bachelder gave me instructions in the art in a Corinna horse-shed at one-cent ante and a dime limit. I paid them for my lessons as the game progressed over an empty egg-crate that served for a table. Now, with the exception of cribbage, poker is the only card game I'm still foolish about.

Dame Fortune smiled on me at poker during those first pleasant days in Camden. In fact I won so often that I was continually ahead of the game and began to think my winnings might soon give me a stake heavy enough for a deep plunge in the New York stock market. But with the time spent at my work and poker, I was not getting the proper amount of exercise in the open air.

Consequently I was in excellent condition to entertain the grip, as it was then called, when it visited Camden that winter, but I

Stop-overs on the Way

managed to duck it until along toward spring. Then it got to me. A doctor was called at once and he stood me on my feet again in a short while.

Previous to that short hiatus with the bugs, I had been corresponding with George Waldo Browne, of Manchester, New Hampshire, a dime-novel writer and also publisher of *American Young Folks,* a juvenile monthly periodical. Seeking more capital to carry his publication, Browne had suggested that I pay him a visit and look his business situation over in view of investing some of my earnings at intervals. I made the trip to Manchester early in July.

Returning, I found myself in Boston with almost three hours to kill before the Bangor steamer, which touched at Camden, would sail. It was raining and the storm was one of those drizzling northeasterlys that can be disagreeably cold in Boston, even in July. Wearing a light top-coat but carrying no umbrella, I pushed around through that chilly storm until my shoes, unprotected by rubbers, were wet through.

In my stateroom berth aboard the steamer that night, I awoke from a dream of being alternately broiled over live coals and packed in ice, while somebody took cracks at my head with a sledge hammer. I was shaking with chills and fever and had a splitting headache. That was one of the longest and most frightful nights of my life. I wondered if I would live until the boat docked at Camden in the morning and almost hoped I wouldn't.

A public carriage carried me up Chestnut Hill and I staggered into the house and went down for the count. The next thing I remember is that a doctor was bending over my bed. Then there were two doctors. It appeared that my first attack of 'flu had left me with some germs lingering in my system, where they had developed a progeny that had renewed the attack in overwhelming numbers.

Those doctors had a job on their hands to help me cheat the undertaker again. They did their part, and I pulled through once more. But I looked like something the cat had dragged in, when I was able to sit up and take more than thin nourishment. Even after I could walk around, I looked like a living skeleton who had escaped from the side show of a circus.

Now there was no chance that I would change my residential address from Camden to Manchester very soon, for doctors' bills and other expenses had left me with nothing but a hole in my pocket. To mend that, I began working again, much too soon, at my typewriter, and something happened that made my hair stand.

About five minutes after I began thumping the keys mornings, I would feel a swelling in my chest and would cough up a mouthful of bright pink blood. With the best of reasons for it, my former fear of tuberculosis returned redoubled.

However, though those small hemorrhages continued throughout the remainder of the summer, they became slighter and further between and eventually stopped when I got rid of a cough that had likewise been nagging me. Nevertheless, I sometimes would cough up traces of blood whenever I caught a heavy cold during the ensuing fifteen years. There was also a sore spot in my left lung that troubled me, and when I took a long, deep breath that lung would wheeze like a cat with the croup.

Seeking to cure that ailment, I went in for open-air exercise, but with discretion at first. I bought a second-hand high-wheel bicycle and pumped it over the dirt roads around Camden. And when my cough had disappeared, I rowed a boat on the harbor evenings, where in pleasant weather there were scores of other boats filled with pleasure seekers. Today practically nobody in Camden seeks either pleasure or health in that manner.

Surely life was simpler then and less hectic. There were joy rides around Megunticook Mountain on buckboards instead of in automobiles, and great ships went up and down the bay under expansive snow-white sails. Traveling over the winding highways, one had an opportunity to behold and enjoy scenery that is barely glimpsed at sixty miles an hour.

There were great clambakes on the shores of the many islands of Penobscot Bay, even on the shores near Camden Village, where clams still could be found but where there are none today. A three-pound lobster, boiled, could be bought for fifteen or twen-

Stop-overs on the Way

ty cents. Human beings carried an air of cheerful serenity that is rare to them now.

Some excellent theatrical companies came to Camden. There I once saw Robert Mantell in Shakespearian dramas, and Sidney Drew, brother of John Drew, appeared with a company of "Famous Broadway Stars," as it was billed.

Thomas E. Shea appeared regularly season after season in repertory, presenting such dramas as *The Bells, Monte Cristo, The Corsican Brothers,* and *The Marble Heart.*

Yearly he showed at the Eighth Avenue Opera House, in New York, and filled that huge auditorium to capacity. Metropolitan critics gave him favorable notices, and one of them pronounced his performance in *Dr. Jekyll and Mr. Hyde* in many respects superior to that of Richard Mansfield.

At Tom Shea's request, I reconstructed and rewrote an act in a new play he had bought in a little more than three hours. The play, with that act as revised by me, formed a part of his repertory for the remainder of that season. After that I seldom met Tom Shea that he did not tell me my forte lay in writing for the stage.

Late in March, after another winter in Camden, I was on the move again, bound, at the continued urgence of George Waldo Browne, for Manchester. Fearing she would never see me again, my mother was distressed by my departure.

In Manchester, where the great Amoskeag Mills were running full blast and business in general was flourishing, Alice and I found a small furnished apartment and settled down with the idea that we might stay much longer than we did. For I soon decided I did not want to sink any of my spare cash in Browne's magazine.

He had previously made a modest success with a similar publication and then sold out to the *Youth's Companion,* published in Boston. Now he was attempting to push another juvenile monthly to prosperity on old lines and with old methods such as giving unframed chromos as subscription premiums.

He was a strange goggle-eyed old bach with a walrus moustache, and he ate pie four times a day, once with each regular meal and once before going to bed. In a way he looked like a fire-eater, but he was actually as meek as the great "Casey" after he struck out. And yet with all that meekness went a streak of stubborness or blindness that would not let him see any other way to success with his publication excepting the way he had once almost succeeded. That was why I quickly became willing for him to go his own way while I went mine—and kept my smackers in my jeans.

About the only valuable thing I learned in Manchester was that rum and molasses is not a sure cure for a cold. The combination worked the first time I turned the dial at the suggestion of my favorite bartender at the Manchester House, where I sometimes dallied at pool and billiards.

Feeling a cold creeping up on me while I was watching Bert Leston Taylor—then a Manchester newspaper man and afterwards a well-known Chicago columnist—absorb a trimming at billiards by a fellow reporter, I hastened to approach the bar and pour my apprehension into the ear of my friend behind the mahogany.

He poured me a shot of rum, into which he stirred a portion of molasses. I drank it and seemed to feel a slight improvement, so I ordered another. Some time after that I lost count of them, but I was feeling very well indeed. I found the place where I lived, with the kindly aid of the cop on the beat.

I went to bed and perspired like a man who sees the horse on which he has bet his bottom dollar running neck-and-neck with the favorite. On awakening the following morning I had a splitting headache but no cold whatever. Thereafter for several years I tried that remedy when I felt a cold catching up with me, but all it ever did was make me need a policeman to show me the way home.

While in Manchester I contributed some little pieces, gratis, to Browne's magazine, but most of the time I rode my typewriter for pelf—and with spurs. The pelf came in but not swiftly enough to make me hoarse from cheering. However, when April wept her way in again I was financially primed for the next shot at fortune. Presently we took another jump which carried us into Manhattan.

21 • NINETY-EIGHT WILLIAM STREET

MORE THAN FIFTY YEARS AGO I stood on the upper deck of a steamer of the Fall River Line and beheld the seemingly endless miles of flat-topped human beehives called New York slipping by on the starboard quarter. There were then no awe-inspiring Towers of Babel in the city.

Packed to the rails with human beings on their way to labor, turtlish ferry boats were swimming from shore to shore, and presently Brooklyn Bridge, which from a distance had looked like a graceful span of cobweb strands, rumbled above our heads. A salty tang came to my nostrils from the Harbor, where great ships, with panting tugs snuggled against their sides, were being escorted past Bedloe's Island, on which then stood no colossal Statue of Liberty.

Past the old Aquarium, on the southern tip of Manhattan Island, we sailed and around into the mouth of the North River, there to reach our docking pier at the foot of Murray Street. I had reached the land of my boyhood dreams at last, and Corinna, behind the Blue Hills, seemed very far away.

Carrying our hand-luggage, Alice and I walked down the gangplank into the dusky dimness of the pier. Cautiously we crossed teeming West Street and headed eastward between the rows of produce markets on Murray Street. We paused when a smoking locomotive, drawing a train of crowded passenger cars, rumbled over steel rails on a great trestle high above us.

Moving on again, we came to City Hall Park and saw on the opposite side the golden dome of the World Building rising high above the roofs of surrounding structures. Now that building is only a pimple amid the towering skyscrapers of Manhattan.

"Now," said I to Alice, "I know where we go from here. The entrance to Brooklyn Bridge is right over there, near the World Building."

We were bound for the home of Addie Maynard, nee Hutchings, who had become the wife of Charles Maynard, of Bangor.

They had moved to Brooklyn, and Maynard had obtained a position as secretary for the head of a firm of New York cotton brokers.

Having decided when I would shake the dust of Manchester from my feet, I had opened correspondence with Addie and she had invited us to become guests in her home until we could get our bearings and find a home of our own. She had suggested meeting us on our arrival but had not done so for the simple reason that I, though stating when we would appear, had not informed her at what point we would arrive.

We took a car over the big bridge, and a policeman directed us to another that would carry us within short walking distance to the Maynard address on Seventh Avenue. When I pressed a button beneath the name of Maynard in the vestibule of a tenement house, the doorlock clicked in response. We climbed two flights and found Addie waiting in an open door. The sight of us made her blue eyes widen.

"Why, Willie Patten!" she cried. "How in the world did you ever find your way here?"

"My dear Mrs. Maynard," said I suavely, "I am now a person who knows his way around."

Addie and Alice fell on each other in an enthusiastic but ladylike manner, and everything was hunky-dory. Thinking Addie looked prettier than ever, I told her so, which made her blush and laugh, her chin twisting in the bewitching way that had always fascinated me. Her husband had departed to perform his secretarial duties, but Addie provided us with a sustaining breakfast to which relish was added by newsy gossip of mutual interest.

Being impatient to feast my eyes on the publishing establishment of Beadle and Adams, I left the ladies still chattering and hurried back over Brooklyn Bridge.

Standing in front of the House of Beadle, at 98 William Street, I thought at first that I had somehow mistaken the address. For instead of a splendid modern structure, I was gazing at a decidedly shabby four-story building of ancient vintage. It did not seem possible that this could be the building from which Erastus Beadle, who had started his business on a shoestring, had re-

Ninety-eight William Street

tired as the head of the company, with somewhat more than a cool million simoleons tucked away for inclement weather.

Recovering my aplomb after some moments of dismay, I climbed three flights of worn wooden stairs to the floor on which the editorial and business offices were located, as well as the distribution department.

In spite of its running-to-seed aspect, there seemed to be still lingering about the place a little of the sympathetic friendliness that had bound Beadle's authors to it with hoops of steel. As long as that aspect lasted, those hacks remained loyal. Even after dry rot and dissolution set in under William Adams' mismanagement of the business, some of them clung fast and went down with the ship.

Given a chair outside Mr. Victor's open door, I could see him, graybearded and seemingly austere, talking with a striking looking man who stood beside the long, slanting desk. The visitor, though not tall, was slim and straight and bore himself with a military air. His longish hair, in which there were strands of gray, touched the collar of his Prince Albert coat. There was also more than a touch of gray in his drooping moustache. In his softly spoken words I fancied I detected the slurrings and elisions of a cultured Southerner.

I was positive that I was at last beholding one of the writing heroes of my boyhood, a man who had fought in wars in many lands and was the friend of Buffalo Bill and author of many dime novel yarns about him.

Presently he came out, his military hat sitting a bit rakishly on his head, and walked past me with a slight limp. Then I knew that the story of his duel over a girl, at the age of seventeen, was not a romantic falsehood. He had been shot through the foot, but I did not know what happened to his antagonist until years after I saw him on my first day in New York. I wanted to speak to him then, but for once in my life, at least, modesty shackled my tongue. I watched him until he disappeared down the old worn stairs.

I presented myself before the venerable editor and was welcomed cordially. As soon as politeness permitted I asked, "Wasn't that Colonel Ingraham who just went out?"

He replied that it was, but, much as I desired to do so, I could not bring myself to ask for Colonel Ingraham's address. Perhaps it would not have been given to me had I asked, for, along with a policy of deferring all payments to authors until publication of their work, William Adams had also given directions against assisting the writers for the concern to become acquainted with one another. He had begun to cut the payment rates of some of them, and I presume he thought the practice might arouse their resentment were they to learn that the payments of others had not yet been reduced.

As he had in my own case, Orville Victor had encouraged and guided many young writers. Himself, he was a writer of no mediocre ability. He had written a life-history of Abraham Lincoln, who had been a reader and admirer of Beadle's publications, and had contributed other biographical works to Beadle's "Lives of Great Americans" series.

Charles A. Dana, famous editor of the New York *Sun*, was his personal friend. For thirty years Mr. Victor read, passed upon, and edited the thousands of publications bearing the imprint of Beadle and Adams, and all that tremendous amount of labor was done without the assistance of a reader or secretary.

Mr. Victor told me he thought I had made a wise move by coming to New York to live. He urged me to drop in often to confer with him regarding future work for which he might have some suggestions. Though not a little in awe of him, I was charmed by his cool magnetism. I think he then had a foreboding of doom for the publishing house for which he had labored so long, for, as I was about to depart, he said:

"Though you have not yet done anything of a striking nature, Patten, I have a feeling that there are fine possibilities in you. Maybe you will live and climb high long after the House of Beadle is dust and tradition."

Well, I have lived. There is now not much time for me to do anything more.

22 · THE NEW YORK THAT WAS

WITH ADDIE MAYNARD'S ASSISTANCE, we found a small walk-up apartment which we furnished, sparsely but passably well, on the partial payment plan, which left us with enough money to carry on until more came in.

When I dropped in to see Mr. Victor again he suggested that I get on familiar terms with the Big Town and sandwich in an occasional detective yarn with my Westerns. Heretofore, with one exception, all my stories had been Westerns, for which I had obtained atmosphere from other dime novels and books like Mark Twain's *Roughing It*. The plots for that kind of work were easy for me to construct from my own imagination.

Now I was glad to turn to the writing of city-life detective tales and gather atmosphere and suggestions for plots from personal observations. This, I thought, would be my first approach to real-life delineation, but the resultant work, aimed at the dime novel market, was still artificial, shoddy, and sloppily written at high speed, the first script always being the final one.

I found much of the face of New York as dirty as that of an urchin who had been making mud pies in a gutter. Everybody seemed to scatter litter, no matter of what nature, helter-skelter on the streets.

In some places old newspapers, cigarette wrappers, empty tin cans, even garbage, lay thick on the sidewalks and in the gutters. Everywhere there was dirt, and dust filled eyes, throat, and nostrils when the wind blew. When it rained, the dust turned to greasy mud. Alleyways were noisomely foul. Persons spat anywhere, on sidewalks, in street cars, even on carpets in homes—believe it or not.

Elevated locomotives, dropping sparks and even red-hot coals into the streets at times, befouled the air with smoke and begrimed buildings, windows, and human dwellers along their way. Sawdust covered the floors of many saloons and filled the small wooden boxes intended for cuspidors, at which drunken patrons sometimes spat and usually missed their aim. Dirty towels hung from hooks under the front rails of bars, and on them the customers wiped their hands and mouths—sometimes blew their noses.

The price for a shot of bar whiskey ran downward from fifteen cents in the better saloons to five cents in the hell holes on the Bowery. A stretch of Eighth Avenue was lined on the west side with meat markets which displayed their goods—butchered cattle, hogs, sheep, and poultry—by hanging them in the open air. The spectacle was enough to make one turn vegetarian.

On the East and West Sides, around the Five Points section, gangs rioted by day and by night, assaulting pedestrians and fighting among themselves with brickbats and paving stones. Though there was rarely any shooting after the custom of laterday gangsters, bloody noses and broken heads were plentiful, and once in a while a hoodlum tickled another hoodlum in the ribs with a sharp piece of steel.

Strong-arm thugs stalked their victims on side streets by day as well as by night, and sometimes cops arrested unfortunates who complained that they had been beaten up and "cleaned." For many of the blue-coated "officers of the law" were grafters who gathered loot from the looters and sneered at the looted.

They protected certain streetwalkers to fatten on the earnings of the wretched creatures. But the women of the streets were small fry compared to the madams of brothels and proprietors of gambling joints, who paid a fixed amount of tribute regularly.

Boss Tweed had been dethroned and jailed, but Richard Croker had stepped into his boots and Tammany was still sitting pretty.

Some of the newsboys of the town were as clever pickpockets as if "Fagin" himself had trained them. I fell victim to one of the young dips.

In those days pockets for loose change were placed on coats outside the larger pocket on the right hand side. Holding his papers spread out on his left arm so that the headlines could be seen by me, a boy placed himself directly in my path and pressed his hidden hand against me, whiningly begging me to please buy a paper. Later I discovered that his concealed fingers had removed about a dollar in change from my change-pocket. I carried my change elsewhere after that.

Other dips worked by twos and threes on the elevated trains and street cars. One or two of them would crowd and jostle an unsuspecting passenger while another was relieving him of his watch or pocketbook—maybe both. There were numberless pawnshops that were "fences" for thieves of all kinds. Women shoplifters prowled through stores and were persistently paroled when caught with the goods and convicted.

Some judges were honest, but many were as crooked as corkscrews. But, after all, it took the Prohibition Era to make crime real big business, not only in New York but from coast to coast—which reminds me not to be too smug in these reminiscences.

Not long before I came to New York a horde of homeless boys had roved the streets like scavengers. On cold nights they slept in cellars and open doorways, often with no other covering to protect their raggedly clad bodies than discarded newspapers or those they had failed to sell.

Some came through the bitter experience and grew up to be honest and successful men, but many more found their way into almshouses and jails. I've never heard of one who found a nickel and ran it up into a fortune after the manner of Horatio Alger's young heroes.

Nevertheless, although I could not read his yarns, Alger may have exerted some influence that led to the opening of the Newsboys Lodging House, in a bare room of which he came to live and write many of his stories.

The old Tenderloin, north of Twenty-third Street and west of Broadway, was a region of sordid carnal sin. Thundering from the pulpit of his church despite the efforts of corruptionists to besmirch him, Dr. Parkhurst started a movement that eventually wiped out that blot on the city.

From nightfall until near dawn the houses of ill-fame in that section were advertised by red lights and the sounds of pianos which were played upon by wretched old men called "professors." If a come-on in town wanted to know how to find such houses, the policeman in that vicinity would direct him unhesitatingly and cheerfully.

And there were restaurants on the stretch of Sixth Avenue between Twenty-third and Thirty-third streets that thrived as pick-up places for streetwalkers. The Haymarket, a dance hall on Sixth Avenue, was notoriously brazen in catering to prostitutes, pimps, and suckers.

But carnal iniquity was not confined to that region only. There were notoriously dirty dives scattered widely below Thirty-third Street and the lower business section of the town. Some of these were the Sans Souci, the Hole in the Wall, and Tom Gould's Place. And there seemed to be hundreds of little "beer parlors" where loose ladies, many being girls in their 'teens, some not over fifteen or sixteen, sat over glasses of suds, hungrily eyeing every man that entered, in hopes of custom that would enable them to live and pay the varlets who thrived on their shame.

From three or four o'clock until after midnight swarms of prostitutes paraded a stretch of Broadway, openly and boldly soliciting. When business was bad they were apt to become almost violently insistent. I never saw one of them arrested. For a well-dressed man after nightfall, they were pests. One of them followed me for blocks one night as I was on my way to catch a ferryboat to Brooklyn. At last she placed herself squarely in front of me.

"For God's sake come with me, Mister," she sobbed, "I've had damned rotten luck today and I'm starving. Honest to God I am!"

I looked into her tear-streaked face and gave her a dollar I could ill-afford to part with. She grabbed my hand and kissed it.

"You've saved my life," she said. "I was going straight to the river if I failed with you."

Perhaps she lied, but I was glad I'd given her that dollar.

The New York That Was

Oh, yes, there was another, quite different, aspect to New York. Thus far I've sketchily depicted the sordid features of the town, but pomp and glitter could be found quite as easily.

There was Fifth Avenue, wide and beautiful, perhaps the most beautiful and amazing street to be seen anywhere in the world. In its myriad of great stores and fine exclusive shops, the wealthy paid hundreds of times the price of a poor man's meal for a fancy bauble or a Parisian bonnet. Golden trinkets were displayed in many windows, and diamonds and rubies and emeralds fit to adorn a princess.

On the Avenue from three o'clock until five in the afternoons of fair days, the abundantly wealthy rode in glittering carriages drawn by richly caparisoned blooded horses. In that showy parade, of course, were parvenus galore.

The original Fifth Avenue Hotel, fronting on Madison Square, was patronized by politicians and business men of power. In its famous "Amen Corner" was the throne of "I-am-a-Democrat" David Hill, then political boss of the state.

The Hoffman House, a little distance to the northward, had a popular bar at which gentlemen quenched their thirst and bathed their eyes in the sometimes-called lascivious beauty of a large painting of fat nude females. This painting was reputedly the work of an old master, and some of those old boys sure did have a taste for beef.

Outside the Grand Opera House and fashionable theaters, hungry beggars could behold fine gentlemen handing down from their carriages splendid ladies swathed in sealskins and ermine and wearing enough precious stones, *in toto,* to sink a ship.

I had found a field too vast and bewildering for any dime novelist to touch it more than superficially in spots—a field that a writing genius—a Balzac—could explore for a lifetime and die with many of its values for literary work still undiscovered.

I felt puny but cheerful.

23 · ALL AROUND THE TOWN

UNLIKE THE MYSTERY NOVELS OF TODAY, the detective dime novels never dealt with crime in "high society." Knowing their clientele, that doubtless was a wise policy by the publishers. To follow in the beaten track of other writers of the kind of city-life stories I would have to knock off, I tried to saturate myself with low-life atmosphere and get at least a glimpse or two of the underworld. So I roamed New York over from Battery Park to the Harlem River. Already Niblo's Garden and Harry Hill's huge joint had disappeared and were beginning to fade as memories.

The theatrical Rialto on Broadway had shifted above Twenty-third Street, from which it extended to Thirty-fourth Street, and practically all theaters were below Forty-second Street. There was then no blazing Great White Way. When a large electrically lighted sign advertising Manhattan Beach, "where cool ocean breezes blow," appeared on the new Flatiron Building at Twenty-third Street it became the talk of the town.

The dome of the World Building and the tower of Madison Square Garden—the latter being situated across Fourth Avenue from the northeast corner of Madison Square Park—were the two highest pinnacles on Manhattan Island. Above the latter the large graceful figure of a nude Diana, her bow drawn to send an arrow after an invisible fleeing deer, was condemned by prudes as being very naughty.

Broadway street cars were propelled by an underground cable that hummed all day and could be heard quite plainly from midnight until morning. Elsewhere the street cars were drawn by horses. The spectacle of a smoke-belching, tooting fire-engine drawn by powerful galloping horses on its way to a fire was something to behold.

In the Italian quarter of the city I once saw a fire-engine pursued by a mob of stark-naked screaming children. There was then another section, called the Jewish Ghetto, where hundreds

All Around the Town

of push-cart peddlers almost blocked the narrow, dirty streets and where I never heard anything but Yiddish spoken.

My new-found friends among writers and artists warned me to keep away from Hell's Kitchen, on the upper West Side. I went there at the first opportunity and rather wished I hadn't when I found I had sauntered into the middle of a street scrap in which twenty or thirty merrily cursing gangsters were indulging. By continuing more or less serenely on my way I was lucky enough to saunter out of that melee with a whole head, the young thugs apparently being too busy breaking each other's, to find time for a crack at mine.

New York was singing "Oh, the Bowery, the Bowery, I'll never go there any more."

So of course I went to the Bowery—not once but several times. I peered into joints and honky-tonks where there were long bars at which frowsy and tough-looking customers were guzzling "suds," and the kind of so-called whiskey that only cast-iron stomachs could take and hold.

In some of those places were stages on which frayed fairies in pink tights and Irishmen with green whiskers curvetted and bemused the patrons with jokes of the unparlor variety. Not satisfied merely to peer in, I entered several of those places, bought beer which tasted like resin, sat amid the dregs of humanity at sloppy tables, and wondered what such forlorn beings could find in life that made it worth living. Very little of that was too much for me.

Drunks reeled along the wide street, above which elevated trains rattled and roared. I saw other drunks booted or thrown out of saloons, some of them to fall in the gutter and lie there.

Wretched women, bedizened and usually intoxicated, leered at me. I pretended not to notice them and do not recall that one of them spoke to me. Yellow lights flared along the Bowery at night, but the shadows in doorways and down narrow alleyways seemed sinister. I fancied I could feel murder in the air.

Likewise I visited cheap saloons along the waterfront, but never at night. I lacked the courage to do that, or possessed enough wisdom not to do it.

As told me by Mr. Victor, it was in one of those waterfront barrooms that "Buckskin Sam" met some gentry who relieved him of carrying around some personal property of more or less weight. His real name was Sam S. Hall. When a mere boy, he ran away from his home in Wilmington, Delaware, and traveled westward into the wide-open spaces, firmly resolved to become a dashing hero.

He actually succeeded in joining the Texas Rangers and became noted for his courage and ability to hit what he shot at. Returning to Wilmington years later, he claimed that he had won the title of major with the Rangers and was familiarly known as "Buckskin Sam."

Touched by the finger of inspiration and urged by the hand of necessity, he wrote an 80,000-word Western novel and sent it to Beadle and Adams; but his grammar and spelling were so bad that Mr. Victor returned it with the statement that it would be acceptable if rewritten by an educated person.

Whereupon Sam formed a partnership with a Harvard graduate who corrected his errors and aided him in constructing his wild yarns. The partnership produced a long list of novels accredited to Major Sam S. Hall ("Buckskin Sam"), all being published by Beadle.

One day Sam delivered a manuscript personally to Mr. Victor. He was adorned in tailor-made clothes and a ten-gallon hat, and he wore a diamond scarf-pin, a finger ring in which another large diamond bedazzled the eye, and a gold watch that was anchored to his vest by a heavy gold chain. His breath bespoke the fact that he had already been bending his elbow.

"Now, Sam," said Mr. Victor kindly, "take a tip from me and keep out of tough saloons if you wish to carry any of your money or expensive knicknacks with you when you go home."

A little man, Sam bristled like a bantam cock. "Don't worry about me, sir," said he. "If any o' these yar city slickers come a-meddlin' with me, I'll chaw 'em up."

All Around the Town

A different looking "Buckskin Sam" appeared before Mr. Victor on the following day. He had a beautiful pair of black eyes but no diamond ring or scarf pin, no watch and chain, no money. Even his ten-gallon hat was absent. Ruefully but wrathfully, he confessed that he had been beaten up and robbed in a waterfront saloon.

"Do you remember where it happened?" asked Mr. Victor.

"I shore do," said Hall. "I can go right back thar."

Mr. Victor called Fred, who was in charge of the mailing department and had never been west of Jersey City. He was a huge raw-boned man with a heavy black moustache and eyes as keen as daggers, and he looked a hundred times more like a Western bad man than Sam did. Mr. Victor asked Fred to go with Sam and try to recover the latter's stolen property.

They returned within two hours. Sam had led Fred to the place and they had found the thieves there, and somehow Fred had awed them into restoring all of Major Hall's property except about one hundred dollars which they claimed to have spent already.

Some time after Mr. Victor told me about "Buckskin Sam's" little adventure in the Big Town, I saw a picture of Sam in the *Police Gazette*.

He was riding a furiously galloping horse along the principal street of Wilmington and shooting into the air with two pistols, like a two-gun man, while frightened pedestrians scampered for the sidewalks. For that Wild West demonstration in his home town, he spent a night in the cooler and coughed up a generous fine at the suggestion of the judge before whom he appeared the next day.

One night Arthur Grissom, who later became the first editor of the *Smart Set Magazine,* went with me and another young man whose name I have forgotten, to visit Tom Gould's cellar dump. Descending a flight of stairs, we entered a smoky room where men and women were sitting around small tables and trying to cheer themselves up or drown their sorrows with glasses or steins of beer.

Everybody present appeared to be under forty, and one girl looked as if she were not more than sixteen. Without exception, the women were dames of the pavement, and most of them had left comeliness behind—if they had ever possessed it. They solicited with appealing glances or stares, sometimes with spoken invitations. Present also were a few slick-haired youngish men who were the pimp-slave-masters of those women of the town; for white slavery was a very real thing in those days.

We were spotted by the ladies as prosperous-looking prospects, but we found seats at a vacant table and ignored all efforts to entice us. A black-haired oldish young man was cuffing the keys of a piano, and presently a young woman joined him and sang. She had once possessed a pretty good singing voice which had become marred by a whiskey huskiness.

She sang a popular song of the day, "The Picture That's Turned Toward the Wall." Near our table, the youngest girl in the place silently wept in her beer.

I had seen enough by the time I'd finished one glass of beer, and we took our departure. The very next night after that, a man was beaten up there and thrown out into the street, where he perversely proceeded to die. The newspapers screamed and the police were reluctantly compelled to do something. A so-called clean-up was started, but it was no more than a superficial wipe at the dirty side of the town's face. However, Tom Gould and two or three other proprietors of similar dumps were sent to the jug for awhile.

Being aware of the value of sharp contrasts in fiction, especially the contrast of squalor and wealth, I sought other scenes than those I've been describing. Lacking entree to homes of wealth, I regretfully viewed the palatial residences of multimillionaires from without and read such descriptions of their inner luxury as I could get hold of. I saw rich old clubmen lolling in the windows of one club on the Avenue and eventually did pass over the threshold of one exclusive club as the guest of a friendly member.

For my own cultural benefit, as well as for atmosphere for fiction, I visited art galleries and museums—the Metropolitan Museum of Art repeatedly. With the aid of catalogs, I learned as much as I could as fast as I could about the great paintings exhibited and the artists who had created them.

I turned to the opera also, but in my haste I made the mistake of attempting to leap too high at a single bound. I should have climbed to grand opera by graduated steps deliberately taken. For good music entrances me. But I was not prepared to appreciate the best at once. I did enjoy *Carmen,* but I fear it was the drama more than the music that gave me pleasure.

Sung by a quartette in a popular restaurant, I thought *Tales of Hoffman* and Mendelssohn's "Spring Song" were exquisite. But it was De Koven and Smith's *Robin Hood* that struck me as near perfection, and I placed most of Victor Herbert's music in the same category. "My Little Gypsy Sweetheart" is still my favorite song of sentiment.

The palmy days of the American stage lasted from the time of my coming to New York until the rise of motion pictures from one-and-two-reelers to shows lasting two hours or more. The famous players of that millennium were held in affectionate regard by regular patrons of the drama.

Many of the stars of that time had received their training with Augustin Daly's stock company in his small theater on Broadway. Daniel Frohman's Fourth Avenue Stock Company followed the demise of Daly's, presenting only excellent American and English dramas and training other actors and actresses to become stars.

Since the day Thomas E. Shea had told me my forte lay in writing for the stage, I had been nabbed by a yearning to test my talent in that direction. Now living in Brooklyn made it possible for me to see the best plays on Broadway, limited only by my ability to buy admission.

At one time or another I saw, with few exceptions, all the leading actors and actresses of the day do their stuff. To my regret, I did miss Edwin Booth, but I saw Joseph Jefferson, Wilson Barrett, John McCullough, Maude Adams, William Faversham, Richard Mansfield, Julia Marlowe, and scores of others—a long list of the great and near-great.

To a degree, my pleasure in playgoing was lessened because I was continually trying to analyze the construction of the dramas I witnessed. I regretted that circumstances prevented me from becoming a super and learning something about the mechanics of the stage from behind the footlights. I read the reviews of William Winter and other dramatic critics and finally found a book on play writing, written by W. T. Pierce, that was a help. Today that book, with its directions for entrances and exits and asides, is archaic.

I entertained no egotistic belief that I could become a great dramatist, but I did think that some day I might construct a play of the caliber of *Blue Jeans* or *In Old Kentucky*.

Again with Arthur Grissom one night, I attended a performance of *Alabama* at Palmer's Theatre, afterwards called Wallack's. Without thrilling me, that play delighted me with its sweet—and possibly false—old Southern atmosphere and charm.

"It's fine," said I to Grissom.

He smiled enigmatically. "Oh," said he, "it's pretty fair for the work of a newspaper cub from Kansas City."

A young man spoke to Arthur as we came out upon Broadway. "Hello, Grissom," he said. "How goes it with the great author from Independence?"

"Oh, how are you, Gus?" said Arthur as they shook hands. "Quite a little play you've knocked off. Yes, really rather good, old top."

"Thanks—so much," said the other dryly.

Then Grissom introduced me to Augustus Thomas, whose first smash-hit we had just witnessed, and I told him, sincerely, that I thought *Alabama* was fine. He gave me a queer look.

"Thanks," he said just as dryly, but he did not add, "so much."

Thomas and Grissom chatted briefly. As Arthur and I walked away together, he said, "That lad's head needs hooping to keep it from busting."

They had known each other back in Missouri, where they had done newspaper work, and Gus Thomas' success in New York had made Arthur green-eyed.

For me *Alabama* was a spur. I wrote a play. Which was produced. Professionally.

---

24 • THE LURE OF BROADWAY

Now, FOR THE FIRST TIME IN MY LIFE, I did a piece of work for which I wrote the climax and knew the characters and the plot complete before I wrote the opening lines. But this was not difficult because I took my theme, characters, and much of the action from a three-part serial I had sold to the *Yankee Blade*, published in Boston.

Having begun on a play, I worked at it and thought about it almost continually when not grinding out pot boilers for Beadle and Adams. Parts of it were rewritten several times before I decided that I had made it as nearly right as I could. It was a comedy-drama in four acts. I christened it "Nan the Mascot."

James M. Hill, a gray-whiskered man familiarly called "Parson Jim," was then manager of the Standard Theater, located on the spot where Gimbel's department store now stands. He was also a play producer.

I had met him one night at Trainor's Bar, next door to the Standard, when he had shown me a photograph of Marie Tempest in tights. And I now induced him to read my play, which had a rural first act and then shifted to New York and Wall Street, with the setting for the final act representing the interior of a Fifth Avenue mansion. As James Hill had come to New York from Exeter, Maine, and made good, I hoped my drama was the kind of thing he would like.

He turned it down politely, even gently. He said it was pretty good, but added that he thought it lacked something to make it a Broadway success.

Elizabeth Marbury had only recently opened a play brokerage office, and I took my comedy-drama to her. She placed it with Eugene Lee, manager of a road repertory company in which his attractive wife played leads. After giving two performances of "Nan," Lee shelved other plays to use mine only—and I began to think that Tom Shea might be right. But even Miss Marbury did not know that Lee was sailing so close to the rocks that he could not buy the proper "paper" to advertise my play attractively. The newspapers along his course gave "Nan" laudatory notices, but Lee's boat went aground in Wakefield, Rhode Island, which, as far as I know, was his finish in theatricals.

Apparently more sore than I was myself, Miss Marbury lost little time about digging up another manager who was willing to take a venture with "Nan." He was Curtis J. Marr, who reputedly had made a killing the previous season with a play called *A Barrel of Money*.

His stage manager, Sedley Brown, had sold one of his own plays outright for five thousand dollars, and together we took "Nan" apart and reassembled it, injecting more comedy into the poor thing, which was renamed "Men of Millions." Still further changes and improvements were made during rehearsals, which were held in a hall on Twenty-seventh Street.

With one exception, Marr had collected a pretty good cast. The exception was a Miss Hopkins, who had been given the part of the scheming cold-blooded wife of one of the principal characters. Having her own ideas about how the part should be played, she gave Sedley Brown plenty of trouble.

"I've been trying to get Marr to fire her and get another woman to play 'Mrs. Baldwin,'" he told me one day while we were lunching in Engle's Chop House, on Broadway. "If she gets cantankerous on the road it'll be bad—and she's just the biddy to do it. I feel that we've got a hit in the play, and Marr has a New York theater he can get into if things shape up right."

Being an optimist and still quite young, I hoped for the best.

The Lure of Broadway

Marr's company ran head-on into trouble on that tryout tour. Grover Cleveland's hat was in the Presidential ring, and a grand political scrap was going into the final rounds. Rousing rallies and torchlight parades were providing the public with free shows that interfered with the flow of cash into theatrical ticket offices.

The pickings were lean for Mr. Marr, and the blow-up occurred in New Haven. There the gallery was packed with college lads who cheered Miss Hopkins on when she began to twitter according to her notion of how the part of "Mrs. Baldwin" should be acted. Delighted and thinking herself vindicated, she twittered still more twitteringly—until the cheering turned to hilarious razzing. Then she went quite off her nut and flopped in a faint in her dressing-room. Sedley Brown frothed at the mouth, and his brother, who played a comedy part, was taken violently drunk. The fourth act of "Men of Millions" was enjoyed by the college students only.

Curtis J. Marr had a broken spirit and a pocketbook as empty as Miss Hopkins' head. He threw in the sponge right there and "Men of Millions" never saw the lights of Broadway.

Still my work on that play was not to be wholly wasted. In the course of time royalties from another repertory company and amateur performances brought me something close to $2,600.

What hurt worse than having a tooth pulled was the necessity of going on with the grind of writing dime novels, which I had begun to loathe. I was sick, too, with another cold, and my bum left lung ached dully but constantly. I longed for a change and a little rest.

So I turned a willing ear to Alice's suggestion not to renew the lease on our apartment but to put our furniture—now wholly paid for—into storage and go back to Maine for awhile. I was not then aware that she was fed up with life in Brooklyn and secretly yearned to return to Corinna to live.

In April we headed back toward the Pine Tree State. My parents had given up the Ogier Homestead and were living in the upper part of a private house on Limerock Street, where there was room for all of us.

Spring was in the air and healing also, for I soon lost my cough and the pain in my lung ceased. Feeling so much better, I did not dislike my work quite so intensely. With the opening of the brooks for trout fishing, I found time to whip the pools and ripples and was both contented and happy.

In the summer Alice went back to Corinna to visit her family. I followed after she had been gone three weeks, and stopped in Asa Grant's hotel. I had wondered how the village would seem to me and that question was soon answered. In spite of many acquaintances and friends in the town, the place still oppressed me with a sensation of loneliness, caused of course by my boyhood days of longing to escape beyond the distant Blue Hills. And so when Alice ventured to suggest our living there again I quietly but firmly informed her that nothing like that would ever happen to me. She did not press the point—then.

When autumn came once more, I was feeling in the pink. We returned to Brooklyn and found quarters in a new apartment house on Munro Street in the eastern part of the city. Ferry boats ran from the foot of Munro Street to Twenty-third Street in Manhattan, and I could reach Broadway in about thirty-five minutes by ferry.

Charles Howard Johnson, a young artist from the West, had joined my circle of New York friends, who were wont to foregather in the Metropole Café on Broadway, which had no connection with the Hotel Metropole.

Already Johnson had become well known as an illustrator for *Puck, Judge, Life,* and *Truth,* and he was soon engaged in illustration work for Harper's and other book publishers. He was a swanky dresser and spent his money as if it grew on trees and shrubbery. It was said that he never walked when he could find another way to get around; even that he took a cab to cross the street.

But Arthur Grissom was even more the dandy than Johnson. He had clothes for morning, afternoon, and evening wear, which included, of course, a glossy silk topper for the latter half of the day. Me, I wore an unfashionable soft hat at all times, but I never stepped into the street without my cane. They said I would catch cold if I forgot it.

Practically every afternoon except on Sundays, at the hour of four, I paraded a turn, north and south, along a stretch of Broadway, bowing in the grand manner to acquaintances, steadily growing more numerous.

I glanced the fair ladies over with an intentionally critical and superior air. I thought quite well of myself and had become more than a little touchy with anybody who did not agree with me—especially anybody who did not keep his fingernails clean.

Talking shop one afternoon in the back room of the Metropole Café, Grissom attempted to take me for a buggy ride. "Say, Pat," said he, (all my friends called me Pat) "why don't you stop grinding out bilge and try to do something better?"

Now Arthur had risen—or fallen—from being a freelance writer and the editor of a trade paper to become a steady contributor to William Mann's *Town Topics,* a literary sheet that dealt also in the gossip and scandals concerning New York and Newport's so-called Four Hundred. But before coming to New York he had written Half-Dime Libraries for Beadle and Adams under the pen name of "Albert Cecil Gaines."

"Have you forgotten your own dime-novel record, Arthur?" said I, feeling my cheeks burn. "And maybe you've had a lapse of memory about writing for a trade weekly in order to live and eat." Then, without pausing, I let him have the toad-sticker full length. "Anyhow, the petrified salacious tripe you're writing for *Town Topics* isn't literature any more than what I write—and it stinks worse."

It wasn't nice between pals, but he had started it and rubbed my sore spot raw. Now his face was flushed.

"The trouble with you," said he, "is that you can't write anything different. You're just a low-rut duffer."

"Listen, Arthur," said I, "I'll bet you a sawbuck—if you can find one in my jeans—that I'll write material for *Town Topics* and sell it there within the next two weeks—just to show you how wise you are not."

We put the money up, and I wrote and sold twelve dollars worth of verse and jokes to *Town Topics* within the time specified. I spent Arthur's ten-spot to treat the Metropole bunch—and Arthur never tried to put the spurs to me again.

Nevertheless, I could not write the sophisticated kind of salacious fiction used by *Town Topics*. That class of work has ever been outside my ability to concoct.

Herbert Grissom, Arthur's younger brother, came on to New York and quickly developed from a shy curly-haired towhead into a gaily promenading Broadwayite. That was not as disgraceful as it is now, when a long stretch of the Main Street has been taken over by shoddy people, crooks, tin horns, bums, and has-beens. Not even in the days of streetwalking ladies was Broadway as ratty as it is now around Times Square.

Occasionally I lingered to dine with my friends, and some times, being flush, we ate in one of the better-class hotels or restaurants. Far more often we patronized small Italian or French table-d'hôte places where one could buy a meal, such as it was, for from forty to seventy-five cents and maybe get a pint or quart of "red ink" along with it, without extra charge. Every one of us was alternately flush or broke, and that goes for Charlie Johnson.

The world was different then. Even in a time of restlessness and trouble, with a vast army of laborers lacking jobs, there was in this country a strong underlying feeling of optimism. Always tomorrow might be a better day. Not many doubted it. Any boy born in the U.S.A. was told that he might become President. And Grover Cleveland had.

Cleveland had been elected, and the Republicans were as raw as dressed turkeys the day before Thanksgiving. They were bleating that Grover would ruin the country. They called him an upstart, an incompetent, a radical, and a dictator. The "interests" railed at him and labor laughed.

He suppressed a savage strike in Chicago and labor howled with rage. There was a grave depression. Strikes multiplied. Business asserted it was being strangled and destroyed, yet many business men predicted that prosperity was "just around the corner." Everybody was right. Everybody was wrong. What a muddled mess it was!

Maybe my memory is at fault, but, in spite of all the hubbub, strife, and anxiety, it seems that then there was more true friendliness and light-hearted laughter than now. Nobody was jittery over the approaching destruction of civilization in the midst of bloody universal madness and carnage. Everybody seemed really to believe that things would be straightened out, somehow, and times would be better than ever.

Even the Brooklyn street car strike, when traffic was halted or snarled in a knot and armed militia men patrolled the streets, while mounted policemen sometimes rode hell-bent through crowds on sidewalks, was something of an exciting joke for me. Surely, there was trouble a-plenty, but nobody feared we were going to be blown to hell because Europe seemed bound for that destination.

Yes, I'm sure that even in America life was then more joyous than it is now.

25 • THE BOTTOM AND THE REBOUND

ON THE FORMER POLO GROUNDS at One Hundred and Tenth Street I saw the mighty Amos Rusie pitch for the New York Giants, but practically all I remember about the game is that Rusie was a big man with dazzling speed. That was the year when Fanny Davenport showed New York her conception of Cleopatra, Alexander Salvini swaggered as Don Caesar de Bazan, and Charlie Hoyt's *Trip to Chinatown* was the laugh-hit at the Madison Square Theater.

It was also the year in which my wife bore me a son in our humble Brooklyn apartment. Likewise it was the year when Beadle and Adams cut my rates, and I was disturbed by a premonition that the zero hour for that establishment was not far distant.

Arthur Grissom was participant in a plot to oust the editor of *Town Topics* and seize the position himself, but when the plot worked it was C. M. S. McClellan who stepped into the departing editor's shoes. Later, under the name of "Hugh Morton," McClellan wrote the books of several musical comedies, one of them being *The Belle of New York,* in which beautiful Edna May starred. He also wrote plays, in one of which, *The New York Idea,* I first witnessed the subtle acting of George Arliss.

I was fed up with Brooklyn as a bedroom, and some time during the year following the birth of my son, we moved into a new apartment house on One Hundred and Sixteenth Street, in New York. Considering that I had received another cut from Beadle and Adams, no cheers are due me for my wisdom. Forced to reef my sails, Broadway and the Metropole Café were seeing me only by using a spyglass, and I was grim and worried in my efforts to stem the tide that was carrying me into the breakers.

I obtained Colonel Ingraham's address—I don't remember how—and called on him in his snuggery on Fifty-eighth street, on the West Side. I found him surrounded by books, photographs, press clippings, and tokens of the various wars in which he had participated.

It was a bit of a shock to see how gray he had become since I had seen him on the day of my first visit to Beadle's Publishing House, but even though he was nearing sixty he was still full of pep and confidence. Taking care not to let him suspect how extremely low-spirited I was, I led him to talk about conditions in our field of endeavor.

"Don't you think the old dime novel days are about over, Colonel?" I asked.

"No, seh," he replied. "The dime novel will neveh die. Maybe some trashy imitations will, but that will leave a wider field for clean yarns like Beadle's."

"But Beadle and Adams appear to be slipping, sir. They have cut my rates."

The Bottom and the Rebound

"Well, they've slashed mine—a little," he admitted, "but that don't mean a thing, boy. It's temporary, caused by the hard times. The squall will blow over before long and the old firm will restore top prices and take ever'thing you can hand 'em. Why, there was a time when I was pulling down twelve to sixteen thousand a year. I had my place in Georgetown then, and my horses and nigger servants. I was living, seh, but the fo'mer depression caught me with mortgages on my property and wiped me out. Ups and downs are the way of life, but if you hang on and keep fighting you're bound to have an up after a down."

He'd made me feel a little better, and I encouraged him to talk about himself. His life had been much like that of some of the dime novel heroes about whom he wrote; so much did it resemble them that many of his adventures seemed unreal. Yet in time I was given indisputable evidence that his experiences on land and sea were not mere figments of his imagination.

For instance, he was an admiral as well as a colonel, and both titles had been won in Cuba, where he had become a colonel in the army and an admiral of the Cuban navy of *one warship!* And he had been captured by the Spaniards, condemned to be shot, and saved by the British Cuban Consul after efforts by the United States Consul had failed.

"My time hadn't come," said he, laughing. "You see, boy, I'm a fatalist. I believe we go over the Range when the clock strikes our hour and not one of us has a thing to say about how he'll go—not even if he shoots himself. Not he but fate ordained that he should do that. Ned Buntline wrote a right fine poem saying he was born in sto'my March, had been a sto'my petrel all his life and would die in battle with his boots on, but the po' cuss had to take it the way fate had arranged it fo' him. He died in his bare feet, on a featherbed."

"But what's the use to struggle if we are such helpless pawns of fate?" said I.

His finely chiseled face lighted up. "In the struggle, my boy," said he, "lies the greatest fun in life. The fun to live in this old world and breathe God's pure air. The fun of meeting one's friends and clasping hands with them. The fun of never quitting." He squinted hard at me. "You don't look like a quitter, not even though you're a damyankee," he chuckled.

When I left that strange, fine gentleman he had put some starch into my backbone, and I was prepared to go on fighting for the fun of it—which was a new angle for me. It is not we, ourselves, who wholly build our characters. We are often greatly influenced and remoulded by those with whom we associate.

Thereafter I opened up a small market for occasional short stories with the American Press Association, which made "boiler plate"—stories, timely articles, and brief items of general interest, type-set and cast into metal columns—to be sold to weekly country newspapers. But I needed a wider field and could not seem to find it in those hard times, when business was taking to cover to weather the storm.

And the day came when, with not even a lonesome copper in my pockets, we were on the point of being evicted from our apartment for non-payment of rent. Pride prevented me from letting any of my friends know about our desperate situation, and now, unable to pay my fare on the Elevated, I walked from One Hundred and Sixteenth to Park Place—at least eight miles—to reach the offices of the American Press Association. There I collected, in advance of publication, twenty-five dollars for a short story.

But I needed—I had to have—more. A novel of mine would be published after another ten days by Beadle and Adams, at which time I was to receive one hundred dollars for it. So over to 98 William Street I trudged and poured my tale of woe into the ears of Mr. Victor.

"I've simply got to have the money now, sir," I told him.

He shook his gray head regretfully. "There was a time," said he, "when I could give you an order on our cashier. I can't now. Mr. Adams has stopped that. You'll have to see him. Tell him just what you have told me."

William Adams was a dour, grim man, but I do not think he was entirely responsible for the fact that the business was going to pot. Unlike Colonel Ingraham, I believed the old-fashioned dime novel had seen its best days. Mr. Adams listened to me in cold silence without having offered me a chair.

"No, Patten," said he when I had finished, "I can't do it. You will have to wait for publication."

I was silent then, but I looked at him hard and long, making no move to depart. Presently he glanced at me and turned his eyes away quickly.

"I don't see how I can break the rule," he said, "but I will talk with our cashier."

He left me standing beside his desk. After some time I saw him returning, and my heart leaped; for he was bringing a check.

"I've got a check," he said, "but I've been compelled to deduct ten dollars for payment in advance. Here's a receipt for you to sign."

The receipt was for "payment in full." He had deducted one dollar for each day up to the time when the payment would have been due!

With contempt and fury flaming in my heart, I signed the receipt. Then I went back to Mr. Victor and told him what had happened.

Never before had I heard O. J. Victor swear, but he blew up then. What he said about William Adams will not bear repeating.

"Well, I'm through, Mr. Victor," said I. "I want to thank you gratefully, sir, for your kindness and help, but, even though I die of starvation, I'll never write another line for this house."

"I don't blame you, Mr. Patten," said he. "And I wish all our authors would quit as you are doing."

I saw him only once after that. He did not long survive the collapse of Beadle and Adams, and I think his death was hastened by the fall of the house that had been his pride and love.

On the street again, I paused for a parting look at the old building from whence had come my first check for six dollars for two short stories, giving me a start as an author. Strange emotions stirred within me. I had traveled an unexpected road since that day, and now I had apparently come to a dead end. Nevertheless, there was relief, almost joy, in my heart.

"Now I'm really through with that stuff," I told myself. "All through! I'll never write another dime novel."

Man proposes, but "there is a divinity that shapes our ends, rough hew them how we will," and I was destined to write almost a thousand more so-called dime novels.

A man may say he'll starve rather than do a thing; but starving is quite disagreeable and he may change his mind, especially if he has a wife and son to support, as I had—and was soon to have an additional load of my parents.

I cashed my ninety-dollar check at a bank that honored those drawn by Beadle and Adams and bought a Brooklyn newspaper. In the For Rent column I found an advertisement that sent me hurrying over Brooklyn Bridge. When I returned I had made arrangements for immediate occupation of a corner flat on Seventh Avenue, not far from our first address in the "City of Churches." The place was old but clean and freshly papered and painted, and it was much more pleasant than the one on Munro Street, where my son Barr had greeted the world with his first wail of dismay.

Alice and I spent the rest of the day and part of the following night hurriedly packing, and in the morning a moving van carried our belongings back to Brooklyn.

As soon as we were settled, I began scouting for markets. William H. Hills, formerly editor of the New York *Dispatch,* for which I had written some Poelike tales purporting to be true revelations of old Manhattan murder mysteries, but which were, in fact, utter fakes, was now editor for the American Press Association. And now he gave me an assignment to write material regularly for a six-column sheet that carried the heading, "Some Odd Stories." My pay was set at five dollars a column, thirty dollars for the sheet. As the material was sold to country papers that used only two columns weekly, my income would be exactly ten dollars a week.

At that time "M. Quad" (C. B. Lewis) and Bill Nye were writing exclusively for the American Press Association, and their salaries were reputedly $12,000 a year for Lewis and $20,000 for

Nye. But I was told in confidence that the former received $8,000 and the latter $15,000.

Continuing to scout, I reached William C. Dunn, who was editing Norman L. Munro's *Golden Hours.* Like James Elverson's *Golden Days* and Frank Munsey's *Golden Argosy,* Munro's paper was a juvenile weekly.

Norman was the brother of George Munro, who had been a clerk for Beadle and Adams at fifteen dollars a week. George had resigned his clerkship to launch his own publishing business with an original capital of $125, and somehow he had raced over the field like Red Grange carrying the ball.

Seeing his brother piling up a fortune—which eventually amounted to several million dollars—Norman had hastened to get into the game. Having opened his own publishing house almost directly across Vanderwater Street from his brother's establishment, Norman was also doing all right, and he eventually became another millionaire publisher who had started on a shoestring.

Further than editing *Golden Hours,* Mr. Dunn was also Norman Munro's printer. Dunn owned his printing plant, which was situated on the upper floor of the building. He had made his start in life as a whiskey salesman, and never have I met a more likeable person or a squarer shooter than Bill Dunn.

"I'm sorry," said he, when I had revealed the nature of my visit, "but all of my writers are under contract and I haven't an inch of room for another."

I felt my face take a tumble, and maybe he saw it slip. For he rose from his desk, saying: "It's my lunch time. Come on and have lunch with me."

Our lunch began with a whole flock of cocktails, and, despite my distaste for hard liquor, I did not back away from one of them. Mr. Dunn had the capacity to take them. I held their potency at bay and kept my head by sheer determination, and wisely refrained from again mentioning my desire to write for him.

Suddenly he said, "Say, Patten, I like you."

Now it comes out. Now you can see what liquor does to human beings. I doubt if Bill Dunn would have said that had he not taken those drinks. Just consider how booze ruins business and everything its vile power touches.

I held my breath for a moment, strong as it was. "Now, Mr. Dunn," said I, "that's pleasant to hear, for I like you."

"Well, then," said he, "what kind of yarn were you contemplating inflicting upon me?"

I had prepared myself for that question before meeting him, so I replied, "Why, I'd wondered if a bicycling story might not fit into your scheme of things."

He took about half a minute to consider. "All right," said he, "go ahead and do it. If it's first class I'll use it and put one of my regular writer's stories into the safe."

I wrote "Bicycle Ben, the Knight of the Wheel," in about three weeks, and he read it the day I placed the manuscript on his desk. "It's all right," said he. "How much do you want for it?"

Fear made me blunder. Afterwards I knew that I should have asked for twice as much. "Oh, how about one hundred and fifty?" said I.

"You'll get your check on Saturday morning," said he.

Though regretting my timidity, I walked away on air.

26 · I CRASH THE GATE

I SOON DISCOVERED HOW BADLY I HAD BLUNDERED in asking such a low price for my first *Golden Hours* serial. Of the writers under contract with that publication, Cornelius Shea received the smallest pay, $300 for stories the same length as mine, 60,000 words, and John De Morgan was pocketing $600 for serial yarns. In between were Harry Irving Hancock and Albert Stearns, drawing $400 each.

Shea wrote Westerns, but I think his knowledge of the West, like my own, was acquired second-hand. However, he wore a ten-gallon hat and the skin of a rattlesnake for a four-in-hand necktie, the snake's rattles serving as a scarfpin. Owning a Staten Island tobacco store, he was not dependent for a living upon his earnings as a writer.

In my estimation, De Morgan, though the highest paid, wrote the poorest stories. In fact he appeared to possess practically no natural fiction writing talent but had acquired an artificial ability to concoct mediocre yarns. He owned a comfortable home on Long Island and appeared to be more financially prosperous than his writing income justified. I never saw anything written by him in any other publication than *Golden Hours*.

Hancock, the youngest of the staff, had done newspaper work, and Mr. Dunn advertised him as "the Boy Reporter." But beyond question, Albert Stearns possessed genuine literary talent, as he eventually proved by becoming a magazine and book writer for the Century Company. For Dunn, he wrote melodramatic serials and slapstick humor under pen names.

Besides *Golden Hours* Norman Munro published the *Family Story Paper* and the Old Cap Collier Library, the latter being in the dime novel field. Laura Jean Libbey, a plump young woman of considerable pulchritude, wrote thrillers for the *Family Story Paper,* and she knew her onions. The vicissitudes of her heroines were harrowing, but the poor things always escaped fates worse than death and married into the highest circles of wealth and culture.

A few men writers of nimble ability whacked out Libbeyish serials for Norman and George Munro and Street and Smith, the stories being published under pen names owned by the firms that bought them. T. W. Hanshew, detective fictioneer, whose yarns about "the Man with a Hundred Faces" were popular at one time, was reputed to have written such serials for the *Family Story Paper*. And John R. Coreyell, whom I met and who—according to a statement made to me by O. G. Smith personally—

was the creator of Nick Carter, sometimes employed his versatile talents upon that type of fiction.

This was while the Victorian Era of sentimentality was strong in its influence upon authors and publishers not only of cheap fiction, but of what was called the best, as may be confirmed by turning to back numbers of *Scribner's Magazine, Harper's* and *The Century*. Those publications were then catering to readers who lapped up honeyed mush and were extremely shocked by anything that might be called realistic.

Perhaps *The Century* provided the worst specimen of such sissified sloppiness, for its editor, Richard Watson Gilder, blushed with mortification over such words as "bosom," "legs," and "belly" and penciled them out of copy submitted by his authors. Gilder was admired by readers of his magazine and cussed, behind his back, by his pet writers.

I had been influenced not only by dime novels but by Dickens and Stevenson. Fortunately I had not read any of the artificial New England tales of Mary E. Wilkins. Unfortunately no red-blooded author like Jack London was then living and writing. Had there been, maybe at least a ghostly shade of his spirit would have appeared in my work.

Happy as I was over selling my first serial to Mr. Dunn, I was made still happier when he soon suggested that I write another for him. Again we were lunching together when he asked me, abruptly, if I knew anything about horses.

"I sure do," I answered unhesitatingly. "My father was a horse fancier, and I have driven and ridden some of the finest high-blooded horses ever seen in the State of Maine."

I did not know, then, that Mr. Dunn was a horse-owner and knew more about the critters than I would ever know, but I thought he looked at me a bit queerly, as if my reply had rung a trifle false.

"Well, then, what do you know about South America?" he shot at me.

Realizing I was on thin ice, I answered somewhat more cautiously: "Not much, but let me read up and I can write about any country down there well enough to give the impression that I've lived in it half my life."

"All right," said he. "Do me another serial with a horse featured in it, and tell what kind of a horse it is, too. If the story is as good as your first one, I'll correct any slips you make. Start the story in North America and about midway carry it into South America. I'll pay for it on acceptance and run it as soon as I can."

Elated, I lost no time in picking up a book about horses and others about South America. Reading them, I covered their pages with penciled markings, and typed several sheets of excerpts. After three days I was ready to start working on the story, the plot having formed in my mind as if doing that part of the job itself. Evidently my sub-conscious mind had been at work, especially while I was sleeping, for knots and problems of days before became clear to me mornings, usually while I was shaving or taking my bath.

With the problems solved and the outline of the story quite clear in my mind, I sat down to my typewriter and typed the title at the head of a page—"The Boy Centaur." Then the story began to caper and romp. Sometimes my thoughts were one or two sentences ahead of the typing. I moved the action logically from the United States to South America by having the horse stolen and sold to a circus that played in South America winters. The boy hero, from whom the horse was stolen, followed and recovered the animal after experiencing many adventures and surviving many perils.

"Man," said Bill Dunn when I placed the manuscript on his desk, "you're a fast worker. It must be poor stuff."

"It's better than 'Bicycle Ben,' " I told him.

I got a check for it four days later.

"Yes, Gil," said Mr. Dunn when I saw him again, "your second story is better than the first. Where have you been all my life?"

He published the opening installment of that serial in the issue which contained the closing installment of "Bicycle Ben."

But he had placed the name of William G. Patten on those stories instead of Gilbert Patten. Maybe he thought the former name had some value, which I doubt. I was sorry, for I was not getting away from the dime novel brand as soon as I'd hoped to—and I was eventually to learn that I could never get away from it.

Alice engaged a maidservant, and we took in two Broadway shows.

My son was beginning to try to talk. Sitting on my knee, he touched a button on my vest with his finger and said, "Buttney." That was his first word. "Moke" was the second, spoken as he reached for my pipe. He was a beautiful boy and life again looked rosy.

But I was far from satisfied. John De Morgan was raking in a hundred dollars a week from *Golden Hours* alone, and I was averaging less than fifty by selling there and anywhere else that I could place a story. So when I turned my third serial in to Mr. Dunn I mustered up courage to say I thought I ought to have a better price for it.

"Well, how much better?" said he, smiling.

Again I blundered. "I think it's worth two hundred and fifty," said I.

"I'll have to put it up to Mr. Munro," he told me. "I'll let you know."

When he let me know he said: "We made a mistake. Munro was in one of his tempers when I told him you wanted a raise. 'How much does he want?' he snarled. I said you had asked for two hundred and fifty. 'Well, why in hell don't you give it to him?' he roared. He was in the mood to have said the same if I had told you wanted five hundred."

Now did that make me feel good? It did not! Even though I had obtained what I'd asked for, I felt like a piker. I told myself that as a business man I was a wash-out.

And still, even though I was selling extra work under several pen names—"Burt R. Braddock," "Lieut. R. E. Swift," and "Harry Dangerfield" being three of them—I felt that I must have another steady market for serial stories. For my mother had written me that my father's lameness had become so bad he was able to earn only a little by picking up odd jobs.

In the meantime, Albert Stearns and I had taken a small office in the Arbuckle Building, on Fulton Street, where we did our writing. Stearns did not use a typewriter, but his hand-written copy was beautifully clear and as easy to read as typewriting. We were congenial office mates.

I told him, one day, that I was going to try to bust into Street and Smith's.

"I don't believe you'll get anywhere with them," said he.

"Well, I can try," was my reply.

On a raw and chilly autumn day I climbed the worn wooden stairs leading up to the editorial offices of Street and Smith, on Rose Street, but little did I suspect that the firm was tottering on the brink of the chasm into which Beadle and Adams had already fallen.

At the head of the stairs I came to a small windowlike opening in a partition. A guard to the inner region surveyed me forbiddingly through the embrasure as I stated the nature of my designs and craved admission. There was arrogance in his voice and manner as he replied:

"We don't want any stories. We've got a safe full of them now and are not buying any more."

I thought he was lying, but, later, Colonel Ingraham told me about that safe full of unused stories. He said there had been a fiction war some years earlier among publishers of the six-cent story papers—Beadle and Adams, Street and Smith, the two Munro companies, Robert Bonner, James Elverson, and a minor Chicago concern—and that much of the fiction bought by them had been taken without proper editorial reading and had proved to be too poor to be used at all.

However that may have been, I was unable on my first call at Street and Smith's to get beyond the portcullis. My arguments, which doubtless were feeble, failed to persuade the beardless guard to admit me. Forced to retire in confusion, I was sizzling hot when I stepped forth again into the chilly air coming over from the East River.

"So," said I to myself, "a beardless lackey turns a capable deserving author away from the door of a publishing house that needs his services! Don't want any more stories, eh? Well, they are going to want mine—and get them!"

I returned to the assault a week later, having loaded my guns better to breach the wall. I had learned that O. G. and G. C. Smith, sons of one of the founders of the concern, were now in command. Presenting my card to the haughty gateman, I demanded to be convoyed into the august presence of G. C. Smith. Beneath my name I had written, "Boston Globe, American Press Ass'n, Golden Hours." A syndicated short serial of mine had recently been published in the Boston paper, but I felt that the name of *Golden Hours,* which was the special rival of Street and Smith's *Good News,* would prove to be my magic talisman. Well, something did the trick, for presently I was escorted into the office of Edward Stratemeyer, at that time editing *Good News.*

Stratemeyer, a slightly parsonish young man, interrogated me concerning my accomplishments as an author and was incredulous when I reluctantly confessed that I had written dime novels for Beadle and Adams under the name of William G. Patten.

"But that's impossible," said he. "You are too young. It must have been your father who wrote them."

A trifle irritated but smiling, I informed him that my father was a house carpenter who had never written a line of fiction. Eventually I convinced him that I was the real culprit.

When I departed I took with me the title for a serial story which, according to his statement, had been given in turn to Oliver Optic and Harry Castlemon, both of whom had failed to deliver satisfactory opening chapters. The title was "The Boy from the West."

I had been asked to write and submit for approval two installments of four chapters each. Not a word had been spoken about how much I would be paid for the story if it should be accepted.

We came to that some time later, after he read the opening I brought him.

"Well, this is pretty fair, Patten," he said, "but not quite up to what I expected from you."

That put me on my guard but did not quite prepare me for his offer. "We will give you one hundred dollars for it if the remainder is satisfactory," said he.

It almost knocked me off the chair I was sitting on. I told him I was getting two hundred and fifty dollars from Munro for stories of that length and that I was the poorest paid of any writer for *Golden Hours,* one of whom was receiving six hundred. He simply did not believe me.

"I happen to know," said he, "that Munro does not pay any such prices."

Now that was calling me a liar and, whether from cowardice or honesty, I have never lied to any editor about the rates paid me by other publishers. Maybe my failure to attempt to better myself by lying stamps me as lacking in cleverness, but at least I have retained my self-respect.

"Mr. Stratemeyer," said I, "you are mistaken—and distinctly insulting." I reached over and took what I had written off his desk. "The title is yours," I told him, "but this much of the story is mine. I shall finish it and sell it elsewhere."

"I'm sorry," said he half apologetically.

Then he began to haggle. He raised his bid to one hundred and twenty-five. I came down to two hundred. There we stuck for a while. Finally and definitely, I told him I would write that one story for him for one hundred and fifty dollars just to show him what I could do, but it was to be clearly understood that I would do no further work for that price.

He said he would have to confer with Mr. Smith. I waited. He came back from the conference and told me to go ahead.

Had I held to my resolution to write no further serials for Street and Smith at that price, Frank Merriwell would never have been born. When my anger had subsided I was not so firm. It is a flaw in my nature that I can never be stiff and determined unless aroused by opposition, and that goes for sport as well as business. Given something well worth scrapping for and let my anger be aroused, I always exert myself to the utmost.

Edward Stratemeyer had made me dislike him, and I was well pleased when, not long thereafter, his position as editor of *Good News* was given to Arthur Dudley Hall. Mr. Hall was a gentleman in the full sense of the word, and to him, as I will show later, I owe the fact that I was chosen to create the Merriwell stories.

I have faithfully described the manner in which began my connection with the firm that afterwards bought many millions of words of fiction written by me, but never one word of all those millions has been written under a pen name not invented by me and not legally and morally belonging to me.

Five of my *Good News* serials were republished as cloth-bound books by David McKay, of Philadelphia, who pocketed a neat little piece of change from them. They led on to the Merriwell stories, which could have been more carefully written had I not been compelled to turn them off at the rate of 20,000 words a week. Dime novels or not, they never hurt any boy or girl, and hundreds of successful and esteemed men have told me that they were their inspiration and guide.

27 · YOUTH AND LAUGHTER

MEANWHILE I MADE A SUMMER TRIP back to Camden, got my parents temporarily settled in a little house on Limerock Street, and managed the Camden professional baseball team for the season—and kept up my writing work at the same time.

Bill Carrigan, a high school lad from Lewiston, was one of my ballplayers that year. His ambition was to become a pitcher, and I tried him in that position, but decided that he was much better behind the bat. Eventually he became a catcher and the manager of the Boston Red Sox, guiding that team to two world championships in succession.

With the additional load of my parents on my shoulders, I never again was able to devote so much time to baseball, though I dreamed of it often.

One day William H. Manning, who had been a steady writer for Beadle for years, called on me in Brooklyn. A modest, pleasant man, he had written Westerns under the pen name of "Major E. L. St. Vrain" and city-life yarns under his own name and the pseudonym of "Ben D. Halliday."

Unmarried, he had lived in one room on Fourteenth Street, in New York, and accumulated a comfortable competence by rigid frugality. But his earnings had ceased with the fall of the House of Beadle and he was contemplating buying a drug store business somewhere, hiring a registered pharmacist for his clerk and ceasing to attempt to write fiction.

He told me some amusing anecdotes about several of Beadle's writers, two of which concerning Edward L. Wheeler, author of the "Deadwood Dick" stories, will bear repeating.

Coming over from Jersey by ferry one day, Manning's attention was drawn to a man adorned in a ten-gallon hat who was swaggering around the deck with a look-me-over air. Presently this person stopped beside Manning at the rail and spoke.

"Waal, pard," said he, "it shore is good to get back to the old town after ranging around out West for months and visiting the Black Hills and Deadwood again."

It sounded a bit phony to Manning. "So you've been out West, have you?" said he. "On business?"

"Wa-al," drawled the stranger, "sort o' collectin' material and color for my writin' work. I'm a born and bred Westerner, but my publishers reckoned I might be gettin' a leetle rusty, stayin' in the East so long."

Now Manning was sure it was a phony. "Might I ask who your publishers are?" said he.

"Shore can," said the other. "I spin the yarns about Deadwood Dick that are published by Beadle and Adams. Dick's a friend o' mine."

Manning could not restrain a laugh. "That's very interesting," he allowed. "Beadle and Adams publish my novels too. I am Major E. L. St. Vrain."

Mr. Wheeler almost stepped out from under his big hat. "Whew!" he breathed. "This shore is coincidence. I'm right glad to meet up with you, pard St. Vrain. I reckon you're a Westerner too?"

"Not yet," said Manning. "I was born in New England, but I've been as far west as West Philadelphia, where you hail from."

The creator of Deadwood Dick swallowed dryly once or twice and then broke into a roar of laughter. "The drinks are on me," he said. "I like to put it over on jays who eat it up, but I certainly made a bad pick in you. May I ask what your real name is?"

Manning told him and they shook hands. "Let's head for the nearest saloon as soon as we land," said Wheeler. "The way you knocked the wind out of me, I need a bracer."

William Manning saw Wheeler several times after that and never saw him sober. The earlier numbers of the Deadwood Dick stories had been dime novel best sellers, but later issues in the series were punk and steadily grew worse. I had wondered what had caused that, and Manning had supplied the answer. It was reported that, in order to get another story from him, Mr. Victor had once locked Wheeler into a room and kept him there until he had written a 33,000-word Deadwood Dick novel.

Around the witching hour of twelve one night, Wheeler rang frantically until admitted to Manning's lodging house. Panting, he burst into the room where Manning was reading the *Evening Sun* before going to bed.

"For God's sake hide me, Bill!" he gasped. "I've just killed a man!"

Now William Manning was a gentle man of peace and his visitor's announcement shocked him not inconsiderably. "What do you mean?" he said when he could speak. "You're joking or drunk."

Gilbert Patten, Frank Merriwell's "father"

Colonel Prentiss Ingraham, dime novelist and adventurer who became Patten's close friend

Patten as he appeared when
Charles Hanson Towne called him "Edgar Allan Poe"

Pencil sketch of Patten by artist Herbert Grissom,
brother of Arthur Grissom, founder of *Smart Set Magazine*

Major Gordon Lillie (Pawnee Bill) and Mrs. Lillie, who almost succeeded in "kidnaping" Patten and his wife

Patten at work

Patten and his home, "Overocks," at Camden, Maine

Patten and his wife, Carol, in 1934

Youth and Laughter

"I'm neither," declared Wheeler. "Look at this!"

He threw open his long black overcoat and exposed a shirt-front smeared with blood, the sight of which made Manning feel sick and faint.

"How did it happen?" he asked. "And where?"

"In a poolroom on Eighth Avenue," said Wheeler. "We had been playing pool. He accused me of cheating and attempted to hit me with his cue. So I whipped out my big clasp-knife and ripped him wide open before I knew what I was doing. Then I ran. I dropped the knife somewhere. They'll be after me. What am I going to do?"

Manning admitted that never before had he been so frightened. "Did anybody see you come in here?" he asked.

"Nobody but the woman who let me in," said Wheeler. "I ran so fast that nobody could catch me, but the police will be notified. I can't go out on the street again—now."

"Then I suppose you'll have to stay here tonight," said Manning reluctantly, "Maybe you can make a get-away in the morning. I don't want to get mixed up in this thing."

Wheeler slept soundly in Manning's bed that night while the latter sat up, catching cat-naps and thinking morning would never come. When it did come and Wheeler said he was broke, the host loaned his unwelcome guest twenty-five dollars, wished him good luck, and was unspeakably relieved by his departure.

Manning bought every city paper issued that day and went through them searching in vain for the report of a murder in an Eighth Avenue poolroom. Nor did he ever hear of such a murder.

"Maybe the son of a gun was really broke and figured I wouldn't lend him any money unless he scared it out of me," said Manning. "And he was right about that. Probably he bought a hunk of raw beef and smeared his shirt with it. Or it's possible he played that trick on me to get even for the way I'd caught him playing a fake Westerner. But whichever way it was, I never got my twenty-five dollars back."

He finished with a laugh in which there was no resentment, and I liked him better for that.

I think I advised him to forget his plan to become proprietor of a drugstore. The last I heard of him, he was living in Massachussetts. He and Oll Coomes, who invested his dime novel earnings in Iowa land and became moderately wealthy, were two of Beadle's writers who were situated to live comfortably after that publishing house ceased to function. Left broke and unable to sell their writings elsewhere, two or three others committed suicide.

Contrary to common belief, not all—or even a majority—of the dime novel writers who wrote Westerns were unfamiliar with the country in which the action of their tales took place.

Coomes lived in Iowa and had seen plenty redskins, and Joseph E. Badger, Jr., was a Kansas ranch owner who had roved the old frontier. William R. Eyster was also a Kansas citizen, and even John H. Whitson, whose pen name was "Lieut. A. K. Sims," had homesteaded in Kansas when a knock on the door might mean that the caller was an Indian.

Both Ingraham and Ned Buntline, whose real name was Col. E. Z. C. Judson, were the friends and associates of such Western characters as Buffalo Bill, Wild Bill, Texas Jack, and other frontiersmen. As before stated, Buckskin Sam had been a Texas Ranger. Captain Frederick Whittaker, an Englishman, had spent time in the Border Country and on cattle ranches before writing Western stories.

I make no apologies for myself. I was a tenderfoot from Maine, living in Brooklyn, where one Sunday I attended a lecture by a large, handsome man who expounded on the "Mistakes of Moses." This man was being roundly denounced as an atheist by ministers of the Gospel.

His name was Robert Ingersoll and he was no more an atheist than some of today's speakers from the pulpits of fashionable churches. An agnostic? Yes, but his beautiful oration at his brother's grave stamped him as one who hoped there lies something for mortal men beyond the brief life we live in this world, now fast becoming a world of universal bloody strife and haunting fear.

My recent summer in Camden had afforded such relief from

city heat and had apparently been so beneficial to my health that I had attempted to buy a little house there in which my parents could be permanently settled and where there would be room for three more, Alice, myself, and our small son, in the summer months. But though she had appeared eager to dispose of the property, the aging widow who lived there alone had asked more than I was willing to pay.

Now, however, I received a letter from my father informing me that the place had been offered for sale at a reasonable figure, and I wired him to get an option on it. Then I made another trip back to Camden and became the owner of a summer house there, mortgaged on terms I felt confident I could meet. Later, my parents moved into that little house on the corner of Bayview and Limerock Streets.

But I had picked up another cold on that trip, and soon my bad lung was again trying to lay me on my back. I fought it with noisome doses of cod-liver oil and kept on doing my work, but the time came when I began to fear I'd lose the decision. One morning I said to Alice:

"Well, we're going to Florida."

Her eyes widened. "When?" she asked.

"Just as soon as we can start," said I.

"But how about the apartment?" she wondered.

"Our lease is up in two weeks. I shan't renew it. We'll put our furniture in storage."

"But the expense of the trip? How———"

"I'm finishing a story for Street and Smith this week and have arranged with Mr. Dunn to do one for him right away. You and Barr can go as soon as we get out of this flat, and I'll join you after I've knocked off the yarn for Dunn."

"But where will we go?"

"I've been corresponding with John Whitson. He's living in Fernandina. I'll write him today to find accommodations for us— a furnished cottage if possible."

"Well," said she, "that doesn't sound too bad. And I hope we never come back here to live."

She was still yearning for Maine.

Two weeks later I put my wife and son, Fernandina bound, aboard a train in Jersey City. Then I went back to my office with Albert Stearns and squared away to write another 60,000-word story for *Golden Hours*.

I had taken a room in the old Pierpont Hotel, on Brooklyn Heights. On the advice of Stearns, I was taking three or four shots of whiskey daily as medicine for my cold, but still using cod-liver oil as well. I don't know that the whiskey did me any good, but it took me down to the Pierpont bar, where I made the acquaintance of the Assistant District Attorney who had been concerned in the prosecution of Carlyle Harris for the murder of his wife. That case had interested me, for I believed Harris had not intended to kill the girl, whom he had secretly married, but had made a tragic blunder..

The Assistant D.A. agreed with me. He thought Harris had given his wife morphine without being aware that she was a dope addict and had already taken a heavy dose of the drug, and that the double dose had killed her. If this theory was right then the law had sent an innocent man to his death, for Harris had been convicted and executed.

Some lively young men foregathered almost nightly at the Pierpont bar, forming a semi-bohemian set into which I was welcomed. We discussed books and plays in a desultory manner. Like myself, one of the group had seen Mrs. Leslie Carter as "Du Barry" on the opening night of David Belasco's ten-strike, and he maintained that she was the greatest living actress on the American stage.

I contended that Julia Marlowe's work in Clyde Fitch's *Barbara Fritchie* made Mrs. Carter look like a ham. Then somebody gave us the bird by ironically proclaiming that Lillian Russell was the greatest living American actress, which raised a howl. Nevertheless, Lillian was vastly admired by all of us, and we proceeded to sing her lovely Weber and Field's hits, "Come Down, My Evening Star" and "Dinah, de Moon am Shinin.' "

Youth and song and laughter! Yes, them *was* the happy days!

28 · MR. SMITH'S LETTER

JOHN WHITSON had found a furnished cottage for us in Fernandina, and my wife and son gave me a cheery welcome when I arrived there late one cool evening in November. A Southern pine fire was crackling merrily in an open fireplace, and the aroma of brewing coffee came from the kitchen. What a pleasure it was to sit down to a meal prepared by a competent State of Maine cook! And what a comforting delight, with appetite satisfied, to smoke a fragrant cigar before the open fire with my little son nestling against my shoulder!

Winter weather in Fernandina, sometimes cool but continuously sunny, put me on my mettle again in short order. I had been there less than ten days when I ceased to cough and was feeling like a colt let out to pasture in springtime.

Aware that I should take more exercise in the open air, I hired a bicycle and pedaled it over the smooth roads and along the stretch of hard sandy beach a mile away. I attempted to take dips in the surf on that beach, but the water, rolling in from the open Atlantic, was, at that time of year, too cold for me to go on with them.

Whitson was a lanky, quiet, Hoosier-born man who had practiced law before turning homesteader in Kansas and soon giving that life up to become a writer. The death of his wife from complications following the birth of their second child, which occurred about three weeks after my arrival in Florida, was a heavy blow for him.

He took his wife's body back to Indiana for burial, left the baby there with relatives, and returned to Florida, where his older daughter had remained with the Pattens. By plunging again into the writing of an ambitious novel that he had been working on he sought to forget as far as possible the tragedy that had befallen him. His novel, *Barbara, a Woman of the West,* eventually was published by Little, Brown and Company, of Boston.

Before leaving New York I had been informed by Mr. Dunn

that he would not be able to buy another serial of mine for some time, but he had not stated why. However, I suspected that *Golden Hours* was on the skids, which, if true, would mean the loss of my most remunerative market. Already the American Press Association, betraying signs of decay, had ceased to buy my page of "Odd Stories," and it seemed that I could faintly hear in the distance the howl of the wolf again nosing his way to my door.

To fend the critter off, I pounded out short stories, jokes, and pieces of verse, some of which were sold to the smaller newspaper syndicates. Fortunately, hard knocks had never beaten self-confidence out of me. I continued to tell myself that sometime, somewhere, and somehow, I would hit the jack-pot.

At that time St. Augustine was the classy Florida winter resort. Taking Barr with us, Alice and I made a trip down there in midwinter. We stopped only one day and a night at the Ponce de Leon Hotel, which seemed palatial with its large open court of flowers, in which a crystal fountain sparkled in the sunshine.

We visited the old Spanish fort, in the dungeon of which many prisoners had perished of torture and starvation, and took a drive over the almost alabaster-white shell road. It was a welcome break from the labor of keeping the home fires burning.

The Florida climate had put my cold to flight and made me feel frisky for a while. I had wondered at the lanquid way the people of Fernandina sauntered or dragged themselves around, but before April came I was dawdling as listlessly myself. Then a mosquito presented me with his bill, and I had an attack of malaria that enabled a doctor to do the same. The doctor fed me quinine, which knocked the malaria out and nearly knocked me out too. That nudged me to move again.

We sailed in May, northward bound, on a Clyde Liner, and Whitson and his daughter sailed with us. After having malaria, I almost enjoyed a short bit of seasickness off Hatteras. But how I did welcome the sight of New York.

Nevertheless, I did not intend to linger there longer than became necessary in order to do a little more market scouting and dispose of our furniture. For Alice and I had agreed that condi-

Mr. Smith's Letter

tions and wisdom demanded that we abandon thoughts of living in the city and retire to Camden—for a while, anyhow.

Alice went on to Camden, taking Barr and Whitson's daughter with her and leaving Whitson and me with a furnished flat and a colored maid, both being hired by the week.

As soon as I could get our furniture out of storage and place it to be sold at auction, I set forth to look up my former Broadway associates and found, to my regret, that practically all of them but George Creel seemed to be on the list of missing persons. And Creel never had been one of the gay Metropole Café set. He'd always appeared to be too serious to fritter away precious hours over the flowing bowl.

In New York, Whitson was like a fish out of water. He was truly rural, and the sights of the Big Town gave him no thrills. Moreover, he was still brooding over the death of his wife. I made him buy an inexpensive hand-me-down suit and brush the Florida dust off his hat before he visited editorial offices in search of work.

Street and Smith appeared to be on the up-grade, and O. G. Smith informed me that they had bought a lot on Seventh Avenue, above Fourteenth Street, where they proposed to erect their own publishing house. Maybe I had brought them luck.

When I received the check for the sale of our furniture at auction, with the selling commission deducted, I was amazed; for that furniture actually had been sold for more than I'd paid for it when it was new! Evidently I had dealt with an honest auctioneering company, too. I doubt if such a thing could happen once in a hundred times.

Having arranged for Street and Smith to buy enough of his work to provide him with a modest livelihood for a while, Whitson made the journey to Camden with me. There he found living accommodations in a private home and seemed pretty well satisfied with everything but the Camden mountains, which annoyed him because—as he expressed it—they obstructed the view!

The money I'd received for the sale of our Brooklyn furniture made it possible for us to complete the furnishing of the house in Camden, which surprised my wife. I now had a den to write in, with windows from which I could look out upon the mountains and the bay, and I began to dream of writing "the great American novel." Maybe I dreamed too much, but nevertheless I wrote and sold enough fiction to prevent the distant howling of the wolf from drawing nearer.

I think it was in June that spring that the Camden newspaper printed three poems written in competition by members of the highschool graduating class, and Edna St. Vincent Millay's "Renascence" was given third place by the "judges."

In Camden, Edna, the small red-haired daughter of a widowed mother, was called Vincent. I barely knew her by sight, but I recognized her poem as real poetry as soon as I read it, while the other two pieces, rated above it, were merely mechanical, uninspired verse such as might be expected of highschool graduating scholars. But when I expressed my opinion of the judgment of the "judges" I found no one who agreed with me but Norma, one of Edna's two sisters.

Norma said, "Well, Gil, you are one person in town with some brains."

When the day came that Edna was acclaimed as perhaps the greatest living poet of the country, dumfounded Camdenites made haste to claim her as their admired own; but, maybe resentful of their former disdain, Edna renounced Camden and snubbed it when it attempted to arrange a "coming-home" reception for her.

My wife was far from fully contented in Camden, but she was pleased when I decided not to spend the winter of '95 in New York, a decision caused by the dearth of folding money in my pockets.

Early in December I received a letter from O. G. Smith in which he inquired if I would like to write a series of stories for boys and girls which the firm contemplated publishing, and my answer was a request for particulars. His reply, dated December 16, 1895, follows verbatim:

Mr. Smith's Letter

GILBERT PATTEN, *Esq.* CAMDEN, MAINE
DEAR SIR:

Replying to your favor of December 13, at hand today, we beg to state that the material of which we wrote you in our last letter is intended for a library that we propose issuing every week; something in line of the Jack Harkaway stories, Gay Dashliegh stories, which are running in Good News, and the Island School Series, all of which we are expressing to you under separate cover, the idea being to issue a library containing a series of stories covering this class of incident, in all of which will appear one prominent character surrounded by suitable satellites. It would be of advantage to the series to have introduced the Dutchman, the Negro, the Irishman, and any other dialect you are familiar with. From what we know of your work, we believe you can give us what we require, and would be pleased to have you write us one of these stories at once. Upon receipt of it, if satisfactory, we will be prepared to make a contract with you to cover twenty thousand words weekly for this new library and a sufficient number of Good News stories to keep them running in the columns of Good News, if you believe you can turn out this amount of work.

It is important that the main character in the series should have a catchy name, such as Dick Lightheart, Gay Dashleigh, Don Kirk,[1] as upon his name will depend the title of the library.

The essential idea of this library is to interest young readers in the career of a young man at a boarding school, preferably a military or naval academy. The stories should differ from the Jack Harkaway stories by being American and thoroughly up to date. Our idea is to issue, say, twelve stories, each complete in itself, but like the links of a chain, all dealing with life in the academy. By this time the readers will have become sufficiently well acquainted with the hero, and the author will also no doubt have exhausted most of the pranks and escapades that might naturally occur.

After the first twelve numbers, the hero is obliged to leave the academy, or takes it upon himself to leave. It is essential that he should come into a considerable sum of money at this period. When he leaves the academy he takes with him one of the professor's serv-

---

[1] The leading character in two of the serial stories written by me for Street and Smith.

ants, a chum. In fact any of the characters you have introduced and made prominent in the story. A little love element would not be amiss, but this is not particularly important.

When the hero is projected upon his travels there is an infinite variety of incidents to choose from. In the Island School Series, published by one of our London connections, you will find scenes of foreign travel, with color. This material you are at liberty to use freely, with our hero as the central character, of course, and up to date dialogue.

After we have run twenty or thirty of this, we would bring the hero back and have him go to college—say, Yale University; thence we could take him on his travels again to the South Seas or anywhere.

If you do the opening stories of school life, you will be able to do them all, as we shall assist you in the matter of local color for the stories of travel.

This letter will, of course, be held as confidential. After you have fully examined the Island School Material, kindly return it to us.

                Yours truly,
(Signed,)   O. G. SMITH

This letter was always held strictly confidential by me. A copy of it was given to James M. Cain by Street and Smith themselves, to be used by him in an article concerning me which was published in the *Saturday Evening Post*.[2] Therefore I am violating no confidence by allowing it to be again reproduced exactly as it was written, even to punctuation.

---

29 · SO CAME FRANK MERRIWELL

HAVING EXAMINED the English stories sent me by Street and Smith, I returned all of them. For I intended to devise my own incidents and plots and did not propose to use anything from the Island School Series, as suggested by Mr. O. G. Smith. Nor did I at any

[2] James M. Cain, "The Man Merriwell," *Saturday Evening Post*, Vol. CXCIX, No. 50 (June 11, 1927)—ed.

time receive assistance from Mr. Smith or anybody connected with his firm in gathering material for "local color" or in carrying out the general plan of the Merriwell stories, other than that contained in Mr. Smith's confidential letter. Doubtless the reason for this was that I did not ask it of them, and maybe I did not ask because I did not wish them to know how utterly unfamiliar I was with military school and college life.

Never in my writing career, with a single exception, have I consciously been a plagiarist. On the occasion of my one lapse from literary ethics I made changes in the plot of a college tale I had read and used it in the altered form, and my alterations weakened the plot more than a little. Nor were they sufficient to prevent John L. Cutler, a University of Maine student, from detecting the crib and exposing it in a brochure written by him and published by the University in 1933—which served me right.

Of course, like many other writers, I adapted and used actual occurrences as reported in newspapers, as well as obtained facts and color from books of travel and other sources. Not a few of my own personal experiences, adapted to requirements, furnished me with material. I confess that the well of my imagination was often pumped pretty dry.

Having decided to make a military academy the locale of my opening stories, as suggested, I wrote to several military schools for catalogs and information which I required. And I picked up a novel written by Captain Charles King, whose hero was a West Point cadet, which gave me some valuable pointers about the lives and duties of cadets in training for army service.

My next step was to manufacture a "catchy name" for my hero. "Frank" leaped into my mind at once, but the rest of it did not come as easily. I covered sheets of paper with penciled names, among them being Merrithew, Merriweather, and Merrifield.

And then, suddenly, I had it—Frank Merriwell! The name was symbolic of the chief characteristics I desired my hero to have —*Frank* for frankness, *merry* for a happy disposition, *well* for health and abounding vitality.

I have been asked many times if there was a living model for my hero. Maybe I should feel pleased by the fact that he seemed so real to a host of youthful readers that they imagined there must be a living person like him whom I knew. But there was no such person, and of course, as I pictured him, he was too perfect to have been a boy of flesh and blood.

There was little of such perfection in my own nature, but I knew I would have chosen to be like Frank had fate made it possible, and I believed all respectable, clean-minded boys felt the same. And so I depicted Frank as an ideal to emulate, and in doing so I may have made him sometimes seem slightly priggish.

I do not wish to give the impression that he leaped into my mind fully visualized. On the contrary, though I pondered over him before starting to write the first story, his development continued for a long while after I began writing about him.

While he had only one besetting weakness, the impulse to gamble, he was tolerant of the weaknesses of others, and the habits of some of his best friends were such as would not be approved by prudes. By surrounding him with such pals I was able to do a little preaching by example, but none of his friends was ever a sneak, cheap-skate or sissy.

Frank was tolerant of human failings, but in one respect he was himself a sap—he always let his adversary strike the first blow. That was sheer stupidity, for often the first blow decided the battle. I had learned this lesson in my boyhood when at last I had fought not only to defeat my enemies but to gain my own self-respect, but I appear to have forgotten the lesson when depicting Frank's behavior many years later.

Believing the old-fashioned dime novel was on its way out, I decided to set a new style with my stories and make them different and more in step with the times. As the first issues were to be stories of American school life, I saw in them an opportunity to feature all kinds of athletic sports, with baseball, about which I was best informed, predominating.

Such stories would give me an opportunity to preach—by example—the doctrine of a clean mind in a clean and healthy body. And also, unlike the old dime novel writers, I would attempt to present even minor characters in such a manner that the readers could visualize them clearly. With me, plot would be secondary to character depiction as far as I could make it and still write a story of interesting action and suspense.

Having pondered over my opening story for a week or more, I sat down to my typewriter and wrote the title, "Frank Merriwell, or First Days at Fardale," on a nice clean page. And I wrote "The End" on another page just four days later.

Although Mr. Smith had not suggested the use of a pen name, I invented the name of "Burt L. Standish" and placed it on the first manuscript.

At that time, I did not know that the stock name of "Hal Standish" was appearing on some of Frank Tousey's publications, any of which I never had read. In my case, I chose the name of Standish because I had liked the sight and sound of it ever since reading Longfellow's *Courtship of Miles Standish* when a boy. I had previously used "Burt" as part of a pen name on some short stories which were printed in *Golden Hours*.

To those who have asked what the "L" in Burt L. Standish stands for, I have answered, "For euphony."

"What ho!" said I when I had finished that first yarn. "I can do these things in four days, and that will leave me two more working days a week in which to bat out other work. It's a cinch."

But now I had to find out if the thing I'd written would go over. I shipped it to Street and Smith and waited somewhat anxiously. If it were accepted I hoped to receive at least seventy-five dollars for it. Ere long I was notified that it had rung the bell, and with the letter conveying that agreeable information came a contract which would bind me to turn out weekly succeeding stories at sixty dollars a week!

The amount offered in payment for the stories let some wind out of my balloon, but it would provide me with a steady, living income for three years, and so—still reckoning on being able to write further yarns in the series in four working days each and having two more days a week to do other work—I put my John Hancock on the contract.

But I was soon to learn that the two extra days I'd counted on would be eaten up by the research and reading required to prepare me for work on one story, which shot my hope of earning extra money to shreds.

At first I carried Frank around in my mind from morning until night, but ere long the weight of him became too much to stagger under. I had to have relaxation; I had to forget him a part of the time. To do so, I began by discarding notebooks and not even allowing myself to carry a pencil in my pockets.

I trained myself to drop my work utterly—to put it out of my mind and refuse to let it creep back until the time came to work again—when I had ground out my daily grist. Also I trained myself to sit down at my typewriter at nine o'clock in the morning *and write* whether the spirit—sometimes called inspiration—moved or not.

I had no time to devote to careful writing. No time to spend in searching for the proper word to express my meaning, as Barrie's "Sentimental Tommy" did. If the proper word eluded me, I used another word as nearly synonymous as possible or reconstructed the sentence with other words to convey my meaning.

Therefore, of course, my style was verbose and sloppy. Writing under such pressure, how could I have done otherwise? Anyhow, Street and Smith were not paying for style; they were buying stories that young readers would enjoy and buy. And of course such composition, indulged in for years, formed writing habits I've never been able to correct.

The first Merriwell story appeared on the news stands April 18, 1896, and was a sell-out. The cover, done in colorwork, was an innovation that drew attention and undoubtedly helped the sales. Thereafter for several years, the volume of issue was steadily increased. No exact statement of the circulation of those stories has ever been made by the publishers, although a total of over 123,500,000 copies has been admitted.

As the Merriwells became the best-selling publication of the kind on the news stands—a fact conceded even by rival publishers—and one of Frank Tousey's publications reached a sale of 425,-

000,000 copies *in toto,* there are logical reasons to believe the aggregate sales of the Merriwells were nearer 500,000,000—which would have meant some feathers for the nest of any publishing concern.

To those who have censured me for entering into the kind of contract I signed with Street and Smith I have replied that beyond a doubt I would have signed none at all if I hadn't signed that one. For they could have—and doubtless would have—obtained another writer for their proposed series, had I refused.

However, I might have seized all rights to the Merriwell stories when it became necessary to recopyright them, as that had to be done in my name or not at all. By a contract agreement, signed by O. G. Smith as president of the corporation and attested by a notary public, I yielded the paper book rights to them and obtained all other rights for myself.

30 · PARTING AND TRAGEDY

WHEN A WRITER FRIEND OF MINE learned that I had signed a contract to turn out a 20,000-word story weekly for three years he said: "You're crazy. A year of that will put you in the bughouse."

Well, six months of it made me apprehensive that he might be right. Feeling that I must spend more time in the open air by day, I began working mornings at eight o'clock instead of nine. That gave me another hour in which I could get outdoors afternoons, and, seeing me idling in the sunshine, one of the townsmen enviously inquired if I never worked!

I marched in my last torchlight parade and cast my last straight Republican vote for William McKinley. Thereafter I became an independent voter, splitting my ticket as my judgment dictated. Learning of this, the local Republican big shot reproved me and hinted that the Republicans had considered inviting me to be a candidate for the state legislature on their ticket. I replied that I had neither the time or inclination to become a political henchman for Republicans or Democrats. In those days an independent voter was called a "mugwump," and thereafter I bore the stigma —with pleasure.

Meanwhile the fame of Frank Merriwell was growing. Fathers and mothers of youthful admirers of my hero were discovering that he was a good example for their sons to try to emulate. Thousands of letters of praise, the best of which were printed in the Applause Department of the *Tip Top Weekly,* flowed in from all parts of the country. To my personal knowledge, one Congregational minister chose his text for a sermon from one of my stories, which he placed beside the Bible on his pulpit.

Of course Merriwell's popularity had an effect upon me, for I saw that I had a much greater opportunity than I had expected to influence the rising generation. At the outset I had looked upon the stories as pot-boilers and a bridge-over until the knock of opportunity should summon me to better work, and I don't recall that I was particularly captivated by Frank Merriwell until I became aware that a multitude of youngsters had taken him to their hearts. That fact made me resigned in a degree, and for the time being, to the kind of ill-paid work I was doing.

With the passing of time, the strain of performing my daily task eased a little as the work became a habit and my principal characters stood forth more clearly. Three years of it did not make me any crazier than at the beginning, and I even found time to rake in some additional dollars by writing a few other stories for Street and Smith. But I never wrote a Jesse James, Buffalo Bill, or Nick Carter yarn, although there was a report that I did.

There was also a rumor that Upton Sinclair wrote some of the Merriwell stories, but no such stories written by him were ever published by Street and Smith. And even comparatively recently a New York newspaper stated that Stewart Edward White collaborated with me on some of the stories! When I advised Mr. White by letter to sue the paper for libel, he most graciously replied that he would be proud if the story were true.

Parting and Tragedy

Even though I became somewhat reconciled to the hackwork I was doing, there were times when dissatisfaction attacked me, and I told myself it would take more than sixty dollars a week to induce me to renew my contract with Street and Smith. And there were also times when regret over the failure of my first play stirred in some dim, sad chamber of my brain.

One day in the early fall of '97 I said to Alice: "I'm stuck in the mud here. I'm going back to New York."

She looked at me, hard. "You'll go without me—or Barr," she said.

"But why?" said I.

"I've told you," she replied, "that I'm sick of the kind of life I've had to lead, always moving from place to place and never really settled anywhere. We've got to be settled in order for Barr to go to school. That's why I wanted you to go back to Corinna."

We had thrashed that out several times and I avoided going over it again. "All right," said I, "then I'll go alone."

But she was opposed to that also, and she had her way—for the time being.

On the fifteenth of the ensuing February, the battleship Maine was sunk by an explosion in Havana Harbor, and the United States became hot under the collar. For, in spite of the failure of the court of investigation to pin the blame definitely upon any person or persons, it was widely believed that the Maine had been blown up by a Spanish mine.

The jingo press, which had been railing at President McKinley for not moving to intervene in the bloody Cuban Revolution, howled for an immediate declaration of war with Spain. And Spain, having tired of the prolonged and costly revolution, which even General Weyler, "the Butcher," had failed to suppress, seemed willing to take on Uncle Sam for a round, which in case of defeat would give her an excuse to drop Cuba like a hot potato. But, as events demonstrated, she was not reckoning on dropping the Philippines into the lap of Admiral Dewey.

Once more the fever to be in New York burned in my veins, and once more it provoked antagonism and family dissension.

With my approval and assistance, my parents moved back into the little house on Limerock Street, but that did not improve matters. Alice and I had reached the stage where incompatability and clashing wills were rapidly making hash of our married life. Both were right and both were wrong, and neither one was more to blame than the other. I think we both felt that the parting of the ways was near.

War had been declared, and the country was in a patriotic ferment when I gave Alice a month in which to make up her mind about living with me wherever I felt it my interest to be, and took an afternoon boat bound for Boston. Boston Harbor had been mined, and the following morning saw the steamer creeping cautiously into port along a channel through the mine field.

When night again came I slept in a large furnished room at No. 4 Temple Street, in the West End, and the following day I banged out my usual twelve typewritten pages of a Merriwell story. I had decided not to go to New York until after returning to Camden at the end of a month to find out if my wife was ready to go with me.

Now even the little change from Camden to Boston had an effect upon my writing, which immediately took a spurt and flowed with less effort and left me less fatigued at the end of a working day; and that was something that invariably happened whenever I made a radical change of environment.

Remaining very long in one locality and environment, I was sure to gravitate slowly toward fallowness and produce with increasing effort; and once I even reached a condition that affrighted me with the thought that I would never be able to write again. Then a complete change of scene and atmosphere broke the shackles of my mind and set what is called inspiration to capering again.

I believe most writers are similarly affected, and for that reason I would not advise a quiet, domestic, home-loving woman to marry a writer. Such a marriage may not go on the rocks as mine did, but the wife is not likely to find the peace and home-stability that her nature desires.

Parting and Tragedy

Two of my friends, former Camden boys, were living in Boston and rooming at No. 4 Temple Street. We dined together often and sometimes took in a show together, and one night we were nearly thrown out of Keith's Theatre because one of us laughed so uproariously at the dancing of a nimble young fellow called George Cohan, who was the youngest member of "the Four Cohans," as they were billed. George not only danced with his feet, legs, arms, head, neck, and body, but his cane and hat also danced.

I also remember seeing Dan Daley in a crazy farce called *Upside Down* that left my sides sore. And I did not fail to drop into the old Howard Theatre, which was the favorite resort of State of Maine visitors in Boston who had left their wives at home. That, however, was my first and last visit to the Howard.

The streets and alleyways of the West End were said to have been constructed along the old cowpaths of the early settlers, and they formed a confusing maze in which one could start for a given point and meet himself coming back, which may account for some of the bewildered appearing persons whom I saw wandering about in that quarter.

Not a few of those wanderers seemed to have an affliction of the lower limbs which made it difficult for them to avoid collisions with other persons or to confine their progress to the narrow sidewalks. Now and then one of them would appeal touchingly for aid, but I remained hard-hearted and was not touched.

The hurdy-gurdys were playing "On the Banks of the Wabash," and Massachusetts boys in handsome blue uniforms were marching off to war, little suspecting they would find their rations of rotten canned beef more deadly than Spanish bullets.

I went back to Camden at the end of thirty days and found my home empty.

Alice had gone to Corinna and taken Barr with her, and she had left a note suggesting that I call on her lawyer, a local attorney, for information. He informed me that she would apply for divorce at the September term of court.

So that was that.

To avoid further reference to an unpleasant subject, I'll state that she obtained her divorce without alimony, for which she had not asked, but with a clause binding me to pay a weekly sum for the maintenance of our son, to which I had willingly agreed.

I did not linger in that empty house in Camden. Closing it up, I gave my father the keys and instructions to look after the property, and headed for New York.

I found my publishers settled in their new business building on Seventh Avenue and was given a welcome that flattered me. For I was susceptible to flattery then; now it rolls off me like rain off a duck's back.

Naturally I am interested if given a spread of publicity in a newspaper, but it doesn't raise my blood-pressure. And I am not interested in opportunities to speak gratis before gatherings of any nature and have declined a dozen invitations to appear gratis on the radio. Only friendship or a desire to help a worthy cause can catch me now, mercenary creature that I have become. Not even a chance to blow my own horn lures me when I know I'm being tempted to boost a fat racket for somebody else.

In the few years since I had climbed the stairs of their shabby old building on Rose Street, my publishers had flourished and prospered as if they were in possession of Aladdin's lamp. Not only were they now publishing the cheaper brand of news-stand fiction, they had launched two successful magazines, *Popular* and *Ainslee's,* and were preparing to launch others.

Although, like many other six-cent story papers, the New York *Weekly* had become defunct, Street and Smith were keeping Mr. Glynn, the old editor, on the job by allowing him to make up new issues from reprints of former stories and printing a single copy of each new paper, which was placed on his desk.

In this manner the fact that the paper was no longer in circulation was kept a secret from Mr. Glynn for quite a while. When he became aware of the kindly deception by his employers the old man closed his desk, went quietly home, and died.

Good News was on its last legs, and Arthur Dudley Hall had been transferred to the editorship of *Ainslee's Magazine.* He told me that O. G. Smith, when contemplating starting the *Tip Top Library,* had asked him whom of his *Good News* authors he considered best qualified to write the stories, and that he had recommended me. I was properly grateful for the recommendation.

I hunted up Arthur Grissom and found him in the editorial chair of the new and sophisticated *Smart Set Magazine,* which he had helped to found. His brother Herbert had become an artist and was doing illustrations for periodicals. With Herbert, I attended a party one night in an apartment of Kate Masterson, a talented writer for a newspaper syndicate. I was then tall and slim, with a shock of curly black hair and a moustache.

When I entered the room where the guests were quenching their thirst, Charles Hanson Towne, a writer of graceful love lyrics, rose up from a chair adjacent to the punch-bowl and gave me a wig-wag.

"Ah, there, Edgar Allan Poe," said he. "When did you come to life?"

It was quite a party.

The weather was hot, and New York can be hot when it is hot. Of course I found time to parade Broadway with my cane, but I missed the old familiar faces and was a bit downcast in spite of the excitement over Theodore Roosevelt's Rough Riders and the war with Spain. I wondered if it were not cooler in Boston, and, after a few weeks, restlessness and a strange, almost lost, feeling sent me back there to stay a while and pound out my stories in the same room I had previously occupied at No. 4 Temple Street.

Late one afternoon, shortly after the first of September, I met Charles Howard Johnson in front of the Bowdoin Square Hotel. He grabbed me, "Pat!" he cried. "What are you doing here?"

"Writing," said I, and made no further explanation. "And you're the last person I'd expect to see in Boston. How come?"

"I need a drink," said he. "Come on."

As usual, he was immaculately groomed in a tailored suit and looked prosperous as a millionaire, but I could feel something strange in his manner. He drank three whiskies at the hotel bar while I was drinking one, and he kept me talking by asking many questions. Presently he said:

"I want you to see a show tonight at the Bowdoin Theatre. Call for tickets which will be in my letter box at the office of this hotel." Then he paused before adding, "You will see my whole life."

We shook hands and parted. I never saw him again.

I took a friend with me to the theater and we sat in the sixth row from the stage and watched Elita Proctor Otis play the star part in *Carmen,* the drama.

She was a large, vital creature with flaming hair, and I wondered what Charlie Johnson had meant by saying I would see his whole life. Later, I learned that he had separated from his wife and was madly in love with Elita Proctor Otis.

Still later, in Camden, I picked up a newspaper in which there was a large cut of a handsome young man and an article about him bearing the heading, "Charles Howard Johnson Dead." Apparently in good health, he had died in his sleep.

---

31 · FALSE MOVES

I HAVE A GRUDGE against Boston Common. As I was strolling across it one day with a friend, he stopped to speak to a girl acquaintance and she introduced us to another girl, a Miss Nunn from Baltimore, who was with her. We sat on a bench and talked. Miss Nunn was petite, not at all hard to look at, and she revealed a mouthful of nice teeth when she laughed, which was often. She amused me.

Mary Nunn and I lunched together the next day, and she told me she was trying to get a job in Boston so that she wouldn't have to go back to school in Baltimore. For the time being she was living in the home of her girl friend with whom I had met her.

False Moves

She had never worked, and she had no training or special qualifications for any kind of employment. Nor had she any conception of the hard and tedious existence of the working girl without vocational ability.

I said I thought she was making a mistake and advised her to go home and complete her school course. She did not take kindly to my advice. She said that what I'd urged her to do was impossible, for she had some pride and she'd told her schoolmates and others before leaving that she would never come back there. She became quite excited and not a little peeved at me for suggesting such a thing.

I saw her at intervals thereafter and took her to one or two shows, but refrained from asking how she was making out in her search for a job. That did not seem to please her either, and one day she let me know it, somewhat indignantly. Then she dejectedly admitted that the only offer of work she'd had was that of a waitress in a cheap restaurant, which was beneath her dignity.

"Well, what are you going to do?" I asked.

She sighed. "I've thought it over," she said, "and I'm going to take your advice. I'm going back home—for a while."

I put her aboard a train the next day and promised to answer her letters if she wrote to me, but I did not expect ever to see her again.

The summer had slipped away, and near the last of October I found myself fed up with Boston. As my contract with Street and Smith would terminate the first week of the new year, I decided that New York would then be the place for me, and back there I went again.

Two weeks after my arrival there, another opportunity to turn my efforts to the writing of plays knocked at my door. How Dore Davidson, an actor and himself a writer of plays, chanced to know anything about me or to obtain my address I am unable to state, but he appeared with a proposition that interested me.

Neil Burgess, who had starred in *The County Fair* for several seasons, had informed Mr. Davidson that he was searching for a new play of a similar rural nature, and for some reason Davidson thought the work of turning out one might be right up my alley. I told him he had made no error and urged him to unfold the program in full.

"Well, here's my proposal," said he. "I want to collaborate with you, with an agreement to split royalties fifty-fifty. You can furnish the story, built around the big scene for Burgess, which must be very melodramatic, and we'll work together on construction and lines. If we hit Burgess with a synopsis we'll be all set to get to work right away, for he'll try the play out on the road and bring it into town before the season is over. It will be a rush job. What do you say?"

Before he asked the question I'd forgotten how to say "No."

I went to bed that night with the play in my mind and awoke in the morning to find the "smash scene" there also. This scene, which would occur just before the curtain fell on the third of four acts, was strictly the sort of stuff that set the gallery gods wild in those days. With the lover of the beautiful leading lady bound, gagged, and helpless, a horrified witness, the dastardly villain would attempt to feed the shrieking lady into a humming, smoking, clanging, and clashing steam threshing machine. And Neil Burgess, playing the part of a sweetly humorous middle-aged country mother, would wallop the villain stiff and cold with the handle of a pitchfork and rescue the lady from the very jaws of death.

"Boy," said I, "that will be something!"

I worked all day on the synopsis, packing it with suggestions for comedy and suspense, but making it as concise as possible. Then I showed it to Davidson.

"Man," said he, "I think you've got what Burgess will grab for."

Mr. Burgess made his decision sooner than I had expected. "I like it," he told Davidson. "Give me the first act in shape to put it into rehearsal, and I'll sign a contract and pay the advance."

Of course I was elated even though I knew that a rush job on the play while still turning out Merriwell stories would double

False Moves

my working hours. But live or die, I was going to attempt to carry the double load.

Then a strange thing happened. After delivering a manuscript to my editor at Street and Smith's, I was met by O. G. Smith as I was about to leave the building and invited into his private office. He was affable and smiling.

"We are preparing to go into the cloth-book field," he told me, "and we want you to write three high-class boys' books for us on a royalty basis. We will make handsome volumes of them, and for each story we'll pay an advance of two hundred and fifty dollars, not to be deducted from your regular royalty payments of ten per cent. When can you give us the first story?"

The proposal stopped me from breathing for a few moments. "Why, Mr. Smith," I faltered, "I—I don't know. With the Merriwells to write also, it might take me three or four months."

"That wouldn't be soon enough," said he. "We must have them all in not more than six months. I believe we can arrange to make the Merriwell work easier for you. John Whitson has written some pretty fair juvenile stories for us, and he's coming to town in a week or two. You can let him do most of the work on the Merriwell, furnishing him with the titles, plots, and suggestions and reading his finished stories before they are delivered to us. That will afford you plenty of time to write all three of the cloth books in six months. There, now that's settled."

Given ten minutes to think it over, I would have thanked him and backed away, but he had decided the whole matter before I could consider it or say another word.

The advance payments and a small cut from the Merriwell stories while Whitson worked on them would mean financial safety for me, and I would be breaking into the cloth-book field as Street and Smith's leading juvenile author. I was caught off base, and tagged.

I can't remember with what words I agreed to Mr. Smith's plan, but I was committed to it when I left his office.

Telling Dore Davidson what had happened made me feel like

a double-crossing swindler, but I tried to redeem myself to some extent in his estimation by giving him the synopsis I'd written, to be used as he pleased. However, he did not succeed in placing an acceptable play with Neil Burgess, and Burgess never found a worthy successor for *The County Fair*.

Feeling sure the way was now open for me to establish myself as a writer of cloth-bound books, I made no attempt to obtain better payments for the Merriwell stories when the time came to sign another contract with the publishers. I believed that somebody else—maybe Whitson—would be writing all of them within a year. And already I had commenced to work on *The Rockspur Nine*, the first volume of the Rockspur Series, when I signed the new Merriwell contract.

It was not easy to break Whitson in to do the Merriwell work, for he was only superficially conversant with previous stories in the series and was wholly unfamiliar with athletic sports. This caused him to make numerous blunders which I had to correct, and I missed one or two of them, as was quickly pointed out by readers of the yarns. Still I doubt if any writer obtainable then could have done better than Whitson.

I finished the first Rockspur book around the first of March and delivered the manuscript to O. G. Smith for his personal reading. He expressed his full satisfaction with it and suggested that I rest up for a week before commencing work on the next book.

That week was eventful for me. I had been corresponding with Mary Nunn and now, suddenly, I received a telegram from her asking me to meet her on the arrival of a train on which she was coming to New York. She was laughing when I met her, and I thought she looked pretty fine.

"Well, this *is* a surprise," said I. "What's the big idea?"

"I'm starving," said she. "Be a good fellow and save my life."

I bought her sustenance and waited for her to elucidate. After keeping me guessing for a while, she said: "I've skipped again. Know anybody who wants to hire a dish-washer?"

"You're loony," said I.

False Moves

"All right, I'm loony," said she, "but some things are too much for my blood. I'd told my girl friends I would never come back to Baltimore, and they spread it that I'd run away. My folks felt disgraced. It was too much for me. So here I am again."

"And I suppose you're broke?"

"Not quite. I robbed a bank. My own, in which I'd saved up some loose change. And I sold my bike for ten dollars."

"I still think you're loony," said I, "but I guess we'd better get married. Then we'll be a pair of loons."

We were spliced in Jersey the following day, where marriage licenses could be obtained and yearning hearts united without agonizing delay. And late in April we went up to Camden and set up housekeeping in the little house that had been empty for a while.

The village gossips gabbled, but Mary was cute and had a way of making friends which caused her soon to be accepted by the leading social ladies of the town. The gabbling subsided.

Whitson followed us to Camden in order to be near me while working on the Merriwell stories, and Colonel Ingraham, now writing Buffalo Bill yarns for Street and Smith, came for a short visit in June while I was doing the third book of the Rockspur Series.

Again I was importuned to manage the local baseball team, but I refused to do more than serve on the board of directors. However, as a director, I engaged a manager for the team who made a success managing the team of the state's leading prep school.

He was studying for the ministry and, by covering up bills contracted and due, he succeeded in leaving the Camden Club several hundred dollars in debt—also at the foot of the Knox County League—when he stole silently away near the close of the season. And several dozens of new baseballs, not yet paid for, stole away with him in his traveling bag.

I shipped my third Rockspur story to Street and Smith before the end of July, and Whitson, again out of a job, became a Baptist preacher and occupied the pulpit of a church for a while in a small town in the western part of the state. Lawyer, Kansas homesteader, dime novel writer, parson and—still later—Massachusetts farmer and instructor of amateur fiction writers, Whitson followed a career at least variform.

I was pleased by the Rockspur books when they were finally issued, for they were, as Mr. Smith had said they would be, really attractive volumes. At last I was a cloth-book writer under the name of Gilbert Patten, and I felt that my days of writing so-called dime novels would ere long be behind me.

But something went wrong. I was told that the established publishers of cloth books were opposed to the invasion of their field by purveyors of dime novels, but I think it more probable that Street and Smith were not properly organized to distribute cloth books widely with retailers. However that may be, their attempt to break into that field somehow miscarried. Nevertheless, I received between two hundred and two hundred fifty dollars each as my royalty commissions on those books, which attested that they were not a complete flop.

When I realized what had happened, I was just as happy and contented as a dog with a tin can tied to his tail. I chided myself severely for failing to ask for a raise before signing my second contract to write the Merriwells. I talked to myself rather harshly.

"Mr. Patten," said I, "you've got the business foresight of an imbecile."

Which was one of the mildest of my confidential comments about myself to myself.

32 · AFTER MANY MOONS

FOR MANY REASONS that I do not wish to specify, I realized before I had lived a full year with my second wife that I had made another serious mistake in my life of errors. Nevertheless, having made

After Many Moons

the hasty cast, I was determined to abide by the fall of the dice.

In one respect, she made no trouble for me. She loved to live in a big city and preferred New York to any other, although there were two winters when we spent much of our time in Boston.

I joined the Authors League and met Jack London and Rex Beach at one of their annual dinners. Following the after-dinner speechmaking, I was talking with London in the midst of a throng of writers when Charles Hanson Towne sauntered lackadaisically up to us.

"Oh, Jack London," said he, "you are a famous man. You're famous for your *John Barleycorn*. But I'm a more famous man. I'm famous for my love poems."

Jack looked at him for a moment before saying, "Oh, yes?" and turning to walk away.

Now Towne was a wit who sometimes scintillated, and a snub was something he couldn't take without a murmur. Gazing pityingly after London's retreating form, he sighed deeply.

"Ah, Jack!" he said, shaking his head. "Poor old Jack. Everybody wants to meet Jack, but when you meet him you find he is dreadfully dull."

Later, I sat long at a table down in the grill room with Rex Beach, Morgan Robertson, and Edwin Milton Royle, the playwright, and drank much beer and heard much interesting talk.

A heavy snowstorm was raging and taxicabs were hard to find when that little party broke up near morning, so Beach and I journeyed to Seventy-second Street by subway and had coffee and hot cakes together for breakfast in a little all-night restaurant. He was then living on West Seventieth Street and I was stopping at the St. Andrews Hotel at the corner of Seventy-second and Broadway. I've never seen him but once since that night.

Men were wearing "toothpick-toed" shoes about then, and the infernal things made me a semi-cripple and permanently crooked-toed before I would admit that they had me licked. Even women in the days of hobble skirts were not such martyrs to style, nor did they suffer such tortures when wearing the ridiculous doodads called hats, in recent years. Now they are wearing men's pants, literally, and dang my eyes if the young and slim ones don't look all right in them.

Street and Smith had changed the name of the *Tip Top Library* to *Tip Top Weekly* and were making a second clean-up with the Merriwell stories already issued by republishing them as fifteen-cent paperbound books in the *Medal Library*.

Each of these issues contained four of the original stories, tied together loosely by a little cutting and rewriting. Also they had sold to David McKay, a Philadelphia publisher, the right to publish twenty-five of the *Medal* Merriwells as cloth-bound books to retail at seventy-five cents each. For these republications I received nothing at all.

When the time came to renew my Merriwell contract again, I asked for one hundred dollars a week—and didn't get it. In this instance I was dealing with Mr. G. C. Smith alone. After some discussion, I was offered seventy-five dollars and told the parting of the ways had come if that was not satisfactory. And I was supporting not only myself and wife but my parents and my son by my first marriage!

Given a day to consider, I could see no way of escaping at the moment. So I returned the following day, and signed. But I blamed no one as much as myself for the jam I was in. I realized that few successful business men do business on a sentimental basis and that by failing to identify myself publicly as "Burt L. Standish," I had failed to put myself in a position to be competed for by other publishers.

"That," said I, "must be rectified."

My first move was to take my light from beneath the bushel where I had hidden it. Although I had no desire to become a writer for Frank Tousey, Street and Smith's chief competitor in the field of five-cent fiction, I found a way, without being my own messenger, to let the information leak through to the Tousey firm that the creator and writer of the Merriwell stories was a person named Gilbert Patten.

Then I waited. Much time passed with no rise to my cast. Meanwhile Edward Stratemeyer was doing all right for himself by writing juvenile books for Lothrop, Lee and Shepherd, Boston publishers. That gave me an idea for another move. I planned two series of books for boys from eight to sixteen years of age, one of school life and athletic sports, the other of Western adventure. That done, I headed for Boston.

There, I laid my typewritten plans, including complete titles for twelve books, before Richard Burton, then editor for Lothrop, Lee and Shepherd. He said he liked both plans but preferred the Western series, the first book of which was to be called *The Deadwood Trail*. He interviewed the head of the firm and came back smiling.

"It's all right, Mr. Patten," said he. "Write us the first book and we'll start the series with it, if it's what we want."

I went away feeling as if I owned the city. There wasn't a doubt in my mind about giving them what they would want.

I remained in Boston a while, plotting the first cloth-book of the proposed series and writing a Merriwell yarn. The latter was a baseball story and I cudgeled my brain to conceive something new for Frank to do on the field. Completely at a loss, I dropped my work one day and went to a baseball game, where I got a seat behind the catcher.

A tall, lean, long-armed pitcher was on the mound, and he had a queer cross-fire delivery that bothered the batters. Shortly after I sat down he threw a fast high ball that curved sharply inward and caromed off the end of the bat, which the hitter had not removed from his shoulder. Down in one of the front rows, a farmerish looking man jumped to his feet.

"I been watching baseball for twenty years," he cried, "and that's the first time I ever see a curve two ways on one pitch."

Well, there it was!

He had given me the idea for Frank Merriwell's "double-shoot," a pitched ball that started to curve outward and then took an in-shoot. In future stories, Frank used that amazing and impossible double curve on dangerous batters in pinches, and over the country boys almost ruined their arms trying to throw it.

But I was also having trouble to find the factual material I needed in writing *The Deadwood Trail*. Eventually, on the advice of a Boston bookseller, I went to the Public Library and searched for an article by Leander Richardson in back numbers of *Scribner's Magazine*, published at the time of the Black Hills gold-rush. I found the article, describing a trip by Richardson over the very ground I wanted my hero to cover, from Laramie, Wyoming, to Deadwood City, and I was all set.

The writing of that book was sheer delight, even though I was compelled to do it piecemeal while dictating the Merriwell stories to a secretary who took down my dictation in shorthand and did the typing at home. I found two drawbacks in dictating my stories; I became verbose, and I could not dictate while sitting down. I walked the floor as I dictated and, no matter how well I was going while on my feet, I ran down and came to a dead stop if I sat down. When the story was flowing fast I walked fast; when it flowed slowly I walked slowly.

I plotted the book a chapter or two ahead of the writing and wrote the story on my typewriter. A final reading of the manuscript in full made me think I had done a pretty good job under the circumstances; but several days after I delivered it to Lothrop, Lee and Shepherd I was called to the office of the editor and informed that it had been rejected.

"But what is the matter with it, sir?" I asked in dismay.

"Personally, I think it's all right," was the reply, "but the head of the firm says it's too fascinating. He thinks it would make boys want to run away out West in search of adventures similar to those your hero experienced."

Astounded, I said, "If that's his reason, he would have refused Stevenson's *Treasure Island* had it been offered here."

"I think he would have," said Richard Burton.

I took the manuscript to New York and ran into unpleasantness there. Editors for book publishers now seemed to know that I had been a writer of dime novels, and the first ones I approached did not even want to see anything written by me.

I felt sunk. And to make me feel more so, I was shocked one morning to read in my newspaper the obituary of Arthur Grissom. Unaware that he had contracted typhoid, he had stuck to his work when he should have been under a doctor's care, and had died quickly on being compelled to quit. He was a talented young man whose future had appeared bright with promise.

With Johnson and Grissom both gone, New York never again seemed the same. I still carried my cane, but Broadway saw less of me, and I'm sure I had lost some of the cocksure jauntiness of former days.

By persistence, I finally placed *The Deadwood Trail* with high-class publishers. It was accepted to be published the following year by D. Appleton and Company. They urged me to follow it up with the second volume of the series I had planned, saying that was the only way to make juvenile writing profitable. I regretfully admit that I never wrote the second book.

A lassitude came over me now, a let-down from high tension and a desire for as much rest as I could get. Camden called, and back there we went again. Once more Colonel Ingraham came on —this time from Chicago—to visit us briefly in the little house that I had named "Cornercot."

Standing with me on the veranda and gazing with apparent pleasure out upon Penobscot Bay, he appeared younger than when I'd seen him last. His cheeks were as smooth as a girl's and softly tinted with what seemed to be the flush of health. I congratulated him upon his youthful appearance.

"Thanks, Gil," he said. "I'm feeling fine and I've got good news to tell you."

"I'll be delighted to hear it, Prentiss," I said.

He laughed then. "Well," said he, "this damned old game foot of mine isn't going to kill me after all."

The bone was decaying in his wounded foot, and the trouble had begun to creep up from his ankle. Reliable surgeons had warned him that he must have his leg amputated at the knee if he wished to live.

"Well, that *is* good news," said I.

He continued to laugh. "No, it isn't going to kill me," he said, again. "I've been examined by one of the best doctors in Chicago who informed me that I've got Bright's Disease and can't live more than six months anyhow."

A brave man looking death in the eye and making a joke of it. But the doctor had miscalculated; Prentiss lived more than a year before he died in a Mississippi hospital.

Another heavy cold bothered me for a while the following winter but did not get me down. We found amusement in amateur theatricals, card parties, and dances. Dictating my stories was a relief from the tiresome labor of pounding them out myself on a typewriter and gave me more time to rest and read. Among other books, I read Owen Wister's *The Virginian,* little dreaming that before many more moons had waxed and waned I would meet a living person who had been the author's model for one of the characters in the story.

Spring came and summer was fading fast away when I received a letter that caused me to sit up and take notice. It was from the publishing house of Frank Tousey and stated that the firm would like to talk business with me.

At last, when I had practically ceased to hope, my attempt to arouse competition for my services appeared to promise success. Without delay, I replied that I would be at the Herald Square Hotel in New York on a certain date, prepared to consider a business offer.

"Now," said I to Mary, "we'll see what we'll see, but this time I'm counting no chickens until they're hatched."

Lu Senarens, Tousey's editor and the author of stories about a steam man, met me at the hotel and felt me out. "I'll do business with your people if the signs are right," I told him.

He took me down to the Tousey publishing house and introduced me to a smallish dark man who was the head of the firm. I did not then know that Mr. Tousey was dead. The small man to whom I'd been introduced talked so straight that he almost scared me.

"We want you to create another hero like Frank Merriwell for us," he said, "and we'll gamble on you at the very start. We'll pay you one hundred dollars a week the first year, one hundred and twenty-five the second, one hundred and fifty the third, and so on up as long as our profits warrant raises, and you can have a contract for ten years if you want it."

Now that was the kind of business talk I'd never before heard from any publisher. Pretty breathless, I asked, "But how can I know your profits warrant raises, sir?"

"It shall be stipulated in the contract that either you or your lawyer—or both—shall have access to our books at any time," was his answer.

It seemed to me that he had placed his cards on the table in a completely frank and honorable manner, and I felt that I should do the same. So I told him exactly how much my publishers were paying me and about the raise I had asked for and been denied. He was silent. He did not attempt to win me over by sympathy or by censuring Street and Smith. Maybe I'm soft, but unto this day I have regarded the man I conferred with as a square-shooter and an honorable business man.

"My contract with S. and S. ends the first week in January," said I. "Mr. G. C. Smith informed me that they positively would not give me a further raise, and that makes it certain they never will, but I do not feel like signing with another firm until I am free and clear of my contract with them."

I do not think clever business men do business that way, but that was the way I was trying to do it.

Now he attempted to rush me, which was a mistake; for I had so often blundered when rushed, that I became stubborn.

"Sir," said I, "if we get together, and I'm sure we will, I will treat you the same. Nobody will be able to buy me off you at any price until I have given you a fair and proper notice of my intention to leave. However, I will not quote your offer to me to Street and Smith or anybody else. I'll simply inform them I am leaving to accept a better offer. My connection with them will terminate when my contract expires, and you've practically got me now."

We shook hands, and I went away from there feeling sad and

heartsick; for I had conceived a strange affection for Mr. O. G. Smith and the firm I was employed by, and I did not want to work for Tousey. But I felt it was a certainty that I would be working for Tousey the following year.

---

33 · IN DENVER

HAVING DECIDED to wait until the first of December before notifying Street and Smith of my intention to sever connections with them at the expiration of our contract—which would give them a full month's warning—I went down to 79 Seventh Avenue to let them know I was in town.

O. G. Smith welcomed me warmly. "I've been thinking about you, Mr. Patten," he said. "How would you like to take a trip across the continent—say, to San Francisco and back?"

His words gave me one of the queerest jolts of my life. "Why—why, Mr. Smith," I stammered, "of course I would like it."

"Well, I think we can make arrangements for you to do so," he said. "We have a way of getting passes over the railroads. It will cost you nothing except for meals and hotels. And I'm sure you can find opportunities in your stories to give the roads you travel over a certain amount of favorable publicity, which would be expected in return for the passes."

I was speechless.

"Of course we'll provide you with passes for your wife also," he went on. "You can take in the big fair at St. Louis on your way, and we would like to have you call at the big depots of the American News Company and boost a little, discreetly, for Street and Smith's publications. You might stop over in Denver a while, which would give you a chance to pick up some real Western atmosphere for your stories."

I didn't know what to say. For a moment I was tempted to upset the apple cart by admitting at once that I had received a most liberal and satisfactory offer to write for another publishing house, but the thought of former blunders through hasty action restrained me.

"But, Mr. Smith———" said I, and could not find words to continue.

"But what?" he asked, surprised by my hesitation.

"Well," said I slowly, "I'm not sure about things. About myself. Traveling so much, I'm not sure I could keep up in my work and give you the best stories I'm able to write."

He smiled. "We'll take our chances on that. If you fall behind a little, you can lay over in Denver and elsewhere and catch up. It will require a little time to make arrangements and get the passes, but I'll start the wheels moving today. You and Mrs. Patten better begin getting ready for the journey at once. I'll let you know when you can leave New York."

Outside the door to Mr. Smith's office, I walked around a few minutes to collect my wits and hide my mental disturbance before going into another office to meet Charles Agnew MacLean, a young newspaper man recently employed to edit my stories.

MacLean was so deliberate and unhurried in everything he did that he appeared lazy, but doubtless he was thoroughly capable and efficient. He won the full confidence of Street and Smith and was promoted to the editorship of the *Popular Magazine* when it was discovered that the original editor was receiving cuts on payments made to certain of his pet authors.

MacLean made the *Popular* the leading magazine in its field and one of the firm's most profitable publications. He published the fiction and won the high regard of many well-known writers, among whom were Louis Joseph Vance, Charles E. Van Loan, Zane Grey, H. C. Witwer, and Jack London. He bought American serial rights to H. G. Wells' *Tono-Bungay* and ran it in the *Popular*.

After leaving MacLean's office I met a tall keen-eyed man who introduced himself to me as Frederick Day, writer at that time of the Nick Carter stories. We left the building together and sat down for a chat in a little café, where he took whiskey and I drank beer. He claimed that he frequently wrote two 25,000-word stories in a week and had once turned out three of them in that time. I asked him for his formula.

"Oh," said he carelessly, "I just tie the plot up into a knot nobody can untie—and then untie it."

I think he was a very capable author of detective yarns who could have written mystery stories equal to the better ones published in cloth books today. Working under such high pressure, he drank heavily at times, and his stories finally became so poor that he was dropped by Street and Smith. Thereafter his downfall was swift. Unable to meet payments on a six hundred dollar mortgage, he lost his home by foreclosure and committed suicide.

When I told my wife of O. G. Smith's offer and my reaction to it she was much annoyed with me. "Can't accept it?" she exclaimed. "Of course you can! It isn't costing them a cent, and you're crazy if you think you wouldn't be entitled to it, if it were, and they were paying our hotel bills too. You ought to have your head examined."

"Maybe you're right," I allowed. "Anyhow, we'll go."

Our transportation came after some delay, and we were off for the journey late in September.

St. Louis was just as cool as a blast-furnace when we arrived there, and the plank walks at the fair nearly made a cripple of me in one day. I bought another pair of shoes in which my feet had room to breathe, and we prowled over the fair grounds two more days, by which time the little woman was limping also and willing to call it enough.

From the train that carried us into Colorado I caught my first glimpse of the Rocky Mountains, lying far-distant like small blue molehills on the horizon. They made me think of the blue hills of Dixmont as seen from Corinna.

Somebody had recommended the Shirley in Denver, a family hotel not far from the Brown Palace, and there we found excellent accommodations at rates I could afford to pay. It was a homelike place, new and immaculate, and the cuisine was praiseworthy.

In Denver

From the windows of our room we could look out over the city to the Rockies, forty miles away and appearing to be not more than twenty.

"Here," said I, "we'll sojourn a while, until I've batted out enough stuff to let Street and Smith know I'm still on the job."

It was then around the first of October, and the following morning I arose to discover, with astonishment and dismay, that about an inch of snow had fallen during the night. I'd never seen anything like that in Maine at such an early date, and the spectacle gave me a yearning to be somewhere else. However, the day was not over before the snow had disappeared.

Paulos Thieman, a young man from Missouri whom I had known in the East, was then editing the Denver *Post,* and I called on him in his office at the first opportunity.

"Well," said I, "how's the gas business?"

When last I had seen him, he was the assistant manager of the Consolidated Gas Company of New York.

"What d'yer mean, gas business?" he barked. Then having obtained a square look at me, he leaped to his feet with a whoop. "Why, Pat, you old Broadway bum!" he cried, getting me by the hand and leaving my fingers so that they had to be pried apart. "What are you doing here—without your cane?"

"I've taken a long and wearisome journey to solve a mystery," said I. "Nobody's been able to tell me why you vanished from Manhattan so suddenly."

He laughed. "Well, ease yourself into a chair," said he, "and I'll sweep the cobwebs from your brain and have it over with. You see, it was this way. Though I was supposed to be the assistant manager of the Consolidated Gas Company, I was actually the manager, and I got too big for my britches. I knew it all. So when Russell Sage told me to follow Consolidated's methods of gas distribution, which I knew were antiquated, I told him he would have to get somebody else if he wanted it done that way. And, a trifle to my surprise, he got somebody else. That's all."

He could laugh about it, which indicates that his downfall had not knocked the high spirits and confidence out of him.

On leaving New York, he had become a reporter for the Kansas City *Star* and, later for the Denver *Post*. Resourceful and utterly fearless, he had faced dangers and obtaind sensational "scoops" for both papers, and Bonfils and Tammen, owners of the *Post* had recognized his value by promoting him to his present position.

After we had chatted a while, he said suddenly: "What's the matter with you, Pat? 'Burt L. Standish' has become famous, but the public doesn't know he is really old Gil Patten, which isn't as it should be. You'll never get your just dues until you take off your mask."

"Maybe you're right," I admitted, "but the time for that hasn't come."

"Oh, yes it has," said he, "and you're going to do it right away. The *Post* will let the blooming world know who you are. Maybe I can get you a full page in a Sunday issue."

"Wait a minute, Paul," said I. "There's a reason why I don't want that to happen now. D. Appleton and Company have just published a cloth book of mine written under my own name, and I may not be writing the Merriwell stories next year."

He looked disappointed. "Well, if we don't do it," he said, "the *Republican* will get you. You can't hide from that pack of hounds if you stay in Denver any length of time."

I promised to give the *Post* the story first if *Republican* reporters got after me.

I was not long in Denver before I became aware that the city was in the clutches of a gang of rotten political grafters. For that was the Denver period depicted by Harvey J. O'Higgins and Judge Ben B. Lindsey in their book, *The Beast and the Jungle*.

The *Post*, always for reform until "appeased," was exposing the reigning racketeers, and for once Tammen, who reputedly had boasted that he had once bribed a grand jury, never seemed to waver in the battle. Maybe he was not offered his price to lay off, but I prefer to think that one Paulos Thieman somehow persuaded him to resist temptation.

In Denver

The Shirley Hotel had a preponderance of lady patrons, many of them the wives of cattlemen who had come in from their husband's ranches to escape the rigors of the approaching winter. Some agreeable young men also were living there, and soon Mary and I were on a friendly footing with a set of pleasant people who played sociable games of draw poker with a ten-cent limit, which couldn't damage losers much.

However, there came a night when the men only were to play, but my wife and another lady were allowed to watch the game. When playing began, Mary sat on a table behind me in a position to see my cards and those of a good-looking young man at my right. The sky was the limit that night, and I drew four sevens on the second deal. I backed that hand teasingly at the start and the young man at my right continued to raise my raises until presently we had the field to ourselves.

Then there was some real betting, and, as the saying goes, the air became tense. Suddenly my wife leaned over my opponent's shoulder and whispered to him.

"Stop betting," I heard her say. "He's got you beat."

Quite naturally, he looked surprised. But, knowing she had seen the cards we both held, he hesitated only a moment or two before putting his cards down, face upward, on the table.

They were four fives and a queen!

There was no murder. There was not even a scene. I gathered the pot in and covered my cards during the rest of the game so that no one but myself could see what I held. When the game broke up I was still a little ahead, although the young man my wife had so kindly warned had taken from me nearly all I had won in that early pot, which placed him, with his other winnings, several hundred dollars to the good.

I never mentioned her action to Mary. Also I never forgot it.

I had written about roulette and faro in my Beadle and Adams stories without ever having seen a roulette wheel or a faro table, but now I had an opportunity to see them. The Navarre was a strange place, both a gambling house and a hotel patronized by a certain class of theatrical people. I found no difficulty in obtaining admission to the Navarre's long gambling room, where I "piked" by placing two-bit bets on the numbered roulette board. The game there was said to be on the square, and it may have been. For with the 0 and the double-0 favoring the house, the chances were against the players.

Always interested in human beings, and always speculating on what makes them behave that way, I finally succeeded in meeting the proprietor of the Navarre and chatting with him. A small, quiet, soft-voiced, pale-faced man, he told me he had come to Denver for his health.

"Lung trouble?" I asked.

"No, lead trouble," said he.

Then he explained. He had been the proprietor of a saloon and gambling houses in Leadville, where one night a man who had lost his last dollar at faro had accused him of running a crooked game and left him on the floor with six bullets in his body.

"I didn't die," said he, "but I've still got some of that lead in me that they didn't dig out. So when I got up and around, I decided that Denver was a healthier place for me than Leadville and came down here to live."

Goldfield, Nevada, hit a boom while I was in Denver, and there was a lot of crazy speculation in Goldfield mining stocks. Paul Thieman took me into the Denver Mining Exchange one day shortly after my arrival in the town and pointed out a Goldfield stock that was quoted on the board at six cents a share.

"Our mining expert says that is a good buy," said Paul.

I didn't buy any, and when I left Denver that stock was selling for almost three dollars a share.

But I didn't leave Denver very soon. In fact, I was doing so many things there that I couldn't get far enough ahead with my work to leave for months. And when I did leave at last, I was headed back for New York instead of for San Francisco.

34 • SHIFTING WINDS

"Lungers," as tuberculosis patients were called, were plentiful in Denver, and I had not been there long before I began to fear that I, myself, would soon be under a doctor's treatment for lung trouble.

The climate affected me peculiarly. Some days I would feel fine and peppy and have no symptoms of a cough; and then suddenly, for no apparent reason, my bad lung would become sore and painful, and I would be doing my best to cough my head off.

Returning to the Shirley after taking a walk one crisp morning, I came upon evidence that somebody had suffered a hemorrhage just outside the door of the hotel. When I reached our room some time later, my wife was surprised to see me unwrap and proceed to open a quart bottle of rye whiskey.

"Now what's the idea?" she inquired.

"This," said I pouring a modest drink into a waterglass, "is for medicinal use. If I don't find a way to cure this foul lung of mine you will soon be happily wearing widow's weeds."

"You are as daffy as ever," she said. "That stuff is no good for what ails you."

"I've heard to the contrary," was my reply. "Anyhow I'm going to give it a whirl and find out. And possibly my greatest ailment isn't what you think it is."

I took another shot of the stuff before going down to breakfast, and still others at intervals throughout the day. I did not like it then and have never liked it at any time, but it stimulated me and gave me a ravenous appetite.

Thereafter during my entire stay in Denver I used whiskey methodically and regularly, and it was not long before I began to take on weight and feel better all the time. Also I did not catch cold as frequently, and my lung gradually ceased to trouble me so much.

Having a social drink one day with a friendly doctor who specialized in tubercular diseases, I asked him how much liquor a man could consume daily without harm.

"That depends upon the man and how he takes it," was his reply.

"Well, how much do you give your patients daily?" said I.

"I don't give some of my patients any," he said. "In some tubercular cases, liquor is harmful. In others, it seems to be beneficial."

"And where you find it beneficial, how much do you give?" I persisted.

"More or less according to how it works in individual cases," said he. "My limit where it seems to work well is about four ounces a day."

I laughed. "Well, I've been taking quite a lot more than that, doctor. Nearer a quart a day. It has stopped my cough and is putting meat onto my bones."

He nodded soberly. "I've noticed you are looking better than the first time I saw you. Apparently it is building tissue for you now, but if you continue to take as much there will come a time when it will destroy tissue faster than it is building it now. Watch yourself."

After that, I cut my daily portion of whiskey to about one pint and added raw eggs and lots of milk to my diet. Also I took long walks in the open air. When I began that self-administered treatment I weighed 167 pounds in my clothes, which is below normal for a man of my height, six feet and one inch. When I returned East, months later, my weight was 182 pounds and I had not been troubled by a cough for a long time. Moreover, my lung, although still sore, had wholly ceased to pain me.

On the day I left Denver I cut liquor out entirely and did not touch it again for more than six months. Yet I continued to gain weight for quite a while, and never again have I raised blood when suffering from a cold. Today my left lung seems to be as sound as the other.

Had I been seeking rest as well as recuperation, Denver would have been a bad place for me; for those were stirring times in

Shifting Winds

Colorado's Capital City. As election drew near, the venal politicians writhed and foamed under the lashings administered by the *Post*. That was duck soup for my friend Thieman, who plied the whip with increasing vigor. However, election day saw no serious rioting at the polling places.

The *Post* had supported Judge Ben Lindsey of the Juvenile Court, whom the political machine had slandered foully and marked for slaughter, and I wondered what manner of man the Judge really was.

The election returns were being projected upon a big canvas screen across the street when Paul Thieman took me into Tammen's private office. The room was well-filled with invited guests, and soon I was less interested in the returns than in a smallish man who could not seem to find a chair that wasn't too hot to sit on. He kept hopping up and walking around and sitting down again.

"What's the matter with that gentleman, Paul?" I asked. "Has he got ants in his pants?"

Thieman chuckled. "That's Judge Lindsey," said he," and he's so happy over the way things are going for him that he can't keep still. Want to meet him?"

Of course I did. So he introduced me to Judge Lindsey, who gave me a quick handshake and went on trying to find a chair that wouldn't let him get away from it. I doubt if he even heard my name, but that made no difference to me; I was for him then and have been ever since.

Paul took me out to see the composing and press rooms. There I beheld a large, florid, and slightly fat, red-lipped person who was smoking a fragrant cigar and watching the returns as they appeared on the screen across the way. He was attired in well-made and expensive apparel from hat to boots, and diamonds big enough to choke a goat blazed on one huge hand and in the pin of his elegant four-in-hand necktie. Something was thrown on the screen that caused the crowd in the street to snarl and boo.

"Dese common people make me sick," said he.

"Now who is that one, Paul?" said I.

Again he chuckled. "That," said he, "is our sports editor. Come over and mitt him."

His name was Otto Floto, and he was a honey. He talked as sweetly as a longshoreman on Saturday night, and it was delight for my ears. He was a character and no snide. I liked Otto.

"But how can he be your sports editor, Paul?" I asked after we had left him still smoking his fragrant cigar at the window. "He's illiterate."

"I'm surprised at you for suspecting such a thing, Pat," said Paul Thieman, grinning. "When the bosses offered him the position he said, 'But I can't spell cat without putting two t's in it and maybe a k.' They told him that was all right, as our proofreaders would correct any words he spelled wrong. Otto knows all the box-fighters and sporting men from coast to coast, and the *Post's* sports department is the best west of New York."

After that I often saw Otto punching his typewriter with one finger of each hand in his "office," which was a doorless and windowless space about four feet wide and four deep, partitioned on three sides. A shaded electric-light bulb dangled above his typewriter at the end of a cord.

I don't know what Otto's salary as a newspaper man was, but he didn't have to depend on it anyway. He owned a saloon in Denver that, patronized by sporting gentry and their followers, was a gold mine. He appeared under his own name in two or three Merriwell stories, but probably was never aware of it.

The election was a debacle for the plundering politicians, who were temporarily stunned and bewildered. For the public was aroused, and the *Post* immediately began advocating the impeachment and trial of the crooks who had held positions of trust in the state and city governments. Panic-striken, the grafters got busy destroying evidence of their depredations.

Meanwhile, I mailed a letter to Street and Smith giving notice that I would not renew my contract with them when it expired, as I had received and practically accepted an offer at a much better salary than they were paying me. I sent a carbon copy of this letter to the Tousey company and asked them to prepare and forward a contract for me to sign on January 1.

I felt cheerful about it as a man unable to swim and overboard in the middle of the Atlantic Ocean.

There was no delivery of mail by air then, and it did not seem that my letter to Street and Smith could have reached New York, when I received a telegraphed reply to it: "We duplicate any offer made you. Please wait for letter mailed today. O. G. Smith."

I sat down and stared at that telegram in amazement. Here I was, caught again in a lovely jam.

35 · AFTER THE BALL

MY WIFE WAS EXULTANT. "Now you've got them," said she. "You can demand two hundred dollars a week and they will pay it. Maybe two hundred and fifty."

"Maybe you're right," I allowed, "but that would be lying. Tousey made me no such offer."

She looked at me with scorn in her eyes. "Don't be a chump," she said. "They'll never know what your offer was, and it's up to you to be smart for once in your life and get as much as you can."

I'll admit I was tempted, but something prevented me from yielding to the temptation. Maybe some persons would call it cowardice, but I feel that it was a desire to preserve my self-respect. We argued over it, and finally Mary said the least I could do was to demand one hundred and fifty a week for the first year instead of one hundred, as I was considering doing. But when Mr. Smith's letter came and I had read it, I wrote him that I would take a hundred and twenty-five the first year and one hundred and fifty thereafter for the term of the contract, which I supposed would be, like previous agreements, for three years.

"And I don't believe they'll agree to that," said I.

But they did, and, instead of three years, the contract sent to me was for five years. I signed it.

Then I had to let the Tousey firm know what had happened, and that was the most difficult letter I ever wrote. I never received an answer, and I suppose the Tousey people felt that I had double-crossed them. I can't blame them if they did.

Shortly thereafter there was a cattlemen's convention in Denver, and cowmen came pouring into the town from all over the grass country. They were a picturesque crew that made whoopee by day and by night, and yet at no time were they—to my knowledge—disorderly or given to brawling. Wind-browned, weather-hardened, and adorned in ten-gallon hats and other trappings which marked them for what they were, they thronged the streets, the hotels, and the saloons, and always they seemed hail-fellow-well-met with one another.

A young man named Parsons, whose father was a widely known Utah rancher, was stopping, with his wife, at the Shirley, and we had struck up a friendship. He took me into places where the cattlemen congregated and introduced me to some of them from ranges as far apart as Texas and Oregon. They knew at a glance that I didn't "belong," but being with young Parsons made me welcome and gave me opportunities to pick up color and suggestions for my work.

One of them told me he had visited New York City and didn't like it. "I couldn't savvy their brogue," said he.

Two special dances were held during the convention, the first at the Brown Palace, the other at the Windsor Hotel. The first one was strictly a dress affair, and, lacking evening clothes, that was "out" for me. However, my lady possessed the required raiment, and I generously escorted her to the ballroom door and turned her over to young Parsons and his wife, who assured me that she would be well taken care of.

But just to satisfy myself that she was not pining as a wallflower, I glanced into the ballroom ten or fifteen minutes later and saw her quite merrily stepping around in the whirling throng with a brownly handsome young man. Thereafter I glanced in again at intervals, and every time I did so I perceived that she was dancing with the same young man again—or still, which did not seem quite considerate for some older and not so attractive men who—there being an excess of gentlemen—were lonesomely looking on.

The dance at the Windsor, on the following night, was different. It had been announced as a costume ball for the cowpunchers, but no one was refused admission because of his attire.

When Mary and I pushed our way in, the floor space of the large ballroom was filled to the last inch by a crush of dancing couples. Nearly all the men were garbed—some of them eye-smitingly—in cowboy apparel, and many of the ladies looked like ranch girls on a spree. The orchestra, also wearing cowboy garb, was making the air tingle with a lively tune, and the couples were prancing right jauntily considering the curbing restraints. And barely were we in the room when it seemed that every man on the floor let out an ear-splitting cowboy yell.

My wife grabbed my arm. "Gracious!" she gasped. "I'll bet they're all carrying guns!"

I doubt if there was a gun in the room.

When the opportunity came, later, we danced until hot and thirsty and then went down to a lounging room and had a cool drink. There we met the Bittingers. A man in the middle thirties, he was a rancher, and his wife was charming. He ordered a quart of champagne and invited us to help them dispose of it, which we did.

Then he danced with my wife and I danced with his. Mrs. Bittinger could waltz. She could waltz like nobody's business. After we had danced until I was again hot and thirsty, we found her husband and Mary, and I ordered champagne in the lounging room. It was very refreshing.

Mrs. Bittinger talked to me, and I perceived that she was not only a superb dancer but also a most intelligent and beautiful woman. My tongue became careless, and I spilled the fact that I was a writer. Then Mr. Bittinger spoke to his wife.

"Tell him who you are, dear," said he.

She asked me if I'd ever read Owen Wister's *The Virginian*. I said I had, whereupon she informed me, a bit hesitatingly, that she was the original of the schoolmistress in that story. She had met Wister when he was gathering material for his novel.

I do not remember dancing again with Mary that night, but I took her with me when I returned to our hotel somewhere around four o'clock in the morning. We agreed that it had been a very agreeable occasion and retired without further comment.

There was a fire somewhere, and somebody was pounding on the door of our room, and it was one o'clock in the afternoon by my watch on the stand beside the bed. Only the pounding wasn't on the door but inside my head, and the fire was in my stomach, as I realized when fully awake. I got up, steadying myself, and rang for icewater to put the fire out. As I was drinking out of the pitcher in which it had it had been delivered by a bellboy, my wife stirred and complained about the noise I was making. I stood beside the bed and looked at her.

"Woman," said I, "why do you haunt me thus?"

She didn't answer. She had gone to sleep again. So I tumbled back into bed and went to sleep again myself—after a while.

---

36 · DANGER

THOUGH BLASTED AT THE POLLS, the political crooks were not resigned to accept defeat lying down; on the contrary, they conspired to use the corrupt courts to sustain them in office. It was a foolhardy scheme by desperate scoundrels. The *Post* exposed it and investigation followed. Then the enraged public talked about marching on the State House and ousting the rascals by

Danger

force. Paul Thieman wrote a causticly humorous story of such an uprising, holding the plotters up to derision as dunderheads and poltroons, and ran it serially on the editorial page of the *Post*. There were subterranean mutterings which reached my ears, and I made haste to see Paul.

"Do you know that you're a marked man?" I asked.

"Well, I had smallpox once," said he.

"There's a rumor," said I, "that the crooks you've been lambasting are going to bump you off."

"Somebody," said he, "is always starting rumors in this town. Bumping me off wouldn't do them any good, and they must have at least enough sense to know that."

To my wonderment, he did not appear even slightly apprehensive. However, as the days slipped by and the defeated officeholders resigned the reins of government to their successors without further disturbance or any harm befalling Thieman, my own apprehension subsided.

Spring was at the door, and the time for me to go back East was drawing near when Paul and I, with our wives, sat down to dine one night in one of Denver's famous restaurants of the goldrush days. The floor of the dining room was tiled, and at every corner of the squares of tiling there were shallow circular vacant places in which, reputedly, twenty-dollar gold pieces had once been set. Also reputedly, those gold pieces had been removed —as many as were left of them—because former customers had fallen into the amusing habit of prying them out with their big knives and presenting them in payment for meals and drinks.

Thieman was light-spirited that night, jovial and witty. His star was in the ascendant, and the future beckoned, smiling.

The occasion was one for mutual congratulations, and we were all light-hearted when a waiter arrived at our table and bent over Paul to whisper something into his ear. I observed with surprise that the waiter was rather pale and appeared to be agitated. Thieman listened, still smiling.

"Thank you, George," he said easily. "I understand. We'll attend to it later."

Our wives were busily chattering to each other, and Paul's manner in replying to the waiter was so undisturbed that they paid no attention to the occurrence.

But my curiosity was aroused, and, under cover of a burst of laughter by the ladies, I asked: "Is anything the matter, Paul?"

He gave me a cautioning wink. "Oh, nothing much," said he softly. "Just a drunk waiting outside to shoot me when we leave."

I don't know that a man's hair ever stands when he is frightened, but I know that I plainly felt a singular crawling sensation go up the back of my neck, and I'm sure my heart missed more than one beat before it began doing a speed-up. I thought of my warning to Paul which he had passed off lightly, even as now. With his life in immediate peril, he was apparently unalarmed. My face must have looked queer, for he spoke to me again from behind his napkin.

"Laugh, Pat," he said. "Pretend I'm telling you a joke."

I think my laughter must have sounded like the croaking of a frog, but his was still smooth and easy.

"Well, what are you going to do?" I inquired out of the corner of my mouth.

"Oh, we'll finish our dinner," said he, "and then we'll go out and see the gentleman about it."

We would! He was going to give me the privilege of walking out with him to face a gunman who would take pot shots at us; for I figured that the fellow, being drunk, was about as liable to hit me as Paul when he went into action.

"Are you armed?" I asked.

"Of course not," said he. "I don't pack a gun around town."

Well, we went on with dinner that I had quite ceased to enjoy, while Paul continued to appear as carefree as ever and grew even more witty. Maybe his composure was contagious, for I, too, became outwardly calm and began to consider what I ought to do if we were to meet a person on murder bent as we were leaving. I could think of nothing better than to make a flying football dive for the legs of any man I might see with a gun in his hand or attempting to draw one.

Dinner over and the check paid, Thieman spoke to our wives. "Toddle on ahead, girls," said he. "I want to tell Pat a naughty story."

There was a small entrance to the dining-room, and there we met the waiter who had warned Paul. "I was just coming to tell you, Mr. Thieman," he said. "The boss called a policeman who chased that crazy galoot away."

"Thanks, George," said Paul, slipping him a silver dollar.

"But what would you have done if he'd been here, Paul?" I asked.

"Well, I reckoned he wouldn't be waiting around with a gun in his hand, and I figured on climbing aboard him before he could draw," was his reply.

But that wasn't the end of it.

The day before we were to leave Denver I walked into Sexton's bar and restaurant, where I was to meet Thieman for lunch. Barely had I entered when he popped out of a small office room at the end of the bar and called to me.

"Come in here, Pat," he said. "I want you to meet a friend of mine."

He was grinning queerly.

I followed him into the office and he introduced me to a man whom I will call Hathaway, which was not his name—for obvious reasons. Mr. Hathaway, slender, dark-haired, and haggard-looking, was sitting at a table on which there were glasses and a bottle of liquor. Obviously he had been drinking heavily, although his face was almost ghastly pale.

"This is the gentleman who came around to shoot me when we were having dinner together the other night, Pat," said Paul.

"I was crazy that night," said Hathaway in a dull voice, "and it's lucky I didn't get to you then. If I had, I'd be a murderer now."

A member of the political machine smashed by the election, he had blamed Thieman for his downfall, and drink had driven him near to committing manslaughter. But a revulsion had followed. Having a wife and two children, he had become thankful of his failure to do the deed, even though he still felt that he was ruined.

I sat at the table with them and heard Paul Thieman advise Hathaway to leave Denver and make a new start elsewhere.

"You never belonged with the rotten gang you got mixed up with here," said Paul. "You're naturally a white man and on the level, and you can make a come-back if you want to—but not in this town."

"That's what my wife has been telling me," said Hathaway, "and by God I'm going to pull myself together and do it!"

The sun was shining in a cloudless sky when we left Denver and the great blue Rockies to go back to my Eastern home beside blue Penobscot Bay.

Part Three

37 · I BECOME A GAMBLER

I BOUGHT MY FIRST AUTOMOBILE in Boston. It was a two-cylinder chain-driven car with planetary transmission for two speeds, low and high, and the engine was under the body.

Starting the motor by hand-cranking near the middle of the frame was excellent exercise for arm and back muscles, if one didn't rupture anything more serious than his suspenders. The spark-plugs were fired by dry batteries, and a carbide generator provided gas for the headlights. To blow the horn, the driver squeezed air into it from a rubber bulb. There was no top or windshield.

A day's journey of fifty miles was good, one hundred was excellent, and one hundred and fifty was front page news!

On a fair morning in April, I settled myself behind the steering wheel of my new car with the little woman at my side and courageously set forth for Camden, two hundred and twenty miles away by the roads we would have to travel.

We bumped and bounced and careened over the highways at such breakneck speed that at twilight and evening star we were actually in Bath, Maine, only fifty odd miles from our destination. There we were informed that the roads beyond the Kennebec River were still absolutely impassable for motor cars.

So I put my horseless vehicle into storage, and we rested and recuperated overnight and made the rest of the journey by train the following day. Two weeks later, we returned for the car and were pulled out of only one "frost hole" by horses before I drove triumphantly into Camden.

Motoring was truly heroic sport in its infancy.

Later, when the roads had settled, I piloted my car up to Corinna, mainly to show the town of my birth that Bill Patten's lazy son was doing all right since going away from there.

Inquiring for former friends and acquaintances, I was shocked to learn that many of them were dead. Herbert Fisher was still making his home there, and he invited us to become his guests for the night. We were in the post-office, where he was waiting for the late afternoon mail to be distributed, when a man sidled up to him and said:

"They are bringing Addie home tonight."

"Oh," said Herbert soberly, "is that so?"

After they had talked a few moments in low tones, I found an opportunity to ask Herbert whom they had been speaking about.

"Addie Hutchings," said he. "She's dead."

His answer made me suddenly ill. They were bringing that lovely laughing little girl whom I had so much admired in my boyhood back to Corinna to bury her there. I walked outside to get a breath of air and wait for Herbert. When he came I thanked him for his invitation to stop at his home that night and told him I was going to get out of the town right away.

"There are so many dead or dying in this place," said I, "that I feel as if I'll die myself if I stay here any longer."

We drove back to Newport, seven miles away, and put up there that night.

What with my work and my new automobile, I was kept busy that summer. I frightened so many horses that I became skittish myself when I met one on the highway.

Pawnee Bill, otherwise Major Gordon Lillie, came to Rockland with his Wild West Show that season, and I presented myself, with Mary, at the performers' gate and sent my card in to him.

On the card I had written, "A friend of Colonel Prentiss Ingraham." (One of Colonel Ingraham's dime novels had carried the title, *Pawnee Bill, the Young Scout*.)

I Become a Gambler

Shortly thereafter we were conducted into the presence of a smallish, long-haired, smiling gentleman in fringed buckskins who said he was always delighted to meet any of Prentiss Ingraham's friends.

He introduced us to his wife, a comely young woman in Western riding togs, who not only could ride but could shoot a rifle as well as Annie Oakley. However, she was not a Western woman by birth but was a Smith College graduate and a lady of charm and culture. The man whom she had married was at that time one of the leading bankers of Oklahoma, and the owner of a horse ranch in that Territory.

"The entire company is going in for the grand entrance in about five minutes," said Major Lillie. "Come with us. I'll give you two good horses and you shall ride on either side of Mrs. Lillie and me."

Now that was something I would have enjoyed, for I knew there would be a large number of Camden people in the audience, but alas! I was compelled to confess that neither my wife nor I could ride well enough to chance it.

"That's too bad," said the Major. "And all the best seats are sold out, so I'll have to give you seats on the side. But we want to see you both in our private car for a little visit after the performance. Wait for us to meet you. Promise."

Of course we did.

Now something odd happened when the cavalcade of Indian fighters, painted redskins, cowboys, cowgirls, and "wild riders from many lands" burst, whooping and yelling shrilly, into the large show tent.

Instead of riding straight forward to the central section of the high-priced seats, they swerved a little as they spread out and came tearing onward to rein their mounts to an abrupt halt. And there directly before us was Major Lillie and his wife, with the former sweeping off his big hat and making a smiling bow in our direction. Thus, although doubtless the other spectators did not realize it, we were recognized as honored guests.

Even though Pawnee Bill's show was of a lesser order than the great Wild West exhibition headed by Buffalo Bill, which I afterwards saw in Brooklyn, it was a highly colorful, fast-moving entertainment from start to finish.

In Major Lillie's private car on a railroad siding near the show grounds, we drank cool beer and ate crackers and Roquefort cheese after the performance. Put at ease at once by a man who was no rough illiterate faker and a lady who was a lady to the tips of her fingers, we soon lost track of time in enjoyment of the passing moments. I can not say how long we had been there when eventually the car began to move, after having been bumped around a little.

Mary cried, "We're going!"

"Oh, they're just shunting the car around some," said Bill. "Don't be disturbed."

I grabbed my wife by the arm. "Come on," said I. "It's time for us to be going, too."

I managed to swing her off safely to the ground and follow her as Pawnee Bill's show train was speeding up to pull out of Rockland.

"Good night, Gil," called Major Lillie laughingly from the platform of his car. "Come again."

He had almost succeeded in kidnapping us.

I sold my two-cylinder automobile in Boston late that fall, after having it repainted, at considerably less than half what I had paid for it, and called myself a lucky guy.

"No more of that stuff for me," said I, "until they get those things so they won't froth at the mouth and bite a man every time he takes them out of the stable."

Before we took a train to return home I bought a magazine in Boston's North Station, and in the magazine I came upon a picture and the floor plans of a beautiful modern Colonial house that somebody in Massachusetts had built for $6,500. I showed it to Mary.

"That" said I, "is my idea of a real house."

It met with her complete approval. "Let's build one just like it," said she.

I Become a Gambler

"And what," said I, "would you suggest we use for money?"

That had her stopped for a while, but some weeks later she told me how she would surmount such a trifling obstacle.

"You are earning one hundred and fifty dollars a week now," she pointed out, "and we can manage to exist without suffering on a hundred and twenty-five. In five years the twenty-five dollars that we do not need would amount to exactly six thousand and five hundred dollars, just enough to pay for the building of our house."

"Fine," said I. "Then we can build it five years from now."

"We can build it right away if you'll listen to me," she declared. "If you ask them for it to build a home with, Street and Smith will advance the sixty-five hundred and pay you a hundred and twenty-five a week for the next five years, instead of a hundred and fifty."

"Woman," said I, "that's a pipe-dream. They'll never fall for it."

But I was wrong again, as usual. Street and Smith sent me a check for $6,500 and a new contract in substitution for the one existing, according to which my weekly payments would be one hundred and twenty-five dollars for the ensuing five years.

With that fat check added to my bank account, I began preparing for the construction of the new house by a local builder, whose office clerk made blueprints and specifications, using for guidance the plans and picture of the house I had discovered in the magazine. I suggested a number of changes which would make the house both larger and more convenient, and, knowing those changes would add to the cost of construction, I began to realize I'd need more money than I had reckoned on.

As I intended to build on the lot I owned, the little house we were living in would have to be moved elsewhere. After trying unsuccessfully to find a purchaser who wanted a house without the land it was standing on, I bought another lot and made arrangements to have the little house moved onto it as soon as the roads were in condition for that to be done. Then, in May, after the moving contractor had the house jacked up and almost ready to travel, a man came along and offered me six hundred dollars for it.

"Mr. Giles," said I, "you have bought a house. Take it away."

And when he had deposited it on his own land, Mary and I lived in it until our new home was ready for occupancy.

Meanwhile I had received a surprisingly cordial letter from Mr. George C. Smith, who wished me good luck in my building venture and urged me to be sure to drop into his office when I came to New York again.

That letter disturbed me, for behind it I seemed to feel something I could not understand, and George Smith was the member of the firm who had said they would never pay me more than seventy-five dollars a week. Curiosity led me to make the trip to New York, taking my wife with me.

G. C. Smith greeted me with so much friendly warmth that I was still more puzzled. Presently, after we had chatted a while, he asked me if I owned an automobile. I told him about my trials and tribulations with the one I had owned and confessed that I had sold it at a sacrifice with great pleasure.

He smiled. "Well," said he, "how would you like to have another car that would be much less troublesome and also inexpensive to operate?"

I took a deep breath. "If there is such a car, I would like it all right," I said.

He nodded. "Very well, we will have one shipped to you. We have an arrangement by which we can pay for it in advertising space. Where do you wish it delivered?"

I told him the nearest railway freight station was at Rockland, and properly expressed my thanks.

When I got back to our hotel and told Mary about it, she did a pirouette. "Well, now you see how it is," she crowed. " 'Ask and ye shall receive, knock and it shall be opened unto you.' "

"Well, I didn't ask for this," said I, "and now I'm fixed so I can't do any knocking."

In the way of celebrating, we saw Donald Brian in *The Merry*

Widow that night and stopped over a day in Boston on the return trip.

I had been watching the quotations on some copper mining stocks that were taking a nose-dive, and a hunch led me to buy a hundred shares of Anaconda at twenty-eight and leave the certificate with the brokers, Hornblower and Weeks. I thought the market had just about hit bottom and for once in my life I was right. The upswing came almost immediately and Anaconda began to climb.

Then I began to gamble in earnest. With that hundred shares held as security by the brokers, I pyramided on every advance of two points made by Anaconda.

The house I was going to build had to be paid for somehow.

---

38 · WHILE BUILDING A HOUSE

THE AUTOMOBILE GIVEN TO ME by Street and Smith was a gray Atlas "runabout," powered by a two-cylinder engine of the two-cycle type that made it a hill-climbing contender with the best motor cars then on the highways. Power—but not speed—was its long suit, and I often found a bit of cheer on hard hills by passing other cars that had been giving me dust to eat on the levels. As Mr. Smith had said it would be, it was easy on the purse and required only a moderate amount of tinkering to keep it tuned up for action.

With an automobile that was not a headache and with laborers starting excavation work for the cellar of our new house, I was wholly unprepared for a squall that broke without warning. My wife informed me that we were not going to build a house!

I thought—at first—that she was joking, but she firmly assured me that no joke was intended.

"It's craziness to put so much money into a house in this town when I've never meant to live here all the time anyhow," she said, "and so I've changed my mind."

We discussed the matter, pro and con, at considerable length with the horns of the dilemma growing increasingly sharper.

Finally I said: "My dear, you don't seem to surmise that I have anything to say about what will be done. What do you suppose Street and Smith will think of me if I don't build a house with the money they have advanced for that purpose? And what do you suppose this town will say if I quit now? And what do you imagine I would think of myself? I never could hold my head up here again. I'd have to get out of Camden, and stay out."

"Well, that's just what I want you to do," she announced, "and the sooner the better. If you don't I'll—I'll leave you flat."

I went to the telephone and called the town's leading lawyer. "Can you come up to my house right away?" I asked. "I have a piece of business for you."

He replied that he would come immediately.

"Now what do you think you're going to do?" my wife wanted to know.

"Why," said I, "as long as you have decided to leave me, I'm going to have separation papers drawn up for us to sign. Then we'll know just where we're at, which will save a lot of bother later."

She laughed. "That suits me."

But when the lawyer came and I had told him why he had been called, she changed her mind again. "I won't sign any papers," she said, "and I'm not going away. I was only fooling anyhow."

I walked down town with the lawyer. "Cheer up," said he, "I've got a temperamental wife, too. Life is never very monotonous with them."

"I'd prefer a little more monotony," said I.

Honey was sour compared to my lady for some time after that little squall.

But now much darker clouds cast their shadows over me. My mother was taken ill, requiring the attention of a doctor and a trained nurse, and when she appeared to be on the way to re-

While Building a House

covery she died suddenly in the night. The shock broke my father, who outlived her only a month.

I have never been a person of great physical strength and endurance, but somehow I succeeded in writing a weekly Merriwell story of 20,000 words throughout that disheartening and burdensome spring of 1908; and I feel that hard work at that time made it possible for me to pull through without cracking. Fortunately, I had the assistance of an unusually efficient secretary, and the physical exercise of walking while dictating tired my body just enough to make it possible for me to sleep well at night.

To be sure that specifications were followed, I watched the construction of the house closely. Mary said I stood around and told the carpenters where to drive nails. She exaggerated sometimes. Lacking the services of an interior decorator, we planned the decoration and furnishing ourselves and made several trips to Boston to order the requirements. Our first trip was by auto, and, after a full day of shopping, we decided to call again on Pawnee Bill, who was exhibiting at Revere Beach.

We had started and were approaching the Parker House, in town, when I said to Mary: "I haven't insured this car and I'm going to stop and wire a Camden agent to cover it now."

She objected, saying we were going to be too late to see the entire performance anyhow, and I did not stop.

Major Lillie discovered us in the audience in the course of the performance and sent a messenger with his "command" for us to be his guests again after the show. I was sorry, for a let-down had hit me and I was feeling dog-tired; but courtesy required that we should make at least a brief call, and we followed the guide who came to escort us after the "Grand Finale." As when traveling, they were living in the Major's private car.

"We won't try to carry you off this time," said Bill, laughing. "We can't. We're staked out on this siding until the season closes."

Mrs. Lillie brought out sandwiches and her husband opened beer again. Relaxed on an easy chair, I was very comfortable; so comfortable, indeed, that presently it became an effort to hold up my end of the conversation, and I found myself struggling to keep my eyes open.

Mary, however, was as wide-awake and chirpy as a sparrow in springtime and quite deaf to any subtle hints from me that we should be pushing off. Finally, I summoned energy to stand on my feet and warn her that she probably would be ditched and killed by a sleepy driver unless we started *pronto*.

Had I waited another twenty minutes before doing that, I would have been much happier on the morrow.

Leaving the car in a garage almost directly across Huntington Avenue from the home of a Mrs. Wilson, where we were stopping, I wasted no needless moments about reaching our room and depositing my weary body in bed. Sleep came almost instantly, and seemingly in another instant I was wide awake again.

I had been aroused by the sounds of whistles and bells and rumblings. Sitting up, I looked out through the window at an angle and beheld the wooden garage, in which I had left the car, apparently wrapped in flames.

Uttering a yell, I bounced out of bed, jerked on my trousers, shot down the stairs, and was out of the house on the run. A crowd of people was watching the fire. Fire engines were there and others were coming. Policemen were there, and fire lines had been established. I went right through them. A fireman grabbed me in the wide-open doors of the burning building. He shouted: "Hey, lunatic, what are you trying to do, commit suicide?"

"My car's in here!" I panted.

"That's just too bad," said he. "Get out of here!"

I found a garage man. "Did they get any cars out?" I asked.

"Three were all we had time to get out," he told me.

"What kind were they?"

"Two touring cars and a gray roadster."

My heart leaped. "The gray roadster must be mine," I said. "Where are they?"

He told me where to find them on the next block.

The gray roadster was not mine!

Mary found me in the crowd that was watching the building

burn and I told her the sad news. "If you had let me send that telegram to Camden, we'd be covered by insurance," I said.

"You always blame me for everything," she said, and began to cry.

"I don't blame you for this mistake half as much as I blame myself," said I, and was suddenly dreadfully tired. "So dry your starry eyes and come on into the house. I'm going back to bed."

"How can you sleep?" said she.

"How can I sleep!" said I.

Resignation had come to me, and when it was apparent that the firemen would confine the flames to the garage building, I did succeed in going to sleep again.

When I arose late the following morning, somewhat rested but far from having a song in my heart, firemen were still watching the smouldering ruins of the garage. I dressed and went out.

The fire had behaved freakishly. It had gutted the first, second, and fourth floors of the four-story building but had jumped the third story, which was still supported by the charred framework. Surprisingly, the structure had not collapsed.

One of the firemen on guard permitted me to get near enough to look down into the water-filled basement, where I could see a mass of destroyed cars heaped one upon another. And there, after a while, I discovered the twisted wreck of a small gray runabout, a sorry sight for my eyes.

"Good-bye, little car," I whispered sadly. "You sure were a good little car while you lasted, but you didn't last very long."

Then I returned to our room and escorted my dejected wife out to a restaurant for breakfast. She picked at her food, but I ate heartily.

"You're a funny man," she said.

"However true that may be," said I, "I don't feel like one."

"But you eat as if starving. How can you do it?"

"What do you want me to do, cry?" I asked. "Seems to me I've heard that it's useless to cry over spilt milk."

I bought a morning paper and read a report of the fire which said that only three cars had been saved.

We were on our way back to Mrs. Wilson's when we met the night hand who had taken charge of the little Atlas on our return from Revere Beach. "You're in luck," he said. "I took your car up to the third floor and it's there now with others that haven't been damaged much by the fire."

It was too good to be true, and yet it *was* true. Later in the day, I got up there over improvised flights of stairs and found my little runabout with those other cars, most of which had been damaged more or less by heat, smoke, and water. The paint on my car did not show a blistered spot anywhere, and a garage man assured me that washing and polishing would make it look as well as ever.

The little woman was waiting for me to report, and what I told her after descending was very comforting. "But how will they ever get it down?" she wondered.

"That," said I, "is their problem. They'll have to do it somehow."

Mary and I went back to Camden by train, and three weeks later I was notified that my car had been returned to Boston from the factory. It seemed as good as new when I went after it and drove it over the road to Camden, but I was to discover in time that even the manufacturers had not been able to restore it to its full pristine vigor.

Meanwhile two ambitious gentlemen named William Jennings Bryan and William Howard Taft had entered upon a race for the White House in Washington, and the air was shuddering with oratory. However, I was too busy to lend an ear to the blandishments of political spellbinders, nor until near the finish of the contest did I imagine that the outcome might affect me. Then Mary came back from another shopping trip to Boston and stated that "the silver-tongued orator" was going to win in a walk.

"The Republicans are frightened," said she. "They say the West will go solid for Bryan and that he has hypnotized the masses all over the country. They predict a stock market panic if he's elected."

"And that scare stuff will make enough voters for Taft to be the one who'll win in a walk," said I. "It's an old gag, but it still works."

Nevertheless, what she had said presently began to make me uneasy. Since my original purchase of Anaconda Copper shares, on which I had been cautiously pyramiding, that stock had risen almost twenty points, but I knew a real stock market panic could wipe out that advance much faster than it had been made.

After talking confidentially with some of my Republican friends and discovering, to my surprise, that they were somewhat fearful that Bryan might be elected, I decided I had rather be safe than sorry. So I telephoned Hornblower and Weeks to sell my Anaconda "at market."

It was sold for forty-seven, which gave me a handsome profit.

But Bryan was not elected, and Anaconda hectically hopped eight or ten points before it paused for a breathing spell.

However, the profits from my only profitable stock market venture, added to what I already had in bank, gave me nearly enough to pay in full for the building of our new home.

39 · FRANK MERRIWELL'S BROTHER

WE WERE SETTLED in the new house on December 23, 1908. To me it seemed the perfect home for a writer, a dream come true. At last my roots were planted deep in the soil of one of Maine's most beautiful coastal towns, never again to be torn free—I thought—by stress or storm.

The snow-white two-story house of ten rooms and two baths stood in the midst of a built-up lawn that was held in place by heavy rough-stone walls. Facing the wooded mountains beyond the village, it also provided glimpes of the harbor and the blue bay that stretched eastward to distant lands. The low roof had a two-foot over-hang, and the wide clap-boarding of the building was in harmony with its gracefully solid general aspect.

On the eastern side, there was a wide veranda, part of which would be shaded in summer by an awning. The window shutters were dark green and there were two outside chimneys of red brick. A wide cement walk led from the street to a pillared porch and a Colonial doorway with leaded sidelights and fanlight.

The central hall, with a Colonial staircase, extended through to a door that opened upon an inset rear porch. All the floors were red birch, and the heavy doors were also red birch stained deep maroon, and the hall and dining room were quarter-paneled. A butler's pantry connected the dining room and the conveniently roomy kitchen at the rear.

Two steps led down from the hall to the large living room on the east side of the house, and this room was paneled and beamed with stained cypress and had folding doors at the rear, beyond which was a billiard room. The tone of these two rooms, which could be thrown into one by opening the folding doors, was dark brown and dim gold, and the lighting fixtures were of hammered iron. There was a handsome fireplace in the living room.

All the rooms on the upper floor opened from a central hall that extended around three sides of the stair-well, and there was an outside sleeping porch at the rear. The maid's room and the sewing room, at the rear on the west side, were cosily sequestered. There were three bedrooms across the front of the house, but the one on the west corner had been made into a library and workroom for me, with three windows, a fireplace, and built-in bookcases. A tiled bathroom connected my den with a master bedroom on the south-west corner and thus formed a suite that could be closed off from the upper hall, affording privacy when it might be desired.

A steam-heating plant kept all parts of the house comfortable in the coldest winter weather.

My accounts showed that I had paid $12,553 for the construction of that house, and it had been built at a time when the cost of materials and labor was paltry in comparison with their cost this day on which I am writing these words.

In attempting to tell the truth about myself—as it seems to me—I am now going to make a shameful confession. Never in my life have I felt even the slightest touch of the Christmas spirit. The cause of this flaw in my nature was an inculcation of my boyhood, when my father called Christmas a pagan holiday that had been adopted by heedless Christians.

There was never a Christmas tree in our home, never shining candles in our windows, and never did my parents give or receive presents on that day. And knowing other children were happy when I was lonely and sad, I came not only to dread Christmas but to hate it. In vain I've tried in later years to feel the glow that others seem to feel at Christmas time; pretending to feel it has always been no more than pretense by me.

Nevertheless, there was music and laughter and feasting and the clinking of glasses in our new home on the Christmas Day of 1908, for we were entertaining guests. It was stinging cold outside but warm and cosy within, and no one seemed happier then than my wife as she played the gracious hostess. Watching her, I thought that here her roots, like mine, might take hold and cling.

And she appeared contented and happy in Camden all that blustery Maine winter. I bought her a new Knabe piano on which she was given lessons by a competent teacher, and she played the ingénue in a drama given as a benefit performance for the local Business Men's Club. Not once did she harrass me in my work by a temperamental outburst, and the star of hope seemed bright before us.

Frank Merriwell's entrance to Yale had made it necessary for me to become at least superficially conversant with college life in New Haven, and I was making frequent short visits to that city, stopping usually at the Hotel Garde or the New Haven House, later the Taft Hotel.

In spite of a statement by a columnist friend of mine, Louis Sobol, that I was never nearer New Haven than Bridgeport, I certainly have sojourned there more than twenty times. But it was O. G. Smith who imposed upon me a problem far more difficult than gathering college atmosphere. Or at least it seemed more difficult when he announced that Frank had grown too old for the class of readers who were buying the *Tip Top Weekly*. He thought they were beginning to tire of him.

"You'll have to introduce a younger hero," he told me, "say, a younger brother of Frank."

I was astounded. "But such a thing is impossible, Mr. Smith," I said. "He has no brother. I have stated in the stories that he is an only child."

He smiled indulgently. "Nothing is impossible for you. You can dig up a brother for Frank."

I stared at him in speechless dismay. He had given me a command to do something that I could see no logical way of doing, and he was plainly in no mood to listen to an argument.

"Well, I'll think it over," was all the answer I was able to make.

"You'll do it," said he as I was leaving his office, and this time there was more encouragement than command in his voice.

Nevertheless, I knew by experience that the young readers of the stories were keen in detecting slips or blunders of any sort and delighted in pointing them out in their letters. Merely to produce a brother for my hero without plausible explanation for his existence would never do; it would surely bring upon me a humiliating storm of ridicule.

For a little while I wondered if Mr. Smith had intentionally put me in a hole by demanding the impossible, but I soon put the thought aside as unfair to a man of his character. Beyond question, he had believed I could do what he had suggested, but the more I wrestled with the problem the more hopeless I became.

I slept badly that night, but a moment after I had opened my eyes to the light of another day I knew the insuperable difficulty was no difficulty at all. Again my subconscious mind had been working and the problem was solved. I laughed aloud at my silly notion that it could not be done.

When Frank made his first appearance in the stories at the age of sixteen his mother was dead, but his father, long separated from Frank's mother, was still living and had appeared several times thereafter. Now, however, he also had died, and Frank would receive the last letter written by him revealing that, after the death of Frank's mother, he had married again and become the father of a second son, Richard by name.

It was so simple and credible that I wondered why I had failed to think of it when Mr. Smith had told me what I was to do.

Relieved and eager, I plotted the story, which would be titled "Frank Merriwell's Brother."

In order for Frank to become his half-brother's guardian and mentor, the death of Dick's mother, a Spanish lady, became a requirement; and, as trouble is the essence of fiction, I decided to have her brother Juan, beset by enemies bent upon his destruction, flee with his family to a hide-out in the Rocky Mountains, taking Dick with them and leaving a broken trail behind, which Frank must somehow follow.

Then, like an inspiration, Shangowah—otherwise "Old Joe Crowfoot"—stepped into the picture. To supply an additional attachment that Frank would have to break when he took his brother away, Dick's cousin Felicia, innocent and lovely, was conceived.

Writing the story, I portrayed Crowfoot as a dirty, evil-eyed, treacherous, bloodthirsty old redskin, a liar and a thief who hated all palefaces except Dick, whom he was instructing in the ways and wiles of the savages, and his first act in the yarn was an attempt to kill Frank. Of course Frank outwitted and baffled Crowfoot, but his failure to retaliate merely made Old Joe contemptuous of what he considered a weakness, even while pretending to be grateful.

Now I was attempting to do something seemingly impossible with such a character. For, instead of a detestable villain whom the readers would hate, I hoped to make Crowfoot a fascinating old hero whom they would admire.

Convinced in time that Frank was fearless instead of weak,

Old Joe grudgingly gave him a new name, "Strong Heart," even though he still nursed his hatred because of the conviction that Frank's purpose was to take Dick away to live among the despised palefaces.

But the time came when Crowfoot's admiration for Frank conquered his hatred, and thenceforth the old redskin fought for him regardless of peril to himself. Nevertheless, he continued to be a cheat, a thief, a liar, and a fraud—and how my readers did love him! They whooped for joy when he played dirty tricks on Merry's dastardly foes and exceeded them in chicanery.

Old Joe was continually complaining that he was going blind, but he possessed the keen, far-seeing eyes of an eagle. He professed to be so badly crippled by rheumatism that he could scarcely hobble around, but in fact he could run with the speed of a deer.

His hands trembled when he fired a gun, but he never missed the target. He did not die. He carried around a dirty and greasy old pack of cards and cheated crooks at poker when they were trying to cheat him. He appeared and disappeared at the least expected times and in the most unexpected ways.

When Dick, following in his brother's footsteps, was preparing for college at Fardale Academy, Frank brought Old Joe in from the West to visit him there, and the redskin "made medicine" at the home plate before a baseball game in which Dick was the winning pitcher.

However, the old redskin could not endure the East; the dishonest, lying palefaces were abhorrent to him. But never did Dick or Frank visit any part of the West that Old Joe did not show up and join them at the moment when he was greatly needed.

Not wishing Dick Merriwell to be the counterpart of his brother, I depicted him as hot-headed and impulsive, yet naturally gentle and magnetic and the possessor of a remarkable faculty—when Frank found him in the Rockies—which made it possible for him to sit beneath a forest tree and call the wild creatures of the wilderness around him.

Birds fed from his hands, chattering squirrels climbed upon his shoulders, timid rabbits played near-by, and the wild deer approached him without fear. He seemed to have a method of communing with them all.

But as this remarkable boy became more like the usual "civilized boy" later on, he slowly lost the ability to charm the wild creatures of nature. Gradually they became afraid of him and drew away, and there came a day when he whistled his birdnotes and sent forth his squirrel calls in vain. No bird or squirrel or any wild thing of the woods or fields would venture near him any more, and he was very sad and lonely.

Attempting to give Dick an accomplishment comparable to Frank's double-shoot, I made him ambidexterous and able to pitch equally well with either hand. But that was not enough. Nor did I succeed in causing Dick to win a degree of admiration equal to that which my readers expressed for Frank.

In spite of my efforts to boost him, he remained secondary to his esteemed brother. Maybe one reason for that was his tendency to preach, something Frank practically never did. And even though he was tolerant, it's possible that he conveyed the impression of thinking himself superior to some of his associates.

Mr. Smith had erred in imagining readers of the stories were tiring of Frank because he had grown too old. This was proven soon after Dick pre-empted the spotlight. By the hundreds, letters began to arrive calling for the return of Frank, and I was literally compelled to bring him back and let him appear fully as often as Dick.

---

40 · AS I REMEMBER

SPRING BROUGHT A ROVING NEWSPAPER REPORTER to interview me. Being in the midst of a daily stretch of work when he arrived, I had him wait in the living room until I could finish a bit of fast action that was going well. With the door of my workroom standing open, he could hear me moving about as I dictated to my secretary. In his write-up, he said:

"Mr. Patten dictates his stories while walking the floor of his study. When his characters laugh he laughs, when they shout he shouts, when the villain jumps he jumps and his secretary jumps also. I don't know what Mr. Patten does when his hero kisses the heroine, but his secretary is a very good-looking young lady."

Now that crack almost deprived me of the most efficient secretary I've ever had, for my wife failed to see anything humorous in it and violently demanded that I fire the girl, who was as modest and decent as she was capable. Although I calmed the storm and retained my secretary, she was henceforth treated with politely chilly hauteur by the lady of the house.

Work and play caused the summer to slip away much too speedily, and, much as I love the summers of Maine, truth compels me to admit that Maine winters are not on my preferred list. Therefore Mary did not have to beg on bended knees to persuade me to close the house late in October and depart for New York.

As usual on arriving there, I improved an early opportunity to appear before my publishers and let them know my town address. On this occasion I was taken out to lunch at a popular club by both G. C. and O. G. Smith, which gave me a feeling of something impending. We chatted pleasantly through the meal, and I was enjoying one of O. G.'s favorite cigars when he began to speak of my stories and expressed the opinion that necessary action was sometimes lacking in them.

"For instance," he said, "in a recent issue you described in considerable detail how Frank stopped to feed and rest his horse after a hard ride. Now that is not what boys want in their stories; they want continuous action and excitement. There was nothing interesting for them in that act by Merriwell."

I tried to think fast. "Did you own a dog when you were a boy, Mr. Smith?" I asked.

His eyebrows lifted slightly. "Yes, two of them," he replied.

"Then you must have liked dogs. And did you like horses also?"

"Of course," he said. "I've always liked horses."

"Many boys like horses," said I, "and they approve of a person who treated them kindly."

"But what has that to do with the lack of action in your story?" George Smith asked.

"Maybe I'm wrong," said I, "but I regarded Frank's treatment of his hard-driven and weary horses a humane action that boys would admire. I have tried by similar methods to make him admired by all decent boys, and I think this has been one of the ways in which the stories have been lifted above the level of the old dime novels and has caused them to be approved by parents as well as boys."

But they were not convinced even when I reminded them of my contentions with editors who had predicted failure for the stories unless I ceased to use so much space for character delineation. Nor did calling attention to the fact that in their enthusiastic letters to *Tip Top,* boys wrote about the characters but hardly ever about the stories. Finally I asked:

"Please tell me one thing: is the circulation of the *Tip Top Weekly* increasing or falling off?"

O. G. Smith looked at his brother, and smiled. "That settles it, George," he said. "I think we'd better let Patten go on writing the stories his own way."

Never thereafter while I wrote the Merriwell stories did I hear a word of complaint from the heads of the corporation. Nor from Frederick Tilney, once a *Tip Top Weekly* editor and afterwards a famous specialist at the New York Medical Center.

Maybe today modern up-to-the-minute juvenile stories depending as much on character delineation as upon impossible hair-raising action, would be wholly lacking in interest for youngsters whose heroes are the unhuman supermen of the so-called "comic books," but I believe that is a misfortune for the youngsters. And I am proud of the fact that no Merriwell story written by me gave its readers a harmfully distorted view of life.

I was again the guest of my publishers, this time at the Union League Club, when I met Frank A. Munsey. O. G. Smith introduced me to him and Munsey seized the opportunity to talk about himself, maybe more to impress the Smiths than me.

I do not remember the exact words in which he hinted that probably I did not know much about him and his rise in life, but I had felt an immediate distaste for him and I promptly offended him by replying that, on the contrary, I was familiar with his career ever since he had been a telegraph operator in Maine. That did not stop him, however.

He gave me a cold, rebuking look and began vaingloriously retelling the many-times-told tale of his struggles and triumphs. In particular I remember his statement that, when launching the *Golden Argosy*, he had walked the floor night after night worrying over how he could meet the bills of his creditors. And I remember O. G. Smith's confidential comment, made to me later, that it was not Munsey but his creditors who worried.

To me, Frank Munsey was about as warm and human as a fish. And I surmised that O. G. Smith liked him no more than I did, for he told me that he expected some day to see the boastful publisher walking the streets on his uppers. But possibly my notion that the wish was father to the thought was an injustice, as O. G. certainly did not appear to be an envious person. However, Munsey was too canny to go broke, as well as too coldly ungrateful to remember in his will many faithful workers who had helped him accumulate his vast fortune.

One night as my wife and I were having an after-theater snack in Jack's famous restaurant on Sixth Avenue, an unusual-looking man stalked into the room. Unlike middle-class New Yorkers, he was wearing a wide-brimmed black felt hat, long black coat, turn-down collar, and a black string-tie carelessly knotted, and he carried himself with an air of unhurried assurance as he looked the place over. Seating himself at a table, he beckoned a waiter to him and spoke in a resonant voice.

"What kind o'likker do you carry in this yar tarvern?" he inquired.

The waiter offered him a wine list which he waved aside. "Just bring me about four fingers o' your best red-eye," said he.

Amused and curious, I asked our waiter who the swaggering gentleman with the delightful Western vernacular was, but the waiter was unable to tell me.

"I'll ask Mr. Dunston," he said, and went away.

Presently Jack Dunston came to our table and bent over me. "The gentleman you inquired about is Mr. O. P. Reed who writes books," he informed me.

I thanked him and smothered a laugh. Then I waited to catch the eye of the old faker who was putting on an act and lifted my glass to him when he glanced my way.

"Here's looking at you, Opie Reed," said I.

He winked at me and lifted his own glass. "Here's howdy, partner," he said, and tossed off his drink of whiskey without a chaser.

The author of *The Arkansas Traveller* and other best-sellers was amusing himself like a boy playing Indian. I wanted to invite him to join us, but Mary objected.

"He's got everybody looking at him," she said. "I don't care to be made conspicuous."

So I missed a chance to chat with a clever writer and a gentleman of the old school, who passed on in Chicago quite recently and left his pioneered field of literature to lesser lights.

During that winter my wife became chummy with a New Jersey lady by the name of Jane whose husband was in the book-publishing business, and they had delightful times together fluttering restlessly from one gay spot to another. Kindred souls, they afterwards were traveling companions on trips to Bermuda, Puerto Rico, and California, and as each trip appeared to make my wife still more restless I began to realize that not even a tendril of her roots had taken hold upon the soil of Maine.

My son, a fine athletic youngster whom I had sent through Hebron Academy, an excellent college-preparatory school, came to visit me in Camden late in the summer of 1909. Not only had he graduated high in his class, he had pitched successfully for the Academy baseball team and had filled a backfield position on the football team.

A frank, forthright lad, he had won the esteem of his teachers and associates, and I was naturally proud of him and wished to see him educationally equipped for future success. For which reason I had already decided to give him a college course to be followed by another at the Massachusetts Institute of Technology, if it became apparent in the meantime that his natural bent lay in the direction of constructive engineering.

However, what training should follow his college course was to be decided by his own proclivities and desires, not by me. Too often had I known parents to force their sons into vocations for which they were inherently unsuited and therefore unable to become anything but plodding drudges or discouraged failures. On that vital issue, I felt that it was a father's duty to advise and guide but not to dictate arbitrarily.

My son entered the University of Maine in September.

There had been talk of the need of a board of trade in Camden but no one had done anything about it, and so I appointed myself a committee of one to canvass the town for members. The citizens responded enthusiastically, and the Camden Board of Trade was organized that fall.

I then suggested a celebration banquet and promised to provide a famous and entertaining after-dinner speaker for the occasion. To fulfill the promise, I telephoned Holman Day, my friend for years and at that time perhaps the most-famous living Maine author. But to my dismay he declared it was impossible for him to come, as he was driving to finish an overdue novel for Harper's.

I pleaded with tears in my voice, pointing out that as he was then living in Portland he could leave his home on an afternoon train, stop overnight with me and get home again by noon the following day.

He yielded and arrived with Mrs. Day, a handsome lady. And

the next morning an old-fashioned November snowstorm, still in full blast, made all outdoors look like the North Pole. They got back to Portland three days later.

A portly, jovial man, Holman Day never prepared a speech, and he usually began one with apparent awkwardness and embarassment which was amusing. It was thus he began at our Board of Trade banquet, and his apparent blundering started the packed hall chuckling, seemingly to his surprise. Gradually, as he warmed up, the chuckling waxed into laughter and in about three minutes the listeners were roaring. He had them going, and he kept them going until he finished in a gale of merriment and applause. I felt that I had done my part in launching the Camden Board of Trade, which is still running as the Chamber of Commerce.

The three days during which Holman and his wife lingered stormbound in our home were delightful days. With a crackling fire on the living room hearth, to which the cup that cheers added a pleasant glow, we kept open house, and many friends braved the snowdrifts to be with us. On the third evening Holman, who had been a roving State of Maine correspondent for the Lewiston *Journal,* offered to relate what he called his "unpublished romances of Maine."

"They have never appeared in print," he explained, "because they involve high potentates and would create disturbing scandals and, in all probability, libel suits. Newspapers usually tell the truth when they tell anything, but there are times when they can not tell the whole truth or even a part of it."

The French clock on the mantle was softly striking nine when he began to relate those suppressed stories, for the truth of which he had obtained sworn statements of reputable citizens, and we listened spellbound while the winter winds howled outside and the fire burned to glowing embers on the hearth. He finished as the clock began to strike the midnight hour. For three straight hours he had held us entranced with true tales more fascinating than fiction.

A night—and a man—to remember.

41 · THE BIRTH OF A MAGAZINE

PROSPERITY FOR PUBLICATIONS like the *Tip Top Weekly* largely depended on their transportation to retailers as second-class mail matter, a privilege the Postmaster General was threatening to abolish, and Street and Smith were active in the battle to retain that privilege. In the way of strategy, they conceived the idea of putting out a new monthly five-cent publication apparently in the same class as the imperiled weeklies and yet of a nature that would compel the Postal Department to grant it second-class entry.

Believing such a monthly publication could not be a financial success, and to produce it as inexpensively as possible, they planned to use as its contents a mass of juvenile stories that had been bought for them by Mrs. Gunter, the widow of Archibald Clavering Gunter, whose novels, *Mr. Barnes of New York* and *Mr. Potter of Texas*, had been sensational money-makers. Should they succeed in obtaining second-class entry for the monthly, they would continue issuing it only long enough to make it appear like a genuine publishing venture. Then it would be dropped.

For a workroom that winter I had an office in Street and Smith's building, where I heard considerable about the battle with the Postmaster General.

The firm's circulation manager, H. W. Ralston, was trying to persuade some one of their editors to shoulder the additional work of editing the proposed monthly and was meeting with polite refusals. Eventually he told me about his troubles.

Being still rashly self-confident, I said: "Of course there's a way to make the Postal Department pass it. I could do it."

I had risen to the bait, and he didn't let me get away. Before he left I had promised to take on the job, even though while doing it I would have to go right on dictating a weekly Merriwell story to my secretary.

But I had no conception of the size of the job I had let myself in for until I examined the stories bought by Mrs. Gunter. Many

The Birth of a Magazine

of them were built around hackneyed episodes, and more than half of them were too poor to be used at all. For I decided to attempt to build a publication that Street and Smith would not want to throw into the discard.

Left short of suitable material, I wrote a series of 10,000-word stories similar to the Merriwell tales, carrying the hero, "Cliff Stirling," through them all. "Julian St. Dare" was a pen-name I invented for those stories.

Then I went up to the publishing house of D. Appleton and Company and bought the serial rights to my book, *The Deadwood Trail,* being confident that installment publication of that story in the monthly would compel the Postal Department to grant the magazine second-class rates. For surely a periodical containing an incomplete serial story could not be classed as a complete book. I also rewrote and improved more than half the adaptable stories bought by Mrs. Gunter.

I was now working at night as well as by day, and it wore me down. By midnight I would be struggling to keep my eyes open a while longer, and yet when compelled to quit by sheer exhaustion I could not sleep. I became wide-awake the moment my head hit the pillow, and all through the remaining hours of the night I tossed and turned and wooed sleep in vain.

But with the light of dawn creeping into the room sleep would also come, and it would be no easy matter to awaken me. Insomnia had me firmly in its grasp when spring came again, and I did not escape until I went on a fishing trip to Moosehead Lake in June.

Having prepared the copy for the first issue of the publication, I made up a dummy and sent it to O. G. Smith for his approval. This was done before a name for the publication had been decided upon, and he sent for me to come up to his office.

"This looks all right," said he, handing me the dummy. "I think we'll call it *Tip Top Magazine.*"

I argued courteously against that. "I believe it will be a success," said I, "and if I'm right the name you've suggested would make it a competitor of the *Tip Top Weekly.* Also the name would stamp it as a juvenile publication, and you may wish to make it something different—perhaps a young man's magazine."

"Well," said he slowly, "what would you suggest for a name?"

Unable to answer immediately, I said I would tell him tomorrow.

Now I felt that the Smiths regarded the name *Tip Top* as having been a lucky strike by them, and in seeking for a similar name I hit upon *Top Notch,* which was accepted at once.

I was told that the first issue of the magazine, which was limited in number, was a sell-out, as was a much larger printing of the following issue. Instead of a liability, the firm had a distinctly promising asset, much to the satisfaction of Mr. Ralston and myself. But when I had prepared the third and fourth numbers for the printer I was obtaining about three hours sleep out of twenty-four and feeling like a dray horse. May had come and Maine was calling me, so I gave notice that I would soon be on my way.

The day before I was to leave the city, H. W. Thomas, one of the firm's minor editors, met me on the floor of the editorial offices. "I'm going to have that magazine, Patten," said he.

"What magazine?" I asked.

"The one you started," he replied.

"Congratulations," said I, and passed on.

But it was not until two weeks after my return to Camden that I received official confirmation of Mr. Thomas' statement. As it would have been impossible for me to continue as an editor while still writing the Merriwell stories, I breathed a sigh of relief and replied wishing Mr. Thomas success. Some time later I was sent a check for five hundred dollars as payment for putting *Top Notch Magazine* on the map.

For many months *Top Notch* continued to bear my pen name, "Burt L. Standish," as the name of its editor, and it was sub-titled "The Young Man's Magazine." Catering to an older class of readers than *Tip Top's* patrons, it harvested a field previously untouched and poured money into the coffers of Street and Smith for more than a quarter of a century.

Released from editorial labor, I found time to rewrite and

expand the "Cliff Stirling" stories into a series of boys' books which were published by David McKay. And I found also that the cloth-book field that I had once coveted was wide-open for me.

Dodd, Mead and Company had published a *Popular Magazine* serial of mine, "Bill Bruce of Harvard," in cloth, and had urged me to submit other stories of that character. Hurst and Company, more insistent, induced me to write a six-book series for them, which I somehow did in the course of time.

They were the "Rex Kingdom" books, published under still another pen name for me, "Gordon Braddock." And for the same publishers I later turned off the "Ben Stone" stories, which appeared as written by "Morgan Scott." However, I was shooting too low and wasting my ammunition; I should have harkened to Dodd, Mead and Company—or, earlier, to D. Appleton and Company.

Months after H. W. Thomas succeeded me as an editor I met him outside his office door one day, and while we were talking O. G. Smith came along and spoke to me. He said: "I've been telling Thomas that we must have something by you in every issue of *Top Notch*, and he says you are not giving him anything."

Now that was putting me on the spot and I defended myself openly and at once. "I'm afraid, Mr. Smith," said I, "that Mr. Thomas has forgotten five unpublished stories of mine which he has bought and paid for."

Of course I could have corrected the misstatement of Mr. Thomas behind his back, but I think my manner of doing so was more manly even though it made him my enemy. In our future relations as contributor and editor, he never failed to give me as much trouble as possible. His criticisms were harshly severe and harshly spoken, and of encouragement and praise there was none.

However, I was not the only writer he caused to suffer; my friend Arthur Somers Roche was another. Before Arthur broke into the real money with the *Saturday Evening Post* and *Collier's Weekly*, he vainly submitted stories to Thomas until the latter said in rejecting one of them:

"It's no good, Roche. You don't know how to write and you never will know."

Arthur Roche told me that before success came to him he had awakened many a night in a cold sweat, with those words echoing in his ears and his mind sickened by the thought that perhaps Thomas was right. But there came a day when he sold all of the stories rejected by Thomas, and some of them were bought by other editors for Street and Smith at prices three or four times above top rates paid by *Top Notch*.

Nevertheless Henry Thomas was one of the most unfortunate, and in some respects I think the most unhappy, men I have ever known. In the course of time he succeeded in making himself thoroughly disliked by every employee of Street and Smith with whom he came in contact, and I doubt if he had one truly close friend in the world. His early success with *Top Notch* did not last, and the publishers let him out when they became convinced that his policy, which had undergone a decided change, was putting the publication on the down-hill grade.

His wife being Italian, he went to Italy to live, and died there.

---

42 · MERRIWELL AND THE MOVIES

O. HENRY WAS EXPLOITING "Bagdad on the Subway," and other writers were trying to duplicate his skill in concocting short stories with "twist" endings. But there was something more to his stories, a peculiar glamor concisely evoked, that was more difficult to imitate than the trick endings.

Two of Street and Smith's editors, Gilman Hall and Richard Duffy, were said to have "discovered" O. Henry, but that seems to have been an unconfirmed report. However, the first stories of many writers who afterwards became famous appeared in Street and Smith's publications.

The "pulps" often were—and still are—the nesting grounds of talent that may ripen into genius. Furthermore, not a few established authors in the higher brackets have purloined ideas and plotgerms from the pulp magazines.

Although I never bothered much about plots for my Merriwell stories, I was beset by a growing repugnance for the task of turning them out, a fact that I did not hide from O. G. Smith. I let him know that I feared my writing ability was threatened with desuetude unless I could make my escape from the rut before long. He laughed at my apprehension.

"Why, you're still a very young man, Patten," he said cheeringly. "You'll be doing your best work ten or fifteen years from now. Take it easy for a day or two and amuse yourself. Have you seen Otis Skinner in *Kismet*?"

I admitted that I had not, and he called up a ticket broker and obtained two tickets for the performance, which I saw, with my wife, the following night.

And of course I went on writing about Frank and Dick Merriwell.

I doubt if anybody foresaw at that time what motion pictures were destined to do to the five-cent weeklies. I'm sure I did not, even though I soon suspected that the sales of my stories were declining for some reason. However, what was happening became apparent later.

Kalem, Lubin, and Selig were making one-and two-reel movies which were being shown at an admission price of five cents for youngsters, and many boys who had been buying *Tip Top Weekly* were spending all their nickels to see those pictures.

But neither writers nor publishers of popular novels in cloth were quick to detect how the wind was blowing when the picture producers began to film best-sellers, like *When Knighthood Was in Flower*, without paying for the screen rights. And many authors were delighted to obtain that kind of "free advertising" for their works.

However, the Authors League soon realized what was happening and warned its members. With the field of copyrighted literature denied them for plundering, the motion picture-makers reluctantly began to pay for film rights of published stories and for the writing of originals.

Talk of big money in writing for the movies led me to go after some of it. Having studied a book of instructions, I wrote a two-reel movie story in continuity and mailed it to Selig, in Chicago.

It was bought for fifty dollars, and I asked and received sixty dollars for two following stories. But when I offered another for seventy-five dollars, I was informed that they were already paying me ten dollars a story more than their other writers were receiving and that sixty was as high as they would go. I let them have the fourth story for sixty but sent them no more, for I was using up ideas around which novelettes that would sell for three or four hundred dollars could be written.

In 1913 I sold the film rights to "The Riddle and the Ring," a *Top Notch* serial that I had written under the pen name of "Gordon MacLaren," to Vitagraph for five hundred dollars. With the title changed to *The Crown Prince's Double,* and Maurice Costello and Norma Talmadge filling the leading roles, it was released as a feature picture and shown at the Criterion Theater, in New York, at the outbreak of the first World War in 1914.

I was given credit for the story, and for the first and only time my name appeared on the façade of a Broadway theater, though not in electric lights. I walked past the Criterion nine times in one week just to read my own name on the building.

That the dime novel was the inspiration for some early movies seems attested by the shorts in which "Broncho Billy" Anderson, a typical dime-novel hero, became the idol of maybe a million American boys.

Later, serial pictures of a like order, every episode leaving the principal character in a situation of hair-raising peril, were pronouncedly similar in patron appeal to serial stories formerly published in story papers owned by the purveyors of dime novels.

Then came Tom Mix and other swashbuckling movie actors in pictures that were screen imitations of Western novels in the pulp magazines, and some times practically unprovable appropriations of their plots.

Many of the earlier movies were "written on the cuff" by their directors, and of course no author's credit was given. In fact, producers seemed to hold mere writers of stories in disdain; credit and glory went to the actors and directors. This eventually led to the formation of the Screen Writers Guild, without the existence of which motion picture writers would still be at the mercy of the producers.

Seeking to add to my revenue from the Merriwell stories, I took fifteen or twenty of the republications in the "Medal Library" to an agent who had been successful in selling picture rights of published fiction to movie producers. A week later, having examined them he said to me:

"There is one good reason why I can't sell the screen rights to your stories."

"And what is that?" I asked.

"The motion picture business has been built on them," was his answer.

Of course that was something more than a slight exaggeration, but he was serious in his contention that so much had been appropriated from my yarns that he could do nothing with them. Nevertheless, the titles of the stories and the names of the characters in them and that of their author were still unviolated, and there came a time when Universal approached Street and Smith regarding the picture rights, and the dickering waxed hot and cold by turns.

There was so much delay, however, that I had practically abandoned hope when I received a letter from H. W. Ralston stating that he thought Universal was about ready to come to terms, as, at the request of one of their representatives, he had shipped fifty "Medal Library" Merriwells to their West Coast Studios.

Following that there was a long silence, and then Universal released a two-reel episode series titled "The Collegians." I saw two of them. The atmosphere was Merriwellian, but I could not see that they were otherwise an infringement that would justify the institution of a damage suit.

Universal slipped, however, in making a picture called *The Cohens and the Kellys*. They were sued for plagiarizing *Abie's Irish Rose* and walloped to the tune of $500,000. I shed no tears.[3]

---

43 · MORE SHIFTING WINDS

MEANWHILE other things were happening, among which was my sudden release from the grind of writing the Merriwell stories.

"You have asked for it," said O. G. Smith one day, "and we have decided that it can be done. Hereafter we will use all you can write in *Top Notch*."

Now that was not quite a full burst of sunshine, for I had sensed the antagonism of the editor and felt that it would continue.

"But, sir," said I, "maybe Mr. Thomas won't want to take all I can write."

"I've told him we need all your stories we can get for that magazine," he replied, "and he'll find room for them. But even if he can't, we have several other magazines, you know. Some of your work could be used in the *Popular* or *People's*. You'll have nothing to worry about, for we'll give you a new contract requiring you to deliver us fifteen thousand words weekly."

But I did not want to be shackled by another contract of that sort, which caused me to tell him I would prefer to go on with only an oral agreement between us.

"But that's not a good business arrangement," said he.

[3] *Abie's Irish Rose* was first produced on May 22, 1922, at the Fulton Theatre, New York, by the author, Anne Nichols. She had almost insuperable difficulties in getting her play on, and the critical reviews were devastatingly bad. Apparently no one liked the comedy except the theater-going public who made it a record-breaking success. It was later moved to the Republic Theatre, where it finished a run of more than four years in New York—ed.

"It should be to your advantage," said I, "for it's my desire to do better work, on which I'll doubtless have to write more slowly and carefully. You will have to pay only for what good work I deliver, and I'll take my checks for it after it has been accepted instead of weekly."

He looked at me sharply. "All right," he conceded after a moment or two, "we'll let it go that way. Now about the Merriwell stories. They are still paying us a profit, though the circulation is dropping. We are going on with them, using another writer or writers."

Plainly that point had been decided without giving me an intimation of their plans, and already I had been placed in a position to make no objection. But not for a moment did I imagine that it would lead to the use of my pen name on stories not written by me, after the Merriwell stories should cease to appear. Nevertheless, I felt a strange uneasiness when he went on to tell me that already they had had William Wallace Cook and William Almon Wolff write and submit specimen Merriwell stories.

"One of them will get the job," he said, "but of course you will continue to use the pen name of 'Burt L. Standish' on some of your work for *Top Notch*."

"Of course I expect to continue to use *my* pen name of 'Burt L. Standish,'" said I promptly.

He appeared to miss the emphasis, and I failed to thresh out with him then the question of my right to the pen name I had invented. Had I done so, I believe he would have conceded to my view, for I think O. G. Smith was honorable by instinct and breeding; but I have yet to deal with a business man who will not take as much as is yielded to him without protest or argument.

Feeling somewhat like a man who has come to the end of a prison term at hard labor, I was quite jubilant for a day or two. And then my wife revealed that she and her traveling companion, Jane of Jersey, had decided to take a winter excursion trip to California, which didn't arouse me to loud huzzas.

"That's fine," said I ironically. "I'm delighted. I've been slipping in my dancing lately, but I'll catch up while you're away. It will give me an opportunity to learn the new dances like the hesitation waltz and do some stepping around with the Broadway chickens. Go ahead, my dear, and don't hurry back on my account."

She clapped her dainty hands. "Oh, goody!" she cried. "I told Jane you would let me go, but I was afraid you wouldn't be so nice about it."

Now what could a man do with a woman like that? Maybe I know the answer, but I didn't do it—then. I stayed in New York and manufactured a baseball serial for *Top Notch* while my lady was absent.

But about a week before she was due to arrive in town again I aroused myself to take daily dancing lessons, and on the night of her return I took her to dinner at Reisenweber's Restaurant near Columbus Circle and put her through the paces of the hesitation waltz. She was not transported, however.

"What have you been up to?" said she. "Who taught you to dance like this?"

"My dear," said I, "they were two charming young ladies I met while you were not around to guard me from temptation."

But I did not tell her that they were teachers at a dancing school I had patronized, and maybe that was why she lapsed into a brief period of meditation. Apparently something had spoiled the evening for her, but for many moons thereafter she was almost abnormally devoted to keeping the home fires burning.

Nevertheless she grew moody and irritable as the following summer revealed that her popularity in Camden was on the ebb, and before the season passed, things happened which led me to sympathize with her growing antagonism toward the town. That feeling of sympathy led me to another impulsive move.

I dropped into the office of a real estate agent one day and asked him if he thought he could rent my house by the season to summer visitors.

"I could have let it this summer, furnished, for a thousand dollars," said he, "and I think I can get as much next year."

"Then put it on your list," said I.

More Shifting Winds

When I told my wife what I had done she almost wept for joy, "Why, I never dreamed you would do such a thing," she cried.

"A thousand dollars, minus the agent's commission, will help pay for the furnishing of a small apartment in New York," said I, "and I must have some place different from boarding houses and hotels in which to do my work."

She went into raptures. It was exactly what she had wanted, and she told me how happy and contented she would be in such an apartment. Life would be one grand sweet song.

We closed the house in the early part of the fall just in time to accept an invitation from Fred Boston, of Gardiner, Maine, to be his guests at his camp in the woods near Moosehead Lake. We motored up there with Fred and his charming wife Ida, and found that a party of other guests, nine men and five women, had reached the camp ahead of us.

The camp was a long building standing high on the side of a clearing in the wilderness that had once been the summer home of horses owned by the great Northern Lumber Company, of which Fred Boston's father was a member. There were a living room, dining room, kitchen, three private bedrooms, and a huge room with curtained-off beds which was called the "ram pasture."

A wide veranda, with couches and chairs to lounge upon, extended the full length of the camp's southern side, and from it one could look out over miles of unbroken forest to the southeastern mountains beyond the unseen lower end of Moosehead Lake. Water was supplied by a windmill that pumped it from a cool well, and all the rooms were lighted by electricity.

There was a private bathroom between two of the bedrooms which were the sleeping quarters of the Bostons and the Pattens. A French-Canadian chef and his Indian wife did the cooking, and the food might have graced the tables of the best hotel in the country. Indeed, such venison and bread and pies and cakes are rarely, if ever, served in any hotel, and strawberries out of season appeared every day.

In the living room there was a huge long chest filled with liquid refreshments, imported champagne as well as bottled ale and something sometimes used for snake bites. I didn't need any of it to improve my appetite; the clear, clean air and the odor of pines and hemlocks and balsam firs attended to that.

Seven days we spent there, seven lazy days for Boston and myself, neither of whom did any hunting. We let others do that while we loafed the time away and grew fat. I fished occasionally in a brook below a beavers' dam and caught a few trout which, it being the closed season, I carefully released from the hook and returned to their native element. Somebody shot a deer on the day of our arrival, but thereafter the most of the shooting was at clay pigeons, and there was enough of that to make any sensible deer seek a quieter neighborhood.

With a cheerful blaze crackling in the fireplace, we played poker in the living room night after night, and my good luck caused one of the players to remark that I must be unlucky in love. He became, some time afterwards, my wife's second husband!

Four guides for the hunters were housed in near-by camps. One of them, Bill Hall, was sixty years old, hairy chested, hard as nails, and toothless. His gums were said to be so hard that he could masticate a tough beefsteak as well as a person with perfect teeth. Looking for color or a good story, I made it a point to become friendly with Bill, and one day he told me how Joe Knowles, the prehistoric-man faker, had been supplied with the skin of a bear, supposedly to protect his nude body from the cold of late September in the Maine wilderness.

Sponsored by a Boston newspaper, Knowles had created quite a hullabaloo by going into the northern wilds as naked as when he was born and taking with him nothing to sustain life, nor a single article with which to defend himself from wild beasts. Somehow he had existed in the wilderness for eight weeks, during which time he was reported to have left at prearranged places brief descriptions of his manner of living and the ingenious methods by which he had avoided perishing of cold and hunger.

The messages were written on birchbark with a stick charred in a fire said to have been started by rubbing two pieces of dry

More Shifting Winds

wood together until they smoked, flamed, and ignited tinder gathered for the purpose. Facsimiles of the messages appeared in the paper sponsoring him.

According to the accounts of the man's amazing exploits, he had trapped a bear in a pit, clubbed it to death, and skinned it with a sharp slice of flint he had found. There were no betraying flaws in his description of the manner in which he had tanned the bear's hide and made it into a protecting coat; it could have been done.

Reputedly, he had fed on roots, wild berries, and bear meat cooked over the fire he had started and carefully kept alive, and he had slept in a brushwood hut of his construction. And these were only a few of his fantastic achievements which set New Englanders agog with wonderment or roaring with derisive laughter.

Scornfully unbelieving, the Boston *American* sent reporters into the woods to catch Knowles and expose him. They failed because the faker was under the protection of two accomplices, Mike McKeogh and a guide by the name of Allie Deming. Knowles was successfully hidden away for two months before he came out of the wilderness, bewhiskered like a wild man and clothed in the tanned skin of a bear and the untanned skin of a deer that he had reputedly also killed.

Stepping triumphantly off a train at Boston's North Station, he was greeted by a roaring crowd that packed the station and overflowed into the streets. A prosperous lecture tour of several weeks followed, but it was brought to an abrupt end by the Boston *American's* full-page accusation of fraud and a challenge to Knowles' backers to institute suit for libel.

"Why," said Bill Hall contemptuously, "that dumb, fat old slob didn't have the brains to think up the funny business all by himself. McKeogh done that and paid Allie Deming to help him take keer of Knowles and steer the reporters away. Old Joe never killed as much as a chickadee while he was in the woods. The stinkin' deerskin he was wearin' when he got up to Boston was the hide of a deer he found dead in the woods, and McKeogh paid me twelve dollars for the pelt of the b'ar, which I shot myself." He chuckled. "But we all come dam' close to being ketched when I went to hand over the b'arskin to Mike."

"Where did you go to deliver it?" I asked as he paused to shift his quid of tobacco into the other cheek.

"Up to Mike's cabin on B'ar Mountain," he replied. "That was where Knowles spent his time while he was supposed to be ramblin' around practically neckid in the woods, and that was where Mike writ them letters on birchbark that the Boston paper printed. I hadn't no more than got the money for the b'arskin tucked away in my pocket before a game warden and a reporter that was after Knowles come in on us."

"But Knowles?" said I. "Where was he?"

Bill chuckled again. "He'd went outside and seen them comin' just in time to crawl under the cabin floor, and he laid there, still as a mouse, and listened to us talkin'. Mike done most of the talkin', and he fooled them birds handsome. They went away believin' we hadn't seen hide or hair of old Joe."

Undiscouraged by his failure in the East, Joe Knowles repeated his "back to the primitive" act in California about a year later, and got away with it. That encouraged another Eastern newspaper to devise an even more sensational scheme in which Knowles figured still later.

Returning to New York State, he went again, stripped to the hide, into the deep woods, but this time he was companioned by a nude woman who was to play Eve to his Adam. And the daring lady was Elaine, the not uncomely daughter of Oscar Hammerstein![4]

The mosquitoes and black flies of a State of New York wilderness enjoyed her stay among them, which was quite brief. Unable to take it, she fled back to civilization, and Adam, left Eveless in

---

[4] Oscar Hammerstein, famous theater man and impresario (1847–1919), was most renowned for having introduced Mary Garden in Massenet's *Thaïs* to the American public in 1907, she being the star of his newly organized Manhattan Opera Company. His daughter Elaine, a dark, lustrous beauty, starred in several early day motion pictures—ed.

his Eden, quickly faded out of the picture, to be heard of no more.

Bill Hall was primed with backwoods anecdotes and lore, and I missed no opportunity to chat with him during my stay at Boston's camp. He gave me color and incidents which I eventually used in "Haunted Land," a *Top Notch* serial of the Maine woods. That lazy outing was not time wasted, and it put me in trim to make the old typewriter hum when I got at it again.

44 · THE CRACK-UP AND AFTERWARDS

THE LIVING ROOM WINDOWS of our apartment on One Hundred and Tenth Street overlooked a pleasant park beyond which loomed the magnificent Cathedral of Saint John the Divine. A shipment of silverware, china, rugs, and other household effects that could be spared from the Camden home, which had been let for the summer months, had made it possible for us to furnish the apartment fully, with an outlay of cash that still left a balance in the bank.

A colored maid, part-time employed, made the housekeeping duties light for Mary, who had at last obtained her professed heart's-desire. But scarcely were we more than fairly settled when restlessness seized her again and sent her flitting away to be absent by day and sometimes overnight at the home of her friend Jane in Jersey.

Now there is in my nature a depressing loneliness at times, bred, I believe, by the lonely days of early boyhood in Maine, and it is only through companionship—the companionship of an understanding person who is near and dear to me—that I have been able to fend off benumbing periods of dejection.

My work is a solitary occupation, and I need someone in whom I take a deep interest to turn to for cheer when the daily task is done. And in that apartment on One Hundred and Tenth Street I found myself more alone and downcast than I had ever been before. My last attempt to sweep away the clouds that were gathering had met frustration, and four words from one of Kipling's poems kept running through my mind, "A fool there was."

At that time other clouds of more terrible portent were gathering over Europe, but as yet nobody seemed to dream, even vaguely, that the storm would hit us, and many persons fatuously proclaimed that the world had become too civilized for another great war to occur anywhere.

Then, abruptly in July, the explosion came and the Great War began.

Germany was on the march to invade France. British troops were on the way to support the French. Russian armies were threatening Germany's eastern border. Italy would be drawn into the mad mess. The Balkan nations would be compelled to take sides. Belgium would be destroyed. All Europe was aflame, but America, sitting pretty and far, far away, would not be involved.

Day after day I read all the war reports in the newspapers. The irresistible rush of the German armies through Belgium and down toward Paris was appalling. My blood-pressure rose. When there was nobody else to talk to, I talked to myself. Propaganda befuddled me until the Black Tom explosion and other events plainly indicated German sabotage.

The sinking of the *Lusitania* on May 7, 1915, made me a warmonger eager for the United States to throw their might against Germany. I was too old to be acceptable for army service when this country declared war, but I put every dollar I could spare into Liberty Bonds.

Meanwhile my marital barque had finally gone on the rocks. Only when the last hope was dead did I abandon the sinking craft, taking with me my personal belongings and what courage disaster had left in me. Bitterness I tried to avoid, but I could not avoid shame for my own folly, nor could I forget many things I wished to forget.

I lived for a time in the Hotel Marlton, on Eighth Street. There

I pulled myself together and went on writing, my first novel being "Haunted Land," in which I used some of the color and incidents obtained in my talks with Bill Hall, and in spite of my troubles that was one of the most popular stories I ever did for *Top Notch*.

I continued to pay the rent for the apartment on One Hundred and Tenth Street and regularly sent my wife thirty-five dollars a week for living expenses, but I closed her credit accounts when I found she was running up bills at several stores.

She wrote me an indignant letter demanding the immediate restoration of her credit privileges. I made my answer through Joseph Warren, then a member of the law firm of Blauvelt, Walker, and Warren, and afterwards Police Commissioner of New York. At my suggestion, he wrote advising her to sue me for divorce in the state of Maine, charging cruel and abusive treatment.

"It will cost you plenty for alimony, Gil," he told me.

"My freedom will be worth it," was my reply.

I believed that, for I was now less lonely than I had been in the apartment on One Hundred and Tenth Street. For the first time I was living in Greenwich Village and mingling with the Bohemians of that quarter. It was a new and strange experience which, added to my matrimonial troubles, banished boredom and kept me on the alert.

The southwest corner room of the Brevoort Café was then a favorite meeting place for Villagers disposed to class themselves as Bohemians, and the management encouraged them to foregather there by practically turning the room over to them. When flush they spent their money freely, and if broke they were made to feel welcome to spend their time there in sociability.

Louie, the headwaiter, knew them all and gave them free rein. Even when Donn Byrne, the Irish novelist who had yet to see Ireland, leaped into the room through an open window, clad only in a bearskin rug, and danced wildly around shouting, "I'm free! I'm free!" he was allowed to depart unescorted by a policeman.

Harry Kemp, "the tramp poet," sandy-haired and rawboned,

allowed me to buy him drinks when he was broke, which was nearly all the time. One day I introduced him to three of my friends from uptown and had a waiter place a chair for him at our table. Sitting down facing a wall-mirror, he casually observed that he had forgotten to change his collar and nonchalantly took it off, turned it inside-out, and put it on again. But he balked when I asked him what he would have.

"You've been blowing me right along, Gil," he said, "but I'm rolling in money today, and it's my turn to do the buying. Name your poison, gentlemen."

He had sold a poem for fifteen dollars, eleven of which he spent for liquid refreshments before departing to attend to a little business, as he expressed it. Leaving the Brevoort some time later, I saw him coming down Fifth Avenue with a bundle under his arm. He was bareheaded, as usual, and in high spirits. Having spent his last four dollars for some books he wanted, he was broke again and normally happy.

My friend Cameron MacKenzie lived a while in the Brevoort before going abroad as a war correspondent for the Curtis Publishing Company. Following the end of the conflict, he lingered and wrote a series of articles on England after the war. He died on shipboard on his way back to America. I had not thought I would never see him again when I bade him good-bye and good luck.

Starting to cross Fifth Avenue at Eighth Street one day, I halted to let pass a swanky roadster driven by a stunning young woman. A sprucely garbed youngish man on the opposite sidewalk also paused and turned to gaze after the roadster. I crossed over and leaned against the iron railing in front of the Brevoort, waiting for him to approach.

"Some car, Mr. Reed," said I as he came along.

"A handsome, clean-cut fellow," he smiled as he replied. "And some baby at the wheel. Let's enter this place and pause at the bar while we raise our glasses in a toast to her."

That was my first meeting with John Reed, whom I had seen around the hotel at times. He had only lately returned from Mexico, where he had interviewed Pancho Villa in the midst of the rebel chief's rabble "army" of outlaws. With no flattering motive, I told him how much I had enjoyed his articles and stories in the *Metropolitan Magazine*.

Cultured, talented, and a brilliant writer, he was one of the young intellectuals who vigorously opposed this country's participation in the European war, which caused him to be denounced as a dangerous radical; and there came a time when he fled abroad to avoid arrest and imprisonment. He died young in Russia. From my point of view, his talents were misdirected, his vision distorted, and his life misspent.

Of course there were anarchists in Greenwich Village in those days. I once saw Emma Goldman, surrounded by a mob of crackpot admirers, in the Brevoort, and even wild-eyed, screw-brained Hippolite Harvell had his approvers. But ninety per cent of those who were called anarchists by stupid people were would-be reformers who imagined themselves crusaders for the betterment of the masses.

Even men like Max Eastman and Art Young were branded as bloody-minded marplots seeking the destruction of law and order. I saw them in Polly's and other Village restaurants now and then and eventually met them and found they were persons of kindly natures, although I was inimical to the use they were making of their talents.

The Liberal Club, on MacDougall Street, was reputedly a hell-hole of iniquity. I dropped in there and found it to be the resort of callow long-haired men and short-haired women who imagined themselves very "advanced" in their ideas. But there was no open iniquity in the place, unless it lay in discussions of inhibitions and Freudian impulses. However the atmosphere was not to my taste, and one visit was enough. That goes also for Romany Marie's dingy little duck-in.

Frankly, I discovered in the Village none of the glamor given it in motion pictures, and I explored it pretty thoroughly. The studio parties which I attended were usually dull affairs at which stupid people assembled to drink beer and gin, smoke cigarettes, and pretend they were quite devilish and different from other stupid people. And such crazy resorts as "The Pirate's Den" were merely sucker traps for gudgeons.

After dinner at the Brevoort one Saturday night I was invited to join Cameron MacKenzie and a group of his friends at a large table in the central room of the café. Besides MacKenzie, I had met only one of the party, Fred Noyes, the stuttering assistant editor of *Adventure Magazine*.

Two of the others were Wallace Morgan, the artist, and a tall, gangling, sandy-haired young man who was doing most of the talking and producing laughter by his bantering of MacKenzie. I think the latter pulled me in to create a diversion.

"Shake hands with Sinclair Lewis, Gil," said Cameron. "He'll tell you how to write your stories. Mr. Lewis, this is 'Burt L. Standish.'"

"My God!" said Lewis. "Not really? Why, Burt, you old wretch, I cut my eye-teeth on your trash, and now look at the kind of people I associate with." He waved a hand toward MacKenzie.

"Tut-tut-two of a kind," said Fred Noyes. "A pair of dud-deuces."

When the party began to break up, Sinclair Lewis asked me where I was going, and I confided an intention of dropping in as a kibitzer on the bunch of poker addicts who gathered regularly on Saturday nights in Dr. George Dorsey's studio apartment, near-by on Eighth Street. He expressed a desire to go with me, and presently we were climbing the stairs to Dorsey's door.

We found seven coatless players, among whom were Arthur Somers Roche, Ewing Galloway, and Ray Rohn, the artist, busily engaged at a crazy game in which the dealer called the wild cards. As Lewis was not then the famous figure he afterwards became, no one gave him more than casual notice, and presently he wearied of watching the game.

"The gentlemen must be thirsty, Burt," he said.

"Me," said Roche, who did not drink, "I'm hungry."

"This hand will be spit-in-the-ocean," said Dr. Dorsey as he shuffled the cards. "Meanwhile"—he glanced toward Lewis and me—"how about a little service for idle hands to do? You'll find the icebox and the liquor in the kitchen."

They went on with their so-called game of poker while Lewis and I repaired to the kitchen. "What can you do best, Burt?" he wanted to know.

"I'm an excellent bartender," was my reply.

"And I'm a fine cook," said he, digging into the icebox, which was stocked to carry Dorsey and a friend over until Monday. "Here's the food—and whiskey, gin, vermouth, and grenadine. Go ahead and whet up their appetites while I wreck the ham and eggs."

Now I really could shake up a mean cocktail at that time, and I was soon plying the card players with seductive and efficacious libations in ample glasses, and I continued to ply them until there was nothing left to ply with.

Meanwhile, Red Lewis shed his coat, lighted the gas-stove, and made sandwiches to the exhaustion of everything from which they could be manufactured. Not only did we serve the party appetizers, we served all the food to be found in the kitchen, save only what we ate ourselves.

Shortly after the stuffed and sluggish poker players resumed their game, Sinclair Lewis and I crept out of the place without saying good-night to anybody. In order not to disturb them, we fastened the door catch back so it would not click when we closed the door softly behind us. On the street again, we enjoyed a hearty laugh.

"I'd like to see Dorsey and his friend when they wake up tomorrow and can't find a drop to drink or a crumb of food in the dump," said Sinclair Lewis. "It'll be a dull Sunday morning for them."

However, he ceased to laugh as we were walking away, and suddenly he grabbed my arm and stopped me in my tracks.

"Do you know what we are, Burt?" said he. "We're a pair of cheap skates. We were Dorsey's guests, and we've pulled a dirty trick on him. We ought to be shot. What time is it?"

I looked at my watch. "Not quite half-past twelve."

"But it's Sunday morning and the bars are closed. Do you know any place where you can get liquor at this hour?"

"Maybe I can knock on the glass in the side door of the Brevoort bar and get in there. I can if Louie's still there and sees me," said I.

"Well, do it," he snapped. "Get a quart somewhere somehow, I'll meet you right here. Wait for me."

Away he went, his long legs taking him toward Sixth Avenue.

Fortunately, Louie was there and recognized me when I tapped on the glass of the Eighth Street door to the Brevoort bar. He let me in, and I had a quart of whiskey tucked under my coat when he let me out. Pretty soon I saw Lewis hurrying back, loaded with paper-wrapped bundles. He was grinning.

"Got plenty from an all-night restaurant," he said. "What luck did you have?"

I told him, and we got back into Dorsey's building by pushing the button to another apartment until the door-lock clicked in response. Tiptoeing up the stairs, we stole back into Dorsey's studio without disturbing the absorbed card players. Then, having deposited the food and whiskey in the kitchen, we stole out again.

Sinclair Lewis took a long breath when we were on the street once more. "Thank God I'm a respectable person again," said he.

---

45 · CAROL

SEEKING TO BREAK THROUGH to the Channel ports, the Germans were storming the staggering British forces in northern France, and in London, Lloyd George was denouncing the English war lords as dunderheaded blunderers. The unarmed Russian Army was collapsing, and the desperate French, who had turned the

Carol

Germans back almost at the gates of Paris, were beginning to be dismayed by the inefficient support of their English allies.

Utterly ruthless and savage in their war methods, the Germans had horrified and enraged American citizens by using poison gas in land battles and resorting to submarine destruction of American ships. Aided by associated dirty workers, Franz von Papen, German Ambassador to the United States, was seeking to paralyze by sabotage and propaganda America's belated efforts for self-defence and the maintenance of her rights on the high seas.

For the time being, our chief concern lay in a Presidential campaign that was approaching a "twist" finish.

Charles Evans Hughes had resigned from the government's Supreme Court to run against Woodrow Wilson, who was seeking a second term. The election was close, but late returns indicated an assured victory for Hughes, who went triumphantly to bed and slept soundly.

When a reporter tried to reach him near morning, his haughty butler stated that the President was sleeping and could not be disturbed.

"Oh, very well," said the reporter, "but don't forget to tell him when he wakes up that he is not the President."

California, reckoned safely Republican, had upset all calculations by going Democratic, and Woodrow Wilson would not have to move out of the White House after all. The shock was terrific for the voters who had gone to bed in the same frame of mind as Mr. Hughes.

"He kept us out of war" was the slogan that had elected Wilson, but he couldn't keep us out much longer.

The unscrupulous savagery of the Germans was working their own undoing by bringing about a revulsion of sentiment in the United States. Peace-loving Americans were getting mad, and peaceful people can become very cantankerous when thoroughly angered. The break, long delayed, came at last, and Wilson declared war upon Germany. Conscription followed.

Meanwhile I had met Carol.

Fed up with the Brevoort set and not feeling like taking part in their screwball antics on New Year's Eve, I went away alone in search of a quiet place to eat and brood the Old Year out and the New Year in over a glass of beer. I finally found myself in a usually quiet restaurant where now everybody was wearing ridiculous paper caps and making a racket with whistles and rattles and horns.

Everyone talked to acquaintances and strangers regardless, and Bobby Edwards stood on a table in the middle of the room and strummed his cigarbox ukulele and sang, "Way down south in Greenwich Village where the old maids come for thrillage"; and I thought a laughing brown-eyed woman with solid strips of silver-white in her black hair was beautiful.

She sat at the next table, very near, with two slightly older ladies, one of whom had snow-white hair, and there was about them an atmosphere and a total lack of gaucherie that stamped them as foreign to the Village. Nevertheless, they were having a wonderful time.

Having lost my desire to brood, I was not drinking beer. A bottle of red wine had come with the dinner I'd eaten at my tiny corner table, and that—or something—had made me sentimental and annoyed at my loneliness.

They called her Carol, those two ladies with the one who sat facing me, and I thought it an appropriate name for her. Carol—a song. I lifted my glass to her but received no response. In spite of evident enjoyment, they were holding themselves aloof from the crowd.

Then it was midnight and whistles were blowing and bells ringing, and everybody shouted as all the lights in the place went out.

After which, during a minute of darkness, there was laughter and little cries. Before the lights came on again I nearly upset my table getting back to it, but I was there in time to raise my glass to Carol once more and wish her a happy New Year. And now, flushed but not so indignant as I'd feared she would be, she lifted her own glass and touched it to her lips.

All around, people were wishing others a happy New Year, and

Carol

presently they sang "Should Auld Acquaintance Be Forgot."

It was the lady with the snow-white hair who invited me to join them at their table. "You look lonesome," she said.

"I have been," said I, "but I'm very happy now. My name is Gil."

"Mine is Ida," said she. "My friends are Dorothy and Carol. Carol is my sister."

"The Three Graces," said I, trying to put my best foot forward. Then I sat down beside Carol. "If you will pardon me," I murmured.

"I don't think I should," was her reply. "I don't think I should speak to you."

"But this is New Year's" I protested. "Don't make me unhappy again."

"What in the world are you two talking about?" said Dorothy.

"Being a gentleman of the old school," said I, "I'll never tell."

Carol laughed. "Then you are forgiven," she said.

They wouldn't let me buy them anything. Instead, Dorothy called a waiter and had him bring another glass and pour it brimming with sparkling Burgundy from their bottle. It was her party, she said, and she was rigid about it.

We chatted, and in the course of the next hour I gathered that curiosity to see what New Year's Eve was like in the Village had led them to give up reservations at a swanky uptown hotel where it would be old stuff for them. I made a mental note of that as the germ for a story to be titled "A Kiss in the Dark," but I never wrote the story.

As the crowd around us grew still more boisterous and unrestrained, Dorothy became uneasy. "I think it's time for us to go, girls," she said, motioning to their waiter.

She paid their check, and I took care of mine. Then I escorted them out, put them into a taxi, bade them good night, and saw them depart, whither I did not know.

I had been told their first names, but apparently that was all the definite information about them that they had wished me to know. Even while being sociable for a hour with a stranger whose background they knew nothing about, they had been discreetly on guard.

A sharp wind cut my face, and I shivered in my overcoat as I walked back across Washington Square. "Well, that's that," said I. "Good-bye, Carol."

46 · FATE OR FOLLY

IN SPITE OF GERMAN SUBMARINES, American troops were at last pouring into France and being rushed to the fighting front. Another drive on Paris had been stopped on the bloody fields around Verdun. But from a distance calculated to be seventy miles, a huge German gun was dropping shells into the heart of the French capital. German Zeppelins had bombed London from the air.

In Russia the Czar had abdicated, and Lenin and Trotsky were pouring oil on the flames of red revolution. Mata Hari, the beautiful spy, had been executed by a French firing squad, and the Germans had evened the score by shooting Edith Cavell in Belgium.

The war news was tremendously exciting, and I still read every bit of it in my morning paper before beginning the day's work at the Robert Treat Hotel, in Newark, to which I had moved from the Hotel Marlton barely in time to dodge a summons server. For my wife had decided to bring me into the Domestic Relations Court, and that was something I wished to avoid if possible.

Though I was still paying rent for the One Hundred and Tenth Street apartment and sending her thirty-five dollars a week for living expenses while waiting for her to accede to my desire for a divorce, she was bitterly determined to humiliate me publicly.

Meanwhile I kept away from the Brevoort, though I went back into New York every Saturday to play pool with a group of my

Fate or Folly

friends at the Hotel Majestic at Seventy-second Street and Central Park West.

At that time the Majestic was the home of many writers, artists, and stage celebrities. Edna Ferber, Arthur Somers Roche, O. O. McIntyre, H. T. Webster, and Lillian Russell were living there, all being granted special rates or courtesies by Jack Heath, the hotel manager, who felt that their presence gave the place an atmosphere to its advantage.

Eventually, at Mr. Heath's suggestion and the offer of a sunny room and private bath on terms within my means, I moved back into New York and lived at the Majestic during the remainder of that winter. Apparently my moves had baffled summons servers, for none disturbed me there.

My room had once been part of a large suite, the rest of which was occupied by Edna Ferber, and every morning at precisely nine o'clock the clicking of her secretary's typewriter was a reminder that it was time for me to drop my newspaper and get to work myself. Sometimes I heard her talking to her secretary, but, singularly, I never even caught a glimpse of her while I was in the Majestic.

I was given a bit of a shock one day when Mr. Heath introduced me to an ample woman with whom he was chatting in the lobby. For it did not seem possible that she could be the same gorgeously beautiful Lillian Russell whom I had many times seen in years remote, on the stage of Weber and Fields' Broadway theater.

It has been claimed that she retained much of her great beauty to the end of her days, but the lady whom I saw and talked to briefly in the Majestic, though buoyantly jovial and full of life, had paid the penalty that the years had demanded. Her spirit, alone, seemed still young.

Needing agreeable diversion, I looked forward to our Saturday afternoon pool games in the basement billiard room of the Majestic. Of course we gambled, but not heavily enough to damage anybody painfully, though Berton Braley sometimes moaned over his hard luck, and "Major" Browder, from Kentucky, cussed amusingly.

One day a strange person, known to all the players but myself, crashed into the game. His light-brown hair rose in a roll from his forehead. He was chewing gum. He peeled off his coat and revealed the most bizarre plaid shirt of many colors that I have ever seen. Ray Rohn led him round the table to me.

"Here is your boyhood hero, Odd," said Ray. "Meet old Gil Patten, the bum who wrote the Merriwell stories."

O. O. McIntyre let his cue fall on the floor and glared at me. "Why, durn your hide!" he barked. "You made a criminal of me."

Said I, "I can easily believe it after seeing you in that jail-bird shirt."

"But I'm serious," he persisted. "You caused me to become a thief when I was merely a tender kid. To get five cents a week to buy your lousy stories I used to gather up old iron and brass to sell to the junk man, and I did it a long while before I noticed that he took the stuff to the rear door and threw it out into his back yard. Next week I climbed the high board fence around the yard, gathered up the junk I'd sold him the last time, took it round to the front door and sold it to him again. I pulled that vile trick on him seven times before he caught me at it and gave me the boot. What you did to me should make you hang your head in shame."

Laughing now, he grabbed my hand and wrung it.

"Odd" McIntyre was a strangely complex character and one of the most sincere friends I have ever known. He was then himself mimeographing and peddling his "New York Day by Day" letter, which was sold to the newspapers that used it for any price they would pay, and some papers failed to pay anything.

His devoted wife helped him with his work and Manager Heath accepted the publicity for the hotel, which he slipped into his letters, as payment for room rent. It was a precarious rub-and-go existence which developed into a brilliant and highly lucrative career after the McNaught Syndicate put McIntyre under contract.

The most astonishing thing about it was that "Odd" was the victim of a nervous affliction, a phobia that at one time threatened to make him a chronic invalid. He was afraid of open spaces and would not even cross a street unless accompanied by another person.

For one engaged in writing a chatty news-letter about New York, this was a frightful handicap. But a method of treatment was found that enabled him to conquer or control his fears, and eventually he made trips to the West Coast and abroad, and apparently accomplished complete self-mastery.

He never knocked. He was a booster, ever ready to give a friend a helping hand up the ladder. His syndicated letter, read with delight by millions, was unique. The thrusts of envy hurt but did not sour him. He is gone, and no one can take his place.

Jensen's Restaurant, on Sixth Avenue near Sixty-sixth Street, was the resort of a small coterie of writers and artists. The food was good and prices reasonable. I ate there often, and it was there I first met a young newspaper artist named Robert Ripley, who was then just a struggler without reputation. A quiet, laughing young fellow with slightly prominent upper teeth, he seemed satisfied to listen and let others do the talking, believe it or not.

Dr. Frank Crane—the uplift writer of syndicated articles—and his wife sometimes dined at Jensen's. He was nothing like what I had thought he would be. Although an ex-parson who had turned to writing flowery, sugar-coated newspaper sermons, he took his whiskey straight, scoffed at prudes and puritanism, cracked risqué jokes, and played poker.

In my mail one morning I found a letter from my wife that had been forwarded to me by my publishers. Expecting something unpleasant, I opened it reluctantly.

It informed me that at last she was willing to divorce me and was making arrangements to do so, charging cruel and abusive treatment, as I had suggested. She stated that she had written a friend in Maine to engage a lawyer for her. Very considerately, she was writing to let me know she would be glad to be free from me!

"And that," said I exultingly, "means that she expects to marry again soon. Boy, what luck!"

Joe Warren's warning that my freedom would cost me a pretty penny in the way of alimony did not worry me. With an apparently assured market for the greater part of my work at Street and Smith's, I was ready to pay the price for past mistakes and hopeful of avoiding future blunders. And I really believed I would never marry again!

After delivering the manuscript of a *Top Notch* novelette one sunny day in February, I set forth to walk up to the Grand Central Station for exercise in the open air and to give me a better appetite for one of the famous oyster stews served at the station's oyster bar.

As I was passing the Public Library, a south-bound Fifth Avenue bus stopped at the curb and several passengers got off, among them being two of the three ladies I had met in a Greenwich Village restaurant on New Year's Eve. The sight of them halted me in my tracks, and my hat came off when they saw me, and they uttered little exclamations of pleasant surprise.

"How do you do, ladies," said I. "It's a lovely day—now."

Carol's smile made the day still lovelier. "Why, you act as if you were waiting for us," she said.

"You have kept me waiting too long," I replied. And then I plunged: "But I'll forgive you if you'll have lunch with me."

"We were going to the library," said Ida, "but we can do that later."

Lunching at the Biltmore, we exchanged cards, and, deciding to be perfectly frank, I confessed that I had a wife with whom I was not living and from whom I hoped soon to be divorced. Ida was a widow, her full name being Ida Kramer Pardee, and Carol, her only sister, unmarried, was living with her on West One Hundred and Sixtieth Street. They were natives of Rochester.

"You see," said Carol lightly, "I'm a chronic old maid. That's why Dorothy and Ida laughed at me New Year's Eve when Bobby Edwards sang about old maids coming down to the Village for thrillage."

"But I don't understand it," said I. "How have you managed to escape? All the men you've met can't have been blind."

The shadow of a cloud fell on her face. "There was one—who died," she said very quietly.

Trying to be complimentary, I had slipped, and my attempt to express regret was bungling. Cleverly she put me at ease again, and before luncheon was over I accepted an invitation to dine with them at their home the following evening.

---

47 · THE ENCHANTED HOUR

THAT THERE MIGHT BE NO DELAY and no misfire in my wife's suit for divorce, I made a trip to Camden to accept writ service and to engage a lawyer to represent me when the case should be called for trial. As far as possible without giving an appearance of connivance, my lawyer was able to help the unpleasant business along to the conclusion I desired.

I knew my wife would demand a third interest in my property, and to meet that I arranged to cash in a paid-up life insurance policy. My lawyer was also to see that a just appraisal of the property was made. To avoid bickering over the furniture in the New York apartment, I let it be understood that I would turn that over to my wife without contest.

Then I returned to New York and waited for the shackles to be broken.

I plotted and began working on a fanciful novel to be called "The Enchanted Hour," in which a famous chemist and surgeon, who had invented a gas for use in warfare which if inhaled one minute would produce deep sleep for an hour, would be the central figure.

In the big scene of the story, the Germans, victorious in Europe, would attack New York from the air and bomb the city to a mass of shattered, smoking ruins. The twist ending of the story would disclose that the German attack upon New York was a dream of one of the characters who had inhaled the surgeon's sleeping gas.

I finished the story, 60,000 words in length, in May and submitted it to *Top Notch*. Feeling sure it was good stuff for that magazine, I was astonished when Mr. Thomas promptly declined it. And I was worried too, for the European holocaust seemed to be approaching its final stages, and I knew the dream climax of the story would make it unacceptable anywhere after the war was over.

I telephoned the editor of the Sunday magazine section of the Hearst newspapers and asked him if he could use such a serial.

"We need a serial," was his reply. "Send it down at once."

None too hopefully, I carried the manuscript down and delivered it at eleven o'clock in the forenoon. At two-thirty that same day I was notified by telephone that my novel had been accepted, and at three-thirty I personally collected a check for it. That stands as my record for a quick sale and receipt of payment.

Relieved and elated, I couldn't refrain from gloating a little. So on my way uptown I dropped in at Street and Smith's to show my check to Charlie MacLean and tell him what had happened. Liking Mr. Thomas even less than I did, MacLean laughingly congratulated me.

"That's what I call putting a fast one over on Tommy," he said.

Previous to that, Charles MacLean, every inch a square-shooter, had helped me prevent Thomas from slipping a fast one over on me. Looking over the latest issue of *Top Notch* one day, I was startled to come upon the announcement of a serial novel "by Burt L. Standish" to begin the following month.

Not having written the story, I hurried down to Mr. Thomas' office to inquire how come. Coolly he informed me that he had bought the story from another writer who had no objection to its publication as written by "Burt L. Standish."

"But *I* object, Mr. Thomas," said I.

"You?" said he. "Why should you object? It's a very good story and was written by a well-known author."

"I don't care if it's a masterpiece and was written by Booth Tarkington, I object to the use of my pen name on it," said I.

He laughed. "Come, come, Patten, three other men have used that name since you quit writing the Merriwell stories."

"But on the Merriwell stories only, and only in *Tip Top Weekly*, Mr. Thomas. This is different."

"I fail to see it," said he. "Anyhow, it's too late to do anything about it now." With which he turned back to his desk with the air of dismissing me.

O. G. Smith had left for the day, and in desperation I told Charles MacLean of my controversy with Thomas.

"It's a good thing O. G. isn't here," said Mac. "You're too mad to talk to him. Leave it to me, Gil. I'll see him first thing in the morning."

The story appeared in *Top Notch* under the name of the man who wrote it, William Wallace Cook, and Mr. Thomas never mentioned the matter to me again. In fact he was unusually affable with me for some time thereafter. Nevertheless I did not kid myself with the notion that he had forgotten or would ever forget.

Charles MacLean had become O. G. and G. C. Smith's right-hand man and therefore a person of power in the concern. His opinion, openly expressed, that my "Big League" baseball serials in *Top Notch* had been the magazine's chief circulation builder, must have carried some weight with his employers. Having retained all rights to those stories excepting American serial rights, I placed them with Barse and Hopkins for cloth book publication on a royalty basis.

I think I was the first writer to make baseball more than incidental in his stories. At any rate, there was quite a while when I had the field almost exclusively to myself. Eventually others—Charles E. Van Loan being among the earliest—turned their attention to baseball as a source of fiction.

I submitted my first baseball novel, "Lefty o' the Bush," to the *Saturday Evening Post* and went over to Philadelphia at the request of a Mr. Williams, then an associate editor on that publication, to confer about it. He told me it was against the policy of the *Post* to use baseball serials, but that Mr. Lorimer had read my story and thought that two, possibly three, short stories could be developed from it. He pointed out the incidents from which the stories might be constructed and urged me, mildly, to write them.

Needing immediate money, as usual, I sold that novel to *Top Notch* and it appeared, after serial publication, as the first book of the "Big League Series," which eventually ran to an issue of fourteen titles. Without remuneration, Christy Mathewson gave them an enthusiastic recommendation which was used by Barse and Hopkins in their advertising.

Although Mr. Thomas' rejection of "The Enchanted Hour" had shaken my confidence in my ability to know what would meet with his approval, the quick sale of the story elsewhere seemed an assurance that I could find plenty other markets if *Top Notch*, which had been my main dependence, should be closed to me.

In spite of my years, I was really healthier and stronger than ever before. I felt young, and strangers inevitably guessed my age ten years less than what it was. In spite of bitter experiences, I had not turned sour or become cynical. I could still laugh, and play, and work like the devil. In spite of everything, I was a perennial optimist in search of treasure at the end of a rainbow.

Elated by my good luck in selling serial rights to my war novel so quickly after it had been turned down by Mr. Thomas, I phoned Miss Carol Kramer and invited her to dine with me that night at Richard's, a restaurant on the Palisades north of Fort Lee, in Jersey.

We arrived at Richard's early in order to sit at a special table on the restaurant's glassed-in veranda while the purple evening twilight gathered over the Hudson and the lights of New York blazed forth like a great constellation of silver stars.

She was different from any woman I had ever seen and any I have ever seen since. I had been attracted to her at first by her striking good looks, but in her I had found something more rare than mere comeliness. It was an indescribable in-dwelling spirit of truth and integrity. There was no single atom of deceit in her nature, and malice was foreign to her. Her pride was intense but wholly without arrogance. Truly unselfish, she was devotedly self-sacrificing with her sister and ever ready to give sympathy and help to others.

Laughingly, she had spoken of herself as an old maid, but although in her mid-thirties, there was a buoyant lightness about her that made her seem—and sometimes look—nearer twenty. Not only had she kept her "figger," youth had not escaped her, and keen enjoyment of life was still within her grasp. She could be very happy, even gay, without being hectic or boisterous.

We danced that night to the music of Richard's three-piece orchestra, and while we were dancing I asked her if she would marry me.

48 · CAMP BY THE SINGING WATERFALL

I WAS FREE AGAIN. Freedom, I had told myself, was what I wanted, but now, having obtained it at a staggering cost and no small sacrifice, I knew it was not what I wanted at all. I knew at last that my nature required companionship, the companionship of a woman, a wife and helpmeet, loyal and understanding and willing to give as well as take. In short, a wife who would play the game.

I sometimes hear or read about "civilized" divorces in Hollywood and elsewhere, after which the parted couples continue to be fast friends and great admirers of their former partners in wedlock, and I wonder. I wonder if such "civilized" divorces are not the most disgraceful and immoral kind, leading to still further discontent and unhappiness for the sundered pairs.

On the other hand, I sometimes wonder if I, myself, am not by nature uncivilized and shoddy. For my heartfelt wish on being set free from my second wife was that I should never behold her again as long as I lived. Far from wishing her harm of any kind whatever, I actually wished her good luck and happiness. But I also desired to forget her as far as possible and to be disassociated as far as possible from every reminder of her.

Carol and I were married in Boston on June 27, 1918, and, having first seen her sister aboard a train for New York, we departed for Bangor, Maine, that same day.

On the night of the following day we were settled—according to our plans—for a stay of three weeks at Bill Early's camps and cabins near Sebec Lake, north of which lay one hundred and fifty miles of Maine wilderness.

Our camp, standing on high ground near the upper of two waterfalls on Wilson Stream, contained a living room with an open fireplace, two bedrooms, and a bathroom with running water and porcelain tub. The living room was sheathed for warmth in cool weather, and there were comfortable chairs for lounging before the open fire. Two windows overlooked the waterfall, which rippled a gay song by day and a soothing lullaby by night.

There was a veranda that nearly always was swept by woodsy breezes which kept black flies and mosquitoes away. We took our meals in the big Main House which Early called a hotel, and the food was the very best of hearty country fare. There Carol ate her first wild strawberries, having never before known that such berries existed.

For she was a city woman with no knowledge of country life, and everything she now beheld was novel and intensely interesting. Daily, sometimes hourly, she encountered new experiences which gave her wonderment and pleasure. When I began to work, which I did from necessity after a few days there, she took frequent walks over the old winding dirt road that led out to the nearest town, fourteen miles away.

She invariably returned bubbling with excitement over something she had seen, a partridge burrowing in the dust, a wild rabbit hopping lazily into the bushes, a chipmunk that uttered chattering screams and disappeared into a hole in the ground, beautiful blue birds that flew in flocks and squawked harshly. And always she came with clusters of tiny wild flowers she had plucked from the roadside grass which she called a hedge. Her capacity for the enjoyment of simple things was tremendous.

I taught her to fish, giving as much time as I could spare to the sport, and within a week, using a light rod, she could handle a leaping landlocked salmon as skillfully as if she had fished all her life for them. And she learned to bait her own hook for trolling if necessary, either with worms or a minnow, sewing the latter on so it would wobble as if wounded. It took her longer to catch on to the knack of fly-casting, at which I, myself, was far from an expert and therefore not a first-class instructor.

The three weeks that we planned to stay at Early's were gone before we realized it, and we stayed on a while longer. In fact, we stayed there four months, lacking four days.

They were four Elysian months, for I had found my woman, the woman of my dreams. Without her, a week at Early's would have been my limit, even though the place was then almost a fisherman's paradise. Using wet flies, I took nine salmon out of the pool below the lower falls the first day I fished there. And when the salmon were not in the pool it was a simple matter to row down the lake, less than a mile away, where fishing of some sort could always be found. For besides salmon, the lake provided trout, small-mouthed black bass, pickerel, and white perch so large and hungry that they sometimes struck at live minnows on a hook.

From the veranda of our camp, early in July, we saw millions of fireflies turn a hillside field across the river into a great waving sheet of silver light, and this happened maybe a dozen times. Whippoor-wills cried their hearts out around the camp in twilight hours, and all night long the restless waterfall seemed to give forth its muted organ notes for our ears only. Day after day a veery sang its cheery song from a small tree in front of the camp, and he lingered to sing there long after all the other songbirds had departed in September.

I wrote my stories on a portable typewriter that was easy to carry when traveling. Plots came at command, the writing was easy, and not one of the stories written at Early's met with a rejection. I seemed to be in a lucky groove, and nothing worried me.

Even the war, over which I had fumed and fretted, now seemed like something taking place on another planet. I told myself that I had cut free and clear of the past and was now entering upon a new and better life.

There was something about Early's camps, an atmosphere, that brought the same patrons back year after year. Even in midsummer when the fishing had grown slack and there was no hunting at all, the Main House was filled to capacity and only a few of the camps were empty. Persons uninterested in either fishing or hunting came there for a rest or to get away for a little while from the monotonous routine of their daily lives.

Three days of pouring rain in mid-July changed Wilson Stream, usually lightly gay and placid, into a wildly tumultuous river that overflowed its banks and turned its two waterfalls into foaming, roaring cataracts. On the fourth day, a crew of husky riverdrivers appeared and plunged into the forest to the north to get out thousands of logs that had been left stranded there by an unexpectedly early shallowing of the erratic stream.

Down came those logs, choking the stream from bank to bank and forming jams that had to be broken by dynamite blasts. As if fleeing from a pursuing demon, the logs crowded and jostled one another and went plunging and whirling over the upper falls, now a miniature Niagara, in tumbling masses that filled the air with crashing sounds like thunder. Each morning that thunderous rumbling began at the crack o' day and often it continued until long after darkness fell.

Carol loved it. Like almost everybody else at Early's, she spent entire days watching the daring loggers working coolly and steadily hour after hour, frequently at the risk of their lives, to keep the logs moving and prevent them from forming a jam in a narrow stretch of white water between the two waterfalls.

Carrying her camera, she got a dozen thrilling shots of the riverdrivers riding the logs into the stretch of boiling water and leaping ashore on a rocky point just in time to avoid being carried over the falls. The boss of the crew told me it was the most spectacular and dangerous drive he had ever seen. He expressed relief when the final run of logs had passed the lower falls without the occurrence of an accident.

To break the monotony, we made two trips away from Early's during the summer, one up to Capen's camps on Moosehead Lake, the other down to Christmas Cove on the seacoast. In both instances Carol became eager to return to Early's. Overnight at Capen's was enough for her, but I thought it would be different at Christmas Cove, where she could dress for dinner at the hotel and for dances. But on the morning of the third day, following an evening of dancing, she woke up begging to go back to our "nice old camp in the woods."

"What's the matter with you, woman?" I cried. "I reckoned you would want to stay here at least a week."

"No can do, man," she said. "I've got a date with a big salmon up at Bill's. Let's hurry."

She was actually *homesick* for our camp near the singing waterfall. So back we went to Early's, and presently I began to wonder if anything short of physical force would get her to leave the place again.

September came, and I took her with me on long tramps into the woods to shoot partridge and visit logging camps. But now, with the fishing season over, the water of the river and the lake had lost its silver blueness and turned harshly dark, and—for my ears—the murmur of our waterfall had become a muted threnody of sorrow.

The first frosts had smitten the feathery emerald green ferns with a brown blight, and the somber trees were sowing the bare ground with dead leaves that whispered of approaching winter, when disturbed by passing feet. At twilight, red deer, seen from the veranda of the Main House, came out of the woods and moved along the far edge of Early's mowing field. Foxes barked and quarrelled in the night, and sometimes blasts of wind smote our trembling camp like threats.

"Come on, Crazy," I kept saying to Carol, "let's get out of this."

And always she replied, "Oh, let's stay just a little longer."

Hiding the sadness that autumn in the country always casts upon me like a somber cloak, I waited for her to cry quits. I waited and shivered, for soon there came freezing nights, and Bill Early was compelled to spend hours each day cutting wood to keep our fireplace running.

All the other camps were empty, and only occasionally did hunters come in to stop overnight in the Main House, and Bill began to look at us as if wondering if we were in our right minds. And one day he told us suggestively that the little steamer that plied between Packard's camps, a mile below on the lake, and Sebec Landing, three miles from Dover, through which the railroad ran, would make its last trip of the year tomorrow.

"All right, Bill," said I. "Get our baggage down to Packard's. We'll go out on that boat."

"Oh," said Carol, "let's———"

"Don't say it!" I shouted. "Don't say, 'Let's stop just a little while longer.' Don't you see Bill has given us notice it's our move? Begin packing, Loony."

"Wa-al, I didn't mean it jest exactly that way," Bill drawled, "but the wood for your fire's gettin' sort of low, and there's liable to come a heavy snowfall anytime now that'll shet us in, and———"

"Oh," said Carol, "I just started to say let's not miss that boat. I'll be ready." And, laughing, she made a face at me.

We left Early's on the twenty-fourth of October, and there were patches of snow in the woods on that day. Long afterwards Carol confessed that our camp by the singing waterfall had put her under a spell she had hesitated to break for fear it would mean the end of our honeymoon.

Our honeymoon lasted more than twenty years.

Carol died the twenty-first of August, 1938.

Camp by the Singing Waterfall

*Once on a barren path I found
  A dainty, flawless flower
That cast a magic spell around
  And charmed me with its power.*

*Long paused I by that blossom white,
  Nor from it wished to sever,
But came at last the stormy night
  That left me lone for ever.*

*At dawn my lovely blossom lay
  All fallen, crushed and broken;
More dark than night to me that day
  When fate's black word was spoken.*

*Since then I've trod a lonely way,
  Yet in its bleakest hour
I dreamed that at its end I may
  Find waiting there My Flower.*

FINALE

NATURALLY IT WAS AN IRISHMAN who was credited with saying that "no man should write his autobiography but himself!"

Which may be one of those supposedly typical back-handed remarks, but the meaning is clear enough. Autobiographies should be written by those who live them. In this case, Gilbert Patten takes us only to 1918, with an added statement reporting the death of his beloved wife Carol, in 1938. He himself lived until 1945.

This is a time lapse which surely clamors to be filled with whatever facts are available. What happened to "our hero" from the age of fifty-two until seventy-nine? And what happened to the dime novel, with which his life was so inextricably interwoven?

For it is indisputable that in the rise and fall of this important phase of American life, Gilbert Patten or "Burt L. Standish" was an outstanding figure.

The tale of one cannot be conclusively told without the other. As the fortunes of the dime novel fluctuated, so did those of their pre-eminent author.

"Romantic sensationalism" is a somewhat high-flown term applied to this type of writing. It was the literature of action to the nth degree and beyond. But "Standish" in his Merriwell saga introduced characterization. His hero and the rest of an almost countless array of personalities became human beings of flesh and blood to youthful readers, not mere stock figures of heroism, villainy, or comedy.

Even after said readers were grown-up men and women, they

Finale

recalled fondly Frank Merriwell and his friends. As the widely syndicated columnist Louella Parsons wrote in her article dated February 9, 1951:

> Shades of my girlhood! Frank Merriwell, whose adventures were read by every boy in America, were also read by this writer. I must say my mother never approved and I used to sneak the books from my brother, but what adventures Frank had! In fact he was equal in popularity to Hopalong Cassidy today. Now Frank is going to be filmed for T.V.

In view of the unquestioned wide and long-lasting popularity of the Merriwell stories and others, what happened to cause the final decline and disappearance from the American scene of the dime novel as such?

Some say, of course, that they are still being written, published and sold—as "pulps"—at a much higher price. But chronologically speaking, the "Dime" and "Nickel Libraries" took the first big dive together, when the Nickelodeon arrived.

Those first motion pictures! Crude, infantile, scorned, the flickers were nonetheless new and fascinating, and they could be seen for a nickel. What redblooded boy wouldn't buy this sort of visible action instead of spending that precious and often only five-cent piece on a book, no matter how highly colored it might be, inside and out?

Thus the sheer novelty of those early silents helped cause the extinction of the dime-novel form of inexpensive mass entertainment. It is interesting to note that as the first "Dime" or "Nickel Novels" leaned heavily on "Westerns," so in turn have motion pictures, radio, and eventually television. They became not only mass entertainment, but in a legendary and stereotyped form, mass history.

Dime noveleers fell on hard times. Some were unable to successfully make the transition from that form to the pulp fiction which followed it. A few failed sadly, ending in poverty and even suicide, victims of the age-old tragedy of falling behind in the parade.

Fortunately this did not happen to Gilbert Patten. As he once put it during those depression days, "I'm broke but I'm happy. Life has always been a grand adventure for me, even at its dullest. It's still the greatest invention I know of."[5]

His third marriage was more than ordinarily successful, and finding happiness with a loyal and understanding wife can carry a man over the greatest disappointments.

It is interesting to reconstruct this phase of his life from the comparatively few hints or direct statements which he set down about marriage in his autobiography. What was his emotional progression through and beyond two divorces into the safe harbor of a lasting relationship with Wife Number Three?

In the first place, he was a New Englander, having undoubtedly the reticence about personal affairs which is more or less inherent in the breed. Too, remember that Gilbert Patten was born and brought up in the Victorian era, when the love-life exposé was much less common than it is today.

Still, he makes it clear that he and his first wife Alice were basically incompatible, and this finally forced their separation.

They were married as a concession to the prejudices of their time and place in a small Maine town, and after he had been more the pursued than the pursuer. According to the girl's watchful parents, she had been "compromised" by spending part of a night sitting beside the bed of her desperately ill school friend, who happened to be male.

He was supposedly dying of typhoid fever, but he recovered and being as he said, "A man of honor," they got married. The groom was twenty, the bride a year or two older and apparently very sure of what she wanted. It might almost be called a shotgun wedding—without the classic cause for such drastic action.

As he relates, Alice helped him greatly in those early days of struggle, when he was trying to find his rightful place in life. Her admittedly more complete schooling came in handy with the "grammer" and spelling in which, like so many natural-born writers, he was always weak to the end of his days. Although ahead

[5] Gilbert Patten, "Dime Novel Days," *Saturday Evening Post*, Vol. CCIII, No. 36 (March 7, 1931), 57.

Finale

of him at the start in some ways, Wife One apparently could not grow and develop as he did, thus following a familiar pattern in many too-youthful marriages. Alice did not fit into the nomadic life he needed then to keep from going stale as a writer.

However, within three years they moved to New York. There, or rather, in Brooklyn, their only child Harvan Barr was born, and years later this father could write to his son:

"Our boy and girl marriage was a mistake. She should never have married me and I should never have married her. . . . But, after all, some good resulted. YOU!"

Then after twelve years the marriage broke up, with Alice and young Barr returning to make their permanent home in small town Corinna, where she felt they belonged.

Which left Gilbert Patten, now thirty-two, a more or less freewheeling bachelor, a formative period that he had been cheated out of by an early marriage. He became one of the convivial crowd of writers, actors, artists, newspapermen, and other high-steppers of the Gay Nineties, who made New York famous and exciting—a "man-about-town."

The "Maine Yankee Boy," as he called himself, developed into a nattily dressed, cane swinging Broadway *boulevardier* and frequenter of the Great White Way of those days—a tall, handsome, dark-haired man whom Charles Hanson Towne, the popular poet, facetiously hailed at a gay cocktail party as "Edgar Allan Poe."

It is surely not unlikely that Patten at this time had chapters in his life, or at least episodes, which would have resulted from his admitted liking for the fair sex. "I like them small and cuddly," he wrote later. But if so, he discreetly left no details in writing, and nothing emerged from other sources.

Yet he did acknowledge he was a man who needed feminine companionship and understanding to save him from recurring emotional depression and even melancholy—which is what may be called an occupational hazard for most creative workers, especially writers, who ply such a lonely, solitary trade.

At any rate, this one soon became involved with Mary Nunn,

a vivacious Southern girl addicted to running away from home, where life was too boresome to endure. Judging from what he tells of their sudden marriage, "let's both be loony together," a strong physical attraction must have been at the controls. Although once burnt, he apparently married a second time on impulse—or perhaps this was just another case of a clever girl knowing her way about and going after what she wanted—while he was still too easy-going or unsophisticated to scent danger.

Listen to him less than a year later in the autobiography, "I knew I had made a serious mistake." But again, as a man of honor, he would try to make the best of a bad bargain. Only now, instead of having a small-town, stay-at-home helpmate, he had at his side a frivolous, flirtatious, restless, extravagant, and apparently untrustworthy woman, one even capable of telling his opponent in a big poker game how to beat her husband!

This he did not speak of to her, but it still rankled years afterward when he wrote, "I never forgot it."

Again, toward the end of this luckless marriage, they played cards with comparative strangers at a fashionable Maine resort, and one man remarked that Patten, being so lucky at cards, "was probably unlucky in love."

This "comparative stranger" must of course have noticed that vivacious Mrs. Patten's writer husband spent hours a day over a hot typewriter, which naturally left her with empty time on her hands. What more natural than for this gentleman of leisure to spend many of those hours with the attractive lady who received his discreet attentions in the charming manner of a Southern woman, brought up to be femininely attractive and graciously receptive to such attentions?

The unlucky husband's concluding statement in the autobiography, on this marital episode, is surely bitterly revealing. "Two years later he became my wife's second husband."

A great deal may be read here between the lines about Wife Two's attitudes, leading to Patten's second divorce.

This cost him more emotionally and financially than the first,

Finale

because he had more to lose in both categories. But he figured it was worth anything it cost to be free of her.

The divorce was delayed by excessive demands and legal complications caused through malice and the desire to hurt. Pretty well stripped financially, he considered his freedom not too dearly bought. And quite naturally he swore, "Never again!"

So here he was, at last cut loose from the too-absorbing Merriwells and from two marriages, fifty years old, and faced with the likelihood of a solitary, womanless old age. Even freedom had its drawbacks, and he was not constituted to endure it for very long.

Besides, surely by this time and after what could be called two strike-outs, he might be clever enough to make a home run and win the Big Game in the last of the Ninth, thus following the famous Merriwell formula—which is exactly what happened.

He did indeed meet and marry his "dream woman." Note again, the college-boy type of romantic idealist emerging once more, at fifty. Two years of freedom, and he was eager to give it up, "living happily ever afterward" in what he thought of as a continual honeymoon.

At a later time he wrote to a friend that Street and Smith considered him their only author who could preach without offense while writing love scenes for boys and girls.

> But in writing this love stuff, I had to make my girls extremely colorless and unreal, which led critics to say I have no understanding of women. However, having been married three times to three different types of women, I believe I have a slight, though far from complete understanding of the far from fair sex.

From the time he married his beloved Carol, the happy bridegroom was to write very few Merriwell stories. After nearly two decades he and Frank, his alter ego, had come to a parting of the ways. But those were years of mutual dependence, during which any wife might well have thought herself crowded out of the marriage bed, as it were. Probably there simply had not been room for three there, even if one was invisible and inaudible!

Now he and his alter ego to whom, as he himself admitted, he had given virtues and characteristics he wished he had possessed in his own youth, were no longer constant companions by day and by night. There was plenty of room in his life for someone else, and he had reached the half-century mark, when the stability of home had presumably more value.

Wife Three's birthplace was Rochester, New York, where she received her early schooling. Her father had been a Union officer during the Civil War, and was of German descent. Daughter Carol was sent abroad to study in Germany, and this European finishing school polish gave her added poise and appreciation of what it means to be a writer. Her husband was always certain of a warmly attentive audience and a wife not flirtatiously interested in other men.

So, like some of his seafaring ancestors, Gilbert Patten had come into safe harbor. His only child Barr was married and living in California, but there was little if any communication between the two men. However in the autobiography Patten does relate how in 1912 he sent his son to the University of Maine, hoping the youth would have the college career he himself never had.

Then in his freshman year, Barr left school "for no discoverable reason," as his disappointed father was to say in a letter to a friend.

During an N.B.C. radio broadcast delivered April 30, 1933, he said in part:

> I have in my life one great regret. I did not go to college.
>
> But I have also a great consolation. Through my writings—especially the Merriwell stories—I have, perhaps, caused thousands of boys who would otherwise not have done so, to obtain a college education.
>
> It is truly said that material wealth is not everything. The young man with a college education, good health, and the world before him is wealthy even though he has not a dollar to his name.
>
> Every boy, every girl, should go to college.

Finale

What an ironical twist of life that he never had the satisfaction of seeing his own son graduate. Barr had walked away from campus, and apparently his father never learned the reason for throwing away a college education.

However, that reason was disclosed after the father's death by Barr Patten himself, to his friend Tony London, the producer who was then planning the Frank Merriwell Television Series.

Barr, at the time a man of middle age, recalled with complete clarity his brief stay in college. Having been a star athlete at prep school, he naturally turned out for baseball practice and easily made the freshman team.

Came the day of the "big game," which he felt sure meant making varsity for next year, and his father had promised to come. It was to be the biggest day in the life of a boy who had spent the previous years with his mother, seeing little of the father who however, had always supported him, and whom he secretly idolized.

Young Barr Patten dreamed of pulling off a real "Merriwell," to win the game not for dear old Yale, or good old Maine—but for his father, author of the famous Merriwell stories and well-known not only in Maine but throughout the whole country—a father any son would be mighty proud of, in front of the whole school.

What happened?

Nothing. The famous father failed to appear and the son, in youthful disappointment and disgust, left college for good and all—without explanations—so that to the senior Patten there was "no discoverable reason" for the action which brought him disappointment, too.

Before the 1920's and into the next two decades, while the dime novel was fading out, Gilbert Patten did as most others of that noveleer brotherhood were forced to do, turn to the fast developing pulp magazine markets, of which there were many opening up and often suddenly closing down.

He continued to write steadily for *Top Notch* and such similar publications as *Telling Tales, Detective Story, The Outlook, Sport Story,* and others. For a short time he also sold stories to Vitagraph, an early motion picture company then located in Chicago.

One of them titled *Temporary Marriage* was shown at the Strand Theatre, Camden, Maine, where he had his summer home. This was in August, 1923, and naturally the local *Courier-Gazette* gave it an enthusiastic review after the big gala opening night.

"Greatest picture of the eternal triangle ever screened . . . a triumph from the standpoint of artistic photography," were some of the phrases used.

In the cast were several future screen stars, including Kenneth Harlan, Mildred Davis, Myrtle Stedman, and Tully Marshall.

Being called upon for a speech by the applauding audience, the author talked mostly about censorship of motion pictures, which he opposed. Among other things he said:

"I admit bad pictures have been made, but there are existing laws against immorality and indecency that will take care of this matter. I believe in letting the picture going public censor motion pictures."

Which problem is still very much with us, more than forty years later!

It was also in 1923 that an enterprising small-time producer tried to cash in on the vast popularity of the Merriwell stories by giving a young actor the name "Frank Merriwell."

It was at about this time that Mr. Norman Taurog, the well-known Hollywood writer-producer was planning a series of two reelers on the adventures of Patten's famous hero.

The writer, the producer, and publishers Street and Smith promptly sued to prevent unauthorized use of the name—and won the case.

It was on January 30, 1927, that the following appeared in the *Courier-Gazette*:

> Gilbert Patten, the talented Camden author, has climbed another rung in the ladder of fame by signing a two-year contract with

Finale

the NEA (Newspaper Editors' Association) which furnishes services for 700 newspapers.

Under the caption: "Frank Merriwell's Daddy Joins NEA," the interesting announcement is given as follows: "From the prolific genius of Gilbert Patten, who for twenty years wrote under the name of Burt L. Standish, has grown a reincarnation of Frank Merriwell, one-time idol-hero of half the youngsters of this country.

So it is that Jack Lockwill, personification of wholesome American youth, is ready to make his bow across the pages of NEA client newspapers. . . ."

In 1930 Patten received nation-wide publicity through the news that he was launching his own publishing company with a string of three pocket-size magazines. The story was carried over Associated Press wires and in many newspapers, and articles appeared in such weeklies as *Time, The New Yorker,* and others.

Time began its article: "High in a Manhattan office building last week, a tall, white-haired man proudly thumbed three dummy paperback books," and went on to tell of the new publisher, Gilbert Patten or "Burt L. Standish" of Frank Merriwell fame.

He became so well-known to the general public that as another interviewer wrote:

> Men stop him in the busy swirls of the Manhattan maelstrom, they step to his table in restaurants and they greet him on trains. In Maine, one even took him to a secret trout stream, where the speckled beauties crowd each other until their very fins crumpled up in the crush. Could friendship stretch to greater lengths?

He spoke over radio on various fine arts programs in Boston, Portland, Bangor, Duluth, New York, and other cities. Relating episodes in his long career, he said about Frank and Dick:

> I wish I had time to tell you of the fun I had writing those stories —about the hundreds of letters I received from Merriwell admirers. Quite a lot of them were written by girls, for at the height of the popularity of the Merriwell yarns, it's probable that fully twenty-five per cent of the readers were girls. Maybe some of them, now mothers with sons and daughters old enough to vote, are listening in.

Reminiscing about his own boyhood, he went on:

Away back there as a young scribbler, a mere kid—a very raw country kid—I had dreams and ambitions. Yes, aspirations. It really is to Dickens, Hawthorne, Poe, and Robert Louis Stevenson that I owe my heaviest debt.

I must have been about seventeen when I began to devour Dickens hungrily ... some day, some fine day I would write a great book—a book like *David Copperfield* or Hawthorne's *The Scarlet Letter*. You see, I hadn't yet fallen under the spell of Robert Louis Stevenson. That was to happen later. Later I was to spend delightful hours over *Treasure Island, The Master of Ballantrae* and *Dr. Jekyll and Mr. Hyde*. I tried to acquire Stevenson's style. Laugh if you want to.

It was at this time that O. O. McIntyre, in his column "New York Day by Day," spoke of Gil Patten as a "two-fisted writing man, a typical drawling-voiced down Easterner," and "the most modest of men." Then quoting George Jean Nathan, "his curious song deserves to be sung, but Gil will never sing it. He is entirely too shy."

"Odd" McIntyre was right.

When finally the autobiography came to be written, it was the work of a typically reticent New Englander who had acquired big town modes and manners over the years but remained always essentially a small-town product. Although not a New Englander, Henry Ford, whose years almost paralleled those of Gilbert Patten, had a boyhood similar to Patten's.

Ford (1863–1947) also lived through that amazing era. He too was a country boy, son of a farmer who tried to make a farmer of him, just as William Patten tried to make his boy follow the carpenter trade. Both youths, in their widely separated ways, were urged on by irresistible inner forces to get clear of narrow though well-meaning parental control and make their imprint upon the times in their own individual manner—Henry Ford to become one of the richest men in the world and Gilbert Patten one of its uniquely successful writers—and both at heart, still country boys!

However, the "shy, modest" Patten did become somewhat ex-

Finale

pansive in talking of future plans, during a 1930 interview concerning his newly launched publishing venture. In taking up the editorial blue pencil, he expected to find new authors and do little of the actual writing himself.

"If writing interferes with editorship, the editorial duties will come first," he was quoted as saying. The famous author smiled broadly. "Why should I write any more? You know Dr. Eliot's famous Five Foot Shelf of immortal books? You ought to see the Frank Merriwell Twenty-seven Foot Shelf! I've got them all bound and stacked at my summer home in Camden. Every time I look at that interminable row of books, I feel like summoning the shade of Alexander Dumas and saying, 'Alex, you must have loafed a lot when you were young. You only wrote a couple of tons of books and plays—while my Merriwell stories would fill not less than 18,000 solid columns of the standard-size newspapers.'"

Trade papers carried announcements from the office of the Gilbert Patten Publishing Company, in what *Variety,* the show business daily, called a "swanky suite in the Salmon Tower Building" at 11 West Forty-second Street, New York. The news release stated:

> *Swift Story's* slogan will be "It Fits Your Pocket." *Dime Novel* will use one complete story an issue, written to order, and from one to two cents a word will be paid on acceptance. The *Pocket Magazine* will use fiction with an appeal to wage earners, edited for both sexes.

Editor-author Patten had decided the field would be well covered! He planned that *Dime Novel* should concern itself with one central character, but knew that with changing times, a 1930 hero must not be patterned too closely after Frank, his 1896 ancestor.

As *Time* put it: "Juvenile readers of today demand something more salty than prep school pranks and last minute football victories."

So the Merriwell author wrote "Ben Hunter, or the Boss of

the Rum Runners," a sort of Robin Hood of the prohibition era. Basically he had Frank's honesty but got himself enmeshed in illegal activities against his will. Many episodes dealt with his valiant efforts to go straight and defeat the gangsters. "Crime must not pay!"

Although the great depression had started, Gilbert Patten, who as he himself admitted later was a poor businessman, refused to see anything but speedy recovery for the land he believed in. What was needed was courage and confidence in the future, and with this he was well supplied—also with some money to invest in his dream.

Again *Variety* for September 10, 1930, had a story on "Gil Patten, who turns publisher this month . . . is reputed to have earned close to half a million . . . and most of that money has gone into his publishing corporation."

This was of course a wildly optimistic figure, but whatever resources the hopeful new publisher had at his command could not save him from the downward wave of depression which was engulfing the country.

His venture was disastrously short-lived, and he never again made a try at the difficult game which he had first played when, as an ambitious youth of seventeen, he had hopefully launched the Corinna *Owl*.

From now on he stayed in the field of fiction writing, though the rewards grew discouragingly meager as his former story markets narrowed or disappeared altogether. But there was one asset which did not decline in value over the years—the loyalty of his readers.

Letters from appreciative Merriwell fans continued to come to Frank's "Father" via the publishers. And in 1931 his two-part reminiscences "Dime Novel Days," appeared in the *Saturday Evening Post* of February 28 and March 7.

The articles dealt largely with various picturesque characters among the dime noveleers, as well as some of his own adventures, and received much favorable attention.

Finale

One reviewer remarked that "Patten eulogizes the great dime novelists whom he admired. Seemingly he doesn't realize that he was the greatest of them all. But he was, and is."

This commentator rather wistfully added that since Patten's writings stimulated interest in college education, "we sometimes wonder why his name is not among those receiving honorary degrees."

One might add that it continues to be a source of puzzlement even to this day.

The appearance of "Dime Novel Days" had been preceded by a June 11, 1927, *Saturday Evening Post* article, "The Man Merriwell," whose author was James M. Cain, best-selling novelist of *The Postman Always Rings Twice*. Mr. Cain's "profile" was generously spiced with wit and anecdote in dealing with the career of Gilbert Patten. And of Frank Merriwell, he wrote, "He was the idol of thousands of boys who kept book on him as closely as thousands of other boys now keep book on Babe Ruth."

Patten's youthful hero was brave, honest, and courageous, but unlike most other fictional heroes of the day, he had a sense of humor! More than this, he could show pity without being weak, forgive his enemies and not be a "sissy," that dread appellation in the world of youth.

By being friendly with characters who happened to be Negro or Jewish or members of other minority groups, Frank helped to erase prejudice and intolerance from growing minds, without preaching. The same was true of the handicapped, as in the case of Harry Rattleton, famous for his comic spoonerisms. He was used for comedy relief, as were various others, but never as the butt of cruel ridicule in Frank's way of life.

So in a sense, Gilbert Patten did become a sort of preacher—by indirection—which might perhaps have pleased his pious mother.

Still, he would have been less than human if he had not been somewhat gratified when several would-be Merriwells failed to score in the publishing game. Even while Street and Smith continued to reap their golden harvest from his stories, they tried to put out imitations, particularly in a series called the "Do and Dare," written by Ernest A. Young, one of their staff.

This author even sent his second-string contender to a "Springvale Academy," in imitation of Merriwell's famous prep school "Fardale." The carbon-copy hero was made to do practically everything Frank did and more besides. But he lacked the Merriwell magic and lasted only two years, having learned the hard way that no one could really compete with the great and only Merriwell!

It was at this period of his long career that Patten was quoted as saying he would never write another Merriwell, "for I feel my mind must now be whipped to that sort of work." His ways of thinking had so changed, "I could not write the Merriwell stories to save my life."

Here might be advanced an intriguing theory about the emotional involvement of an author with his "brain child" to a depth and degree which may lead to a perhaps unrecognized split in personality. A writer, having invented a character, might find his imaginary creation practically taking over its master's life!

The classic example of course is "Frankenstein," Mrs. Shelley's scientist, who in 1818 created a mechanical monster, that was to become the prototype of other such fictional sub-human creatures which grew stronger and more cunning than their creators.

Frank Merriwell was in no sense a monster, but from another angle he could be considered a benevolent despot, governing the actions and thoughts, in fact the entire life of the man who first dreamed him up. They lived closely together for nearly twenty years—but which was master and which the servant?

Patten relates how Merriwell became an actual obsession, an alter ego, controlling practically every waking thought, and working constantly in the subconscious mind. For Frank was concerned only with the turning out of a new story each week, rain or shine, in sickness or in health, almost "until death do us part!"

A minimum of twenty thousand words a week must be pro-

Finale

duced, with new locales, many different characters, and adventures in all parts of the world, the stories to be first imagined, then set down on paper. It was a truly Herculean job, because this intensive drive for wordage was continued not during six months nor twelve, but for over seventeen years, practically without interruption!

"Once or twice I thought I was going crazy," Patten later commented. It became a question of "saving my reason and my job."

He forced himself to try getting away from Merriwell for a few hours a day, but that was really impossible. The actual daily stint of writing was almost the lesser part.

> ... I would have to be continually reading along the lines of my work and making rather copious notes from that reading in order to give the stories an essential color of verity—the atmosphere of being written by one who knew all about military-school life, college life, railroad life, the sea, woods, horses, dogs, wild animals, birds of the air, trees, plants, sports of all kinds, America, foreign lands, and a thousand other things with which no one man could possibly be familiar. . . .[6]

After years of this, it would become difficult to distinguish the mental dividing line between creator and creation, so closely were they merged. Eventually, Patten, in sheer self defense, had to stop driving himself so relentlessly along this road.

He entered into no more long-term contracts, regaining his status as a free lance writer after such a long stretch of meeting that weekly deadline with a complete, exciting, and "authenic" novelette.

It was in the August 12, 1931, New York *World-Telegram* that the brilliant columnist Heywood Broun devoted his entire space to Gilbert Patten, in the form of a letter from the latter.

In a previous column, Broun had written a eulogy on "those good old Merriwells" of his youth, "but I never did know the author's name."

Said author quickly supplied the deficiency and also objected

[6] *Ibid.*

humorously to Broun's remark that he had allowed Frank to remain at Yale for eight years.

'Tain't so, Heywood, 'tain't so! Either there was malice in the assertion or your memory played you a bum trick. He got only the usual four years, much as I would like to have stretched it. Of course, in a later yarn he did go back to Yale as a coach.

Dang it all, Heywood, I fitted for college myself, though I didn't make it, because I got to writing pieces and selling 'em, which led me to decide that I couldn't afford to waste time around a college. I allowed Frank to do a lot of things a college man couldn't do, even away back in those pre-historic times, but I didn't keep him in Yale eight or ten years, honest I didn't.

Everybody knows it's no job at all to turn off a column a day. That seems a loafer's job to anybody who ever wrote dime novels.

Broun went on to comment that "Mr. Patten's working requirements while in the Merriwell business were enough to make any columnist seem a slacker."

Then, no doubt with a grin, Heywood Broun admitted that he didn't know whether or not dime novels influenced him directly. But "after spending five or six of the most impressionable years of my life reading Merriwells—I went to Harvard. When I began to actually see Yale teams, I realized that the Merriwells were just fictional."

Louis Sobol in his New York *Evening Journal* "Voice of Broadway," devoted an entire column to telling a story about "Burt L. Standish." He was assigned by King Features Syndicate and International News Service to do a special reporting job on the upcoming Yale-Harvard final clash of 1931, in the hope that someone would "pull a Merriwell."

Sure enough, in the final moments of play, Albie Booth, the diminutive Yale star, kicked the final winning field goal and as the *Literary Digest* phrased it later, "brought Frank Merriwell to life," while sixty thousand spectators roared!

So Gilbert Patten or "Burt L. Standish" got his story.

But these were depression years, and the mortality rate among popular magazines was high. Many markets were closed, and, like other writers, Patten felt the pinch. On a February day of 1933, a reporter saw him in his favorite Greenwhich Village café, Lee Chumley's place, and asked for an interview. It went like this:

> He still likes fishing and "a car that will step," although he has been in several auto wrecks, and feels it would be wiser if he left "stepping cars" entirely alone. He lives with his wife and sister-in-law on Washington Heights and has a son who with great foresight has been looking for gold to mine in California, during the past several months.

It was about this time that a party was given at Chumley's honoring Gil Patten, and among other guests was Eddie Eagan, former outstanding Yale athletic star and college boxing champion, now Assistant United States Attorney of New York. As reported, "Eagan spoke to Patten with all the reverence of a disciple at the feet of his master. 'I lived 'way out in Colorado,' he said, 'where Yale was something you did when you shouted good and loud—that's all it meant to us—and college was a place where sissies went. It wasn't until I began sneaking in your novels on Frank Merriwell that I got the big yearn to be like him, and that's how I came to go to Yale—something I'll never regret.' "

Another one of the many who became college-minded through the Merriwells was William C. Lengel, Associate Editor of *Cosmopolitan*, who wrote: "What finer literary companions have I met with? What pleasanter hours has any reading given me? How I fought and bled for dear old Yale! In the pages of *Tip Top Weekly*, Frank Merriwell was my hero. Tom Brown was milk and water compared to him.... Oh, Burt L. Standish, creator of Frank Merriwell, all-too-faultless hero, you made me see the color and glory of college life! You made me long for the higher education. You influenced my life at eleven!"

It was in 1934 that Merriwell and his creator entered on a new phase. Not only was a comic strip being widely syndicated by King Features in some two hundred newspapers, but also a radio series of fifteen-minute plays was broadcast nationwide, three times a week, sponsored by the manufacturers of a popular toothpaste.

As reported in the New York *Evening Journal* of March 17, 1934, "The Merriwell brothers are coming to the air after all these years. The adventure heroes who strutted through the nickel novels make their debut March 26, and Gilbert Patten, the 'Burt L. Standish' who created the characters, will do the 'scripts. . . . He gets more per story via radio than twenty of his novels of yesteryear would have netted him. . . . Mr. Patten is 68 years old. . . ."

The *Eastern Gazette* published a letter from that old Maine man Gilbert Patten, dated from Hudson View Gardens, New York City, March 15, 1934.

EDITOR OF THE GAZETTE
DEXTER, MAINE
DEAR EDITOR:

Maybe you'll remember me as the poor bum of a boy who was born in Corinna and ran there, many long years ago, a poor, dinkey little newspaper called The Owl. We have had one bit of pleasant correspondence and I believe you were kind enough to mention me in your paper.

Well now—at last—I've put over my Merriwell air program, a fifteen-minute dramatic broadcast that will come from Chicago over N.B.C. network, starting March 26th at 6:15 P.M. Your nearest station will be Boston.

If you see fit to mention this in your paper, I shall fully appreciate the free publicity. And it should be news up there, as it will occupy plenty space in hundreds of big-town dailies all over the country. The J. Walter Thompson Co., through whom I sold the program, has just sent up here to my New York home, two photographers who shot something like twenty-five pictures of me. Sorry I can't send you a newspaper cut.

If you do mention it, I wonder if you would be kind enough as to see I get a copy of your paper? I didn't see your other notice but it brought me several letters. You might make something of a story of it, as I am somewhat widely supposed to be dead—and I have only recently escaped from a hospital after two severe cutting operations,

Finale

which, thank God, did not necessitate the removal of any of my innards.

I shall be at my home in Camden, Maine, in time to start north for a fishing trip at Moosehead, early in June.

With very best wishes,
GILBERT PATTEN

There was a steady build-up of national publicity on the new radio series and its author, who admitted he enjoyed bringing Frank up to date, sending him on airplane jaunts instead of buggy rides, having him use the radio and speak the language of modern boys. But juvenile programs which frightened children were deplored by Mr. Patten.

"I don't believe the words of gangsters or gunmen or similar expressions will ever creep into the Merriwell broadcasts," he was quoted as saying. "However, you've got to give the kids some excitement, suspense, and thrills. They look for such fast moving episodes, and what's more, they will do the kids no harm."

The author had already prepared seventy scripts for broadcasting, but at the same time he was again quoted in a New York *Evening Post* article as saying he would rather be writing a serious novel which had been kicking around in the back of his mind for many years, a "semimodern work with sentiment in it but not sentimentality. But it has to be postponed now."

It was also in 1934 that announcements were made about a series of short films to be done in Hollywood, as featured in a *Film Daily* column of May 9, by-line, Phil M. Daly:

> GOOD NEWS . . . the famous Frank Merriwell, hero of Young America when we were a lad, is to be brought to the screen at last. Why the long delay is a mystery. Burt L. Standish, Gilbert Patten in real life, has written over 1000 of these Merriwell novels. . . . he started 40 years ago, Street and Smith have constantly reprinted them since. . . . we're tickled silly to welcome Frank Merriwell to the screen . . . in a series of 3-reelers. Frank's exploits thrilled us till we were out of our 'teens, and millions of other American youths . . . and grown-ups too . . . a fine, clean, upstanding hero such as our Boy Scouts of today emulate. The screen can stand this injection of Youth and Wholesomeness.

So it was that the Merriwells took on a new lease of life. In their beginnings millions of the small, gaudy-jacketed books were sold in those little combination cigar and candy stores that were so common in the United States at the turn of the century. Now the kids of the country could see and be thrilled by them via the far-flung airwaves of radio and the screen magic of motion pictures.

After some lean years Frank Merriwell's "Father" now seemed all set for a successful and financially comfortable seventh decade of his varied career. His apartment in Hudson View Gardens, uptown at One Hundred and Eighty-third Street and Pinehurst Avenue, gave him a comfortable city home with a fine view of the noble river which flows by New York City. And the heat of summer could be avoided by going north to Camden and "Overocks" or "Freedom's Shore," the big white colonial home to which he liked to proudly refer as "the house that Frank built."

He was receiving much pleasant acclaim in the public prints, even to being "cover boy" on the issue of *Radio Art* of June 15, 1934. It was a picture of a good-looking man with snowy hair but the clear, smiling eyes of invincible youthfulness and the laugh wrinkles of one who likes and is liked by his fellows. An ardent sportsman, when the picture appeared he was already in Maine, once again enjoying sport fishing on Moosehead Lake and in nearby trout streams he had known for half a century.

No doubt he agreed with Izaak Walton that "angling is an art worthy the knowledge and practice of a wise man." As Walton's friend and fellow angler Sir Henry Wotton put it, fishing is a "diverter of sadness, a calmer of unquiet thoughts...."

Gilbert Patten was not a "prophet without honor" in his own state, for he had attained the stature of a favorite native son, well-known and admired in Camden and throughout all of Maine. He became the subject of a thesis written by a Maine University student who wrote of him:

> In person Patten is a big, broad-shouldered man, well over six feet in height. His most distinguishing features are a ruddy complexion, snow-white hair, an aquiline nose, and piercing brown eyes.

Finale

In conversation he talks fluently and rapidly, with a pleasant, well modulated voice. His laugh is hearty and infectious. His guest, however, is most aware of his searching gaze, which apparently misses no detail of its object.

A healthy, vigorous man, Patten keeps his weight well below the two hundred mark by diet and exercise, confessing to "one hundred and seventy-five pounds in the nude." Gayety is his panacea, though he feels it is the resource only of a superficial mind. "I need as a minimum one good hearty laugh a day," he remarks. "Yet it is said that the man who can laugh heartily, especially in these times, is shallow. Well, then, I'm very shallow, and that's no surprise to me. I've long more than half-suspected it; in fact, I've been quite sure of it. But laughter is my medicine, my safety-valve, my entrenchment against the assaults of melancholy."[7]

As for his religion, he was "a firm believer in a Creative Force and Intelligence usually called God," and "would give much to be firmly convinced of an individual life after death." But since his rebellious youth he had never been a member of any orthodox church or sect, he was quoted as saying.

Upon his return to New York in that autumn of 1934, he had occasion to build up even stronger entrenchments against "the assaults of melancholy." The comfortable and financially secure future to which he had looked forward began to be shadowed. A letter to his son Barr, who was then living permanently in California, tells the story:

Hudson View Gardens
New York City, Oct. 30, 1934

Dear Barr:

Sure, Boy, I'll be sending you a coupla Merriwell books, autographed, as soon as I can get 'em. Think I have two or three down at my office on 44th Street.

And I'm glad you're in such good spirits. When a man is working and accomplishing something for himself he ought to be in good spirits. I'm naturally damned lazy, but I believe I'd die of dry rot

---

[7] John Levi Cutler, "Gilbert Patten and His Frank Merriwell Saga" (University of Maine *Studies*, Second Series, No. 31), *The Maine Bulletin*, Vol. XXXVI, No. 10 (May, 1934), 80–81.

in a year or two if I couldn't work at something that interested me and held some future promise for me. I've seen others quit—and die.

Just now I'm bucking up against a bum condition caused by the decision of the sponsors of my radio program, on Aug. 10, not to go on the air again this season. Up to that time they had talked of putting the program on five times a week in Sept. Then in conference, they decided to spend their ad. budget in other ways. And we haven't been able to hook another sponsor yet.

Also I had to cancel my Merriwell strip because my contract didn't give me what I ought to get from it, and I haven't yet placed it again. That is, I did place it with United Features, accepting a vaguely worded letter of agreement, only to have United finally hand me a contract, in September that violated the original understanding and tied me up for twenty years! Twenty years! My God, they were optimistic! I'm getting up toward seventy. They would have owned and controlled the name of Frank Merriwell if I had signed that paper. I didn't sign it. Though staggering with the blow and disappointment and anger, I told them where they could put that document, and walked out.

Now something's got to break pretty soon or I'll be in the bread line. But it'll break. I can't live on the beautiful letters I've received from Rudy Vallee, Fredric March, Al Smith, O. O. McIntyre, Congressman Carl Moran, the Governor of Maine, and others. These letters feed nothing but my vanity. But this slump has got to break, and it will pretty soon.

Now that you've written so freely about your Aunt Cora, I can speak my little piece. I never had any use for that lady. She was a snob, always. In fact the only persons in your mother's family I ever had any use for were your mother and her mother. Your Grandmother Gardner was a real person. I believe she was fine and intrinsic. The others whom I knew were the commonest of common clay who mistakenly thought they were superior. Your mother must have acquired the really superior qualities of her mother. SHE was not a Gardner, and I don't believe there was very much Gardner in your mother. She was, as I remember her, distinctly different from the rest of the tribe. Our boy and girl marriage was a mistake. She should never have married me and I should never have married

Finale

her. And it would never have happened had we not entered into a pact to bedevil the rest of the family who were trying to break up a schoolboy and schoolgirl friendship.

But, after all, some good resulted. You! For in spite of the fact that we have not seen each other in all these years, I have a strange and abiding belief that you're a son I have every right to be proud of. Oh, I've heard about you from people who have been out there and, with no foreknowledge on my part, have made inquiries concerning you.

And speaking of family relations, I cut away from mine . . . and thus it happens that in the last twenty years or more, you're the only one in whose veins the Patten blood flows who has commanded a particle of my interest.

Not that I've found out the Patten blood is bad. Quite the contrary. Prof. Milton Ellis, of the University of Maine, who traced my genealogy for John Levi Cutler's booklet in the U. of M. Studies, entitled "Gilbert Patten and his Frank Merriwell Saga," places my ancestors among the prominent ship-builders, agriculturists, and landowners of my native state—and yours. Two of them were military men who bore the title of Colonel. The Town of Surry was once called "Pattensborough," and there are still Patten's Bay, Patten's Point and Patten's Pond, named after my Great-great-grandfather Patten. Northward in the state is the Town of Patten, named after another distant relative. In pioneer days practically all the Pattens were prominent and leading citizens in their communities. My father, it happened, was one of the less-ambitious and poorer Pattens. Probably I inherited my lazy streak from him, though at times he could work like a beaver.

So I want you to bear in mind that you have good blood in you on your Grandmother Gardner's side and on your father's. You don't have to be a snob to be conscious of that. . . .

As for your dime-novel-writing father—well, he's the only living person who has received the honor of being included in the University of Maine Studies. So you see Frank Merriwell is at last being recognized as a semi-classic—if not literature, at least sub-literature that should be studied in college. Or if not studied, of sufficient importance to command the interest of students. And that's more than I ever dreamed would happen.

By the way when I spoke at Augusta on Summer Visitor's Day last August, I met a chap by the name of Tobey, I think, who said he went to Hebron with you. He's now one of the fish and game wardens of the State. He wanted to know where you were and how you were getting on. It was there that I met Rudy Vallee, who wrote me the fine letter I've mentioned. Rudy introduced me to the 15,000 persons present, and I managed to get through a four-minute speech without choking. I got five or six good laughs, too. Old Wash Perry, of Camden, said I made the best speech of the day—but that was hooey. I didn't orate, I just kidded, and that, I guess, was a relief from the orators who had preceded me, among whom were Secretary Morgenthau, Senator Wallace White and the Governors of Mass. and Rhode Island. Morgenthau and White were so long-winded that, as I afterward learned, the audience was bored to death with them. Probably that was what made my short kidding talk sound better than it really was.

Anyhow, I afterward received a letter from Governor Brann thanking me for my participation in the program and for my support of his candidacy. Maybe you noticed that he, a Democrat, was elected by a majority of 25,000 in that rock-bound Republican state.

What are you going to do about Sinclair and Merriam—throw your vote away? Cussed if I don't believe I'd have to if I were voting in that state.

There, I've batted along through all this mess of drivel and you must be bored stiff. I'm sorry. I'll stop.

Write again when you can, Son.

Carol and Ida (her sister) send their very best wishes, and we all hope some danged movie producer will buy my stuff and want me to jog out that way for a while before this winter wanes and passes. But I'm not *too* hopeful.

I'm on the wagon—and for good, I'm afraid. The stuff doesn't use me right at all, even one little teenty drink of it, since I came out of the hospital. I feel fine when I let it alone, so I'm letting it strictly alone.

Alas! And I looked forward to Repeal! Only to become a teetotaler when it came!

My best to you in every way.
DAD

Finale

At the finish of this revealing letter, we have a sample of Patten's ability to laugh at himself. Having been a rather good social drinker during prohibition, now that hard liquor was legal again, Frank's "father" was forced to become a teetotaler—and to cut down on his chain-smoking cigarette habit, too. For since those earlier days when Frank was a paragon of abstinence from tobacco and alcoholic beverages, his creator was humanly far from abiding by the rules he advocated for American youth.

As the years went on, Gilbert Patten no longer looked at life through the necessarily rose-colored glasses of his immature dreams. He had too often come up hard against bitter reality and disappointment to accept the world at face value any longer.

It was in this mood he wrote that first adult novel of 140,000 words, finished early in 1934. Of this he later said:

> In the novel I have, for the first time, written as I wished to write, that is, as honestly as possible. Even in that, however, I may have failed largely because of my acquired habit of conforming to conventions and seeking the dramatic and over-emphasizing it. It is certainly not a juvenile novel, and I have a hope that it may be lucky enough to attract some attention—if I ever get it published.
>
> I am now mulling over the plot of another novel gathering material and preparing for the writing of it, which I probably shall not start before next June or July. . . .[8]

This novel was never published, and before the second could be written, financial difficulties after a tragic personal loss made work impossible for many long months of ill-health.

For several years Mr. and Mrs. Patten had lived in Hudson View Gardens, one of New York's first co-operative or own-your-own apartments. It was in a delightful semisuburban section of upper Manhattan, where existence could be more pleasant than in crowded downtown areas, and they enjoyed their city home with its tree-shaded neighborhood immensely.

But in 1938 his devoted wife died, leaving him indeed bereft and desolate—as witnessed by the poem to her which concludes

[8] Letter to John Levi Cutler, January 23, 1934.

the autobiography—as if, to all intents and purposes, life had really stopped for him in that year.

With narrowing finances, he found himself unable to maintain the necessary payments on the apartment. When it became known that the popular author of the Merriwell stories was threatened with loss of his home, there was talk of a benefit fund. In fact, the famous columnist, Franklin P. Adams, started one.

Persons from here, there, and everywhere began mailing in contributions, but this hurt Patten's sensitive pride. He asked that no further donations be made and insisted upon returning every dollar he had received, even though it did mean giving up his home.

The strain of this difficult situation brought on a nervous breakdown from which recovery was slow after leaving Hudson View Gardens. It was about two years before he was seen again in his familiar downtown haunts frequented by artists, writers, and other professional folk who were his friends and colleagues.

At a luncheon held in a New York hotel he was described by one who met him then as "a tall, erect gentleman with thick white hair and extremely pleasant manners. A fine conversationalist, with an easy flow of excellent talk."

Life had dealt him some hard body punches, as Merriwell might say, but his creator was meeting them courageously.

Evidence of his "gameness," in the true tradition, is the short article, "Frank Merriwell to the Rescue," which appeared in 1940.[9]

Part factual but mostly fantasy as the article is, the author showed himself still possessed of a grim sense of humor when looking at recent events in his life, including bankruptcy, serious illness, and the loss of his wife.

As 1940 rolled around, he was living in a New London, Connecticut, hotel back at work on that second novel. This dealt with his youthful hero grown to wealthy, well-established middle age. He was married to Inza, dark-haired heroine of the Merri-

[9] See Appendix.

Finale

well series, and they had a daughter named Bart—after Frank's greatest friend of college days, Bart Hodge.

Title of the book was *Mr. Frank Merriwell, a Novel of Today.* The jacket blurb stated that during the many years since the last Merriwell story appeared, Patten had often been asked the question: "What would Merriwell be like today?" Or again, "What would Frank Merriwell be able to do against some of today's problems?"

The blurb continued:

> Here is the answer to all of these questions. In *MR. FRANK MERRIWELL*, Patten has created a vital, adult Merriwell, for adult and young readers alike. It is a fighting, two-fisted story of adventure in modern America. But Frank Merriwell is still the clean, honorable and kind personality he always was. The story of the struggles of the Merriwell family will give all his old friends many hours of thrilling reading.

There had been nerve-wracking delays and several postponements of the publication date by the Alliance Book Corporation of New York. The harassed author went to southern California on a visit to his son Barr, then residing in Vista with wife Maybelle and his daughter Gilberta, named for her grandfather.

Finally the book came out in April, 1941, and according to the author, "the press notices were more than kind, some were of the finest sort and several reviewers called the book 'a must' item."

Nevertheless *Mr. Frank Merriwell* was not a success, and this was the final disappointment of Gilbert Patten's long career. He never wrote another book, although he did work on polishing the autobiography.

When endeavoring to make *Mr. Frank Merriwell* modern and up-to-date in its attitudes toward sex and other aspects of life now treated so much more blatantly than in the past, the author seemed ill at ease. As his own son later remarked, "he didn't know how to write about risqué situations."

Having returned to New London, Patten fell ill again, and probably the fate of the novel helped push him into another sickness. Barr convinced his father he should come back to California and make his permanent home with the family. Leaving the East would not be easy, especially since most of his surviving friends lived there.

Finally he decided to make the change, and his daughter-in-law Maybelle came to New London and made the train trip back across the continent with him.

This was the sort of thoughtful thing Mrs. Barr Patten would do, and she spared no effort to make her husband's father feel he was a welcome addition to the family home. Barr was in business for himself there at Vista, a pleasant town in the heart of the southern California avocado orchards. A friend described Barr as a big, hearty man and good companion, interested in sports, an ardent hunter and fisherman, and "proud of his father's works."

So now Gilbert Patten became a settled resident in a lush, semitropical section of California, about forty miles north of San Diego and eight miles inland from the Pacific Ocean. As he wrote to an Eastern friend, "This is a marvelous climate for persons with thin blood and a poor circulation."

Here was peace and evergreen natural beauty, the affection of family, new friends, plus pet dogs and cats of which he was very fond.

Lonely he must undoubtedly have been for old homes and old companions, but again, his genial, philosophic nature helped in the adjustment to a different sort of existence.

Weather being so mild, almost every day there could be a stroll to the local public library, with the handsome old gentleman walking always straight and tall, still carrying a favorite cane, just as he had at the turn of the century when strolling Broadway with other picturesquely successful personages of his earlier days.

Although he was absent from former haunts, there were many left there to drink a toast to Gilbert Patten. The "Friends of Frank Merriwell," an informal group of men mostly in the public relations field, used to gather in a certain off Madison Avenue tavern for a quick one or two after the rush of busy days. Here,

Finale

as Frank's friends, they stopped for a drink of fellowship and a joke or two, remembering no doubt, that Patten's panacea for life's troubles was laughter.

"Laughter is my medicine, my safety-valve. I need a minimum of one good laugh a day."

Certainly an excellent prescription for anyone!

In California, as in New York or Maine, Gilbert Patten became a familiar, well-liked figure in the community where he lived. His health improved, and the strain and struggle of a war-torn world had little or no impact on his possibly monotonous but peaceful twilight years. He could still say, as he had long ago, "Life has always been a grand adventure for me, even at its dullest. It's still the grandest invention I know of."

The final phase can best be described through a letter written recently by his granddaughter, Gilberta Patten Richmond, to Mr. Tony London:

March 14, 1961

DEAR TONY:

Here are some more things about Grandy that Maybelle thought you might like to have.

He found a great deal of pleasure in the company of the family pets, a Persian kitten and a schnauzer ladydog. Often, when relaxed in his big chair the kitten would curl up on his shoulder and the dog would sit on his knee. It was a real storybook sight to see.

Tootsie (the schnauzer) accompanied him on his daily trips to the library, and looked forward to the outing with a great deal of enthusiasm. It was a sorry day for her when weather or activities denied her this pleasure. She would droop for hours all the way from her whiskery nose to the tip of the long tail.

The night before his death he played cribbage with the men who were taking part in the golf tournament the next morning. He enjoyed cribbage very much and there was usually a running score kept by him and his opponents from visit to visit. On this particular night he retired earlier than the rest of the household, pleading weariness.

About eight o'clock the next morning he came out of his bedroom, told Maybelle he had slept well and felt the doctor had helped him. As she was busy preparing baked beans with all the trimmings for the men at noontime, he said he thought he would go back to bed for a while. Maybelle went to his room about ten to get her heavy coat and he appeared to be sleeping soundly, so she did not disturb him. Barr came home a short time later and when the housekeeper told him his father was still in bed, he immediately went to the bedroom to find the old gentleman had passed on.

Gilbert had an aversion to funeral eulogies, caused by a long-drawn-out service for his mother. When his father passed away six weeks after the mother, he informed the minister that there would be no fee if the service lasted over twenty minutes. We passed this aversion on to Mr. Silas Sibley, an elderly retired minister who officiated at Gilbert's funeral, but to no avail. He was a great admirer of Gilbert's and spent one hour comparing him to David. If Grandy was around, I'm sure he was very restless before it was done.

Sincerely,
MAYBELLE AND GILBERTA

Gilbert Patten's ashes rest with those of his wife Carol, in New York. Born in Maine, he died in California, his long lifetime covering the westward trek of an expanding nation, from the Atlantic of his boyhood to the Pacific of his final years.

In one of his last letters written eleven days before his death, he said:

> My tide is fast ebbing to flood no more. Fifty years from now—maybe twenty-five—I'll not even be a faint smear on the sands of time. I watch the setting sun with interest and wonder what—if anything—lies beyond the swiftly contracting horizon.[10]

When he was no longer here to read it, an article appeared in the *Boston Sunday Post* "Your World" for April 22, 1945, which would no doubt have brightened that "swiftly contracting horizon."

By-line, Wendell Hazen:

> The man who took me through prep. school, who took me through college, who taught me the wonders of baseball, football, basketball,

---

[10] Letter to David C. Adams, published later in *Dime Novel Round-Up* (March, 1945).

hockey and track athletics, who carried me on fascinating vacation trips spanning the continent, who taught me good sportsmanship and fine manly habits of courage, honesty and perseverance, died recently, and men of my age throughout the land were shocked by his passing.

His name was Gilbert Patten, creator of the fictional character Frank Merriwell. But he was known to me as Burt L. Standish, the name he took to write under when he began the series of five-cent novelettes, known as the *Tip Top Weekly,* in 1896, which was to endure for 17 years.

My name is Legion, that great legion of boys who for nearly twenty years read with eagerness each successive weekly issue ... readers of the gaudy, paper-covered books were liberal with them. Few of these extraordinarily successful publications can be found today and when located they are collector's items. One reason for this is the number of hands through which each number passed, finally wearing out in service.

It is difficult today, with the vast store of reading matter available, to realize just what these simple, homely stories of one boy's life and adventures, meant to us youngsters of that faraway era.

In spite of his modest personal appraisal, so characteristic of Gilbert Patten, there is convincing evidence of the permanent place Frank Merriwell and his "father" will continue to have in the field of Americana. One example may be found in *American Heritage* for February, 1956.

An article on dime novels concludes that they have more than a nostalgic interest for historians, because they "teach us a great deal about our nationalistic ways ... and reflect however crudely, the American spirit of an earlier and perhaps more innocent age."

APPENDIX

Foreword to "Frank Merriwell to the Rescue"

New York Sunday Mirror Magazine Section, March 24, 1940

LAST, AND PERHAPS THE GREATEST FIGURE in the history of the dime novel, Gilbert Patten, author of the famous Frank and Dick Merriwell tales under the pen name of Burt L. Standish, today at 74 is still indebted to the renowned characters he created in 1896.

Numbered among the world's most prolific writers of fiction, he was a veritable "fiction factory" and completely dominated the field of juvenile fiction.

A few years ago Mr. Patten began to modernize the Merriwell stories but ill health halted him. Upon recuperating he faced new difficulties, and two deaths in the family brought a second nervous breakdown.

More recently financial reverses and possible eviction from his cooperatively owned apartment have beset him. In the article below, the Merriwell author tells how Frank indeed came to his "rescue."

FRANK MERRIWELL TO THE RESCUE
by Gilbert Patten
(The Original "Burt L. Standish,"
Creator of Frank and Dick Merriwell)

ROUND TEN. The bell! I came out of my corner crouching and more than a little groggy from the wallops Fate had given me in the last three rounds.

I'd been romping through the scrap and more than holding

Appendix

my own up to the seventh. Then—wham!—something exploded in my brain and I barely managed to struggle to my feet at the count of nine. The bell had saved me then, but I reeled rather than romped through the next round and Fate handed me another sock on the jaw. I was hanging on the ropes when the bell saved me again. The going was swiftly becoming very bad.

But I wasn't licked yet. I wouldn't give up. I came back for more in the ninth—and got it. Plenty! That was a killing punch, a deadly stab that dropped me to my knees, sick, weak and gasping. I thought dully that I was done for at last. I was all through and didn't seem to care. Washed up! Licked! Finished!

Then a voice seemed to whisper into my ear. It said, *"This is the Battle of Life. Are you yellow? Can't you take it? Get up! Get up from your knees, you poor fish, and fight as long as there's a spark of strength left in you. Your great hero never quit. Are you weaker than the brain child you created?"*

That brought me to my feet again.

Now it was the tenth round and for the first time, as I came out reeling and groggy, I saw the true face of my adversary behind the false, smug mask he wore. It was a cold and cruel face in which there was no trace of human sympathy or natural kindness. His eyes glamed with covetousness, with greed, as he sprang at me suddenly—and struck!

I woke to find myself in a courtroom. For a little while I was puzzled and bewildered. Then I realized that what I've just related was a symbolical dream of what life had been doing to me of late. The smashing blow in the seventh was a nervous breakdown that had prevented me from earning a dollar for two years.

The one in the eighth represented the death of my wife's sister. The lethal stab in the ninth, which had dropped me to my knees, typified the sudden and shocking death of my wife. The final savage wallop in the tenth was an order of eviction from the home in which I had spent fourteen of the happiest years of my life.

The judge was speaking. His voice was not unkind and I thought I saw regret and sympathy in his eyes.

"You have not denied that you owe the money charged to you for upkeep," he was saying. "According to a stipulation in the lease signed by your sister-in-law, which states that one dollar a year shall be collected for rent, you can be legally evicted as a tenant in arrears from the apartment you inherited through the death of your sister-in-law and your wife. Therefore it is incumbent upon me, in compliance with the law, to order you————"

A clear, electrifying voice rang through the courtroom:

"Wait, your Honor! Just a moment, please!"

A young man, clean cut, finely built, supple and graceful yet distinctly athletic, came hurrying down the center aisle. His was the strong yet keenly intelligent face of a person of breeding and culture. Yet it was also the face of one in whose heart the flame of human kindness and understanding glowed warm and steady. Something indescribable, like a magnetic aura, seemed to surround him.

"Here, your Honor," he said as he reached the judge's bench and placed something before the silent and staring magistrate, "is a full amount of cash to pay all arrears owed by the defendant."

In the moments of the deep hush that followed his words, a dollar bill dropping to the floor would have sounded like the fall of a sledge hammer. Then the judge asked, "Well, who are you?"

A faint smile flickered at the corners of the young man's lips before he answered quietly:

"I? Why, I'm Frank Merriwell."

Pen Names of Gilbert Patten,
Cited in Dime Novel Round-Up
Article by David C. Adams, March, 1945

WILLIAM G. PATTEN
WILLIAM WEST WILDER
WYOMING WILL
LIEUTENANT R. A. SWIFT
BURT R. BRADDOCK
WYL PARTON
STANTON L. BURT
HARRY DANGERFIELD
JULIAN ST. DARE
MORGAN SCOTT
GORDON MACLAREN
HERBERT BELLWOOD
BURT L. STANDISH

INDEX

Adams, Franklin P. (columnist): 316
Adams, Maude (actress): 142
Adams, William (publisher): 152–53
Adams, William T. ("Oliver Optic"): 101
Adventure Magazine: 268
Advertiser (Corinna, Maine): 111
Advertiser (Cottsfield, Maine), Patten works on: 100–102
Ainslee's Magazine (Street and Smith publication): 186
Alliance Book Corporation (publishers): 317
American (Boston): 261
American Heritage: 321
American Press Association, Patten writes for: 152, 154
American Young Folks (George Waldo Browne publication): 123
Appleton and Company (publishers): 199, 206, 249, 251
Arliss, George (actor): 150

Badger, Joseph E. Jr. (dime novelist): 168
Barrett, Wilson (actor): 141–42
Barse and Hopkins (publishers): 281–82
Beach, Rex (writer): 195
Beadle and Adams (publishers): 32, 110, 143; buys Patten's first story, 104; buys Patten's first dime novel, 109; Patten's first visit to, 128–30; cut Patten's rates, 149; Patten leaves, 153
Biddeford, Maine: 73, 77
Bonner, Robert (publisher): 161
Booth, Albie: 306
Boston, Fred: 259–60

Brian, Donald (singer and actor): 228
Broadway, description of: 148
Brooklyn, New York, Patten moves to: 131, 146, 154
Broun, Heywood (columnist): 305–306
Browne, George Waldo (publisher): 123; description of, 125–26
Bryan, William Jennings: 234–35
"Buntline, Ned": see E. Z. C. Judson
Burgess, Neil (actor): 189–90
Butters, Jack (boyhood acquaintance): 54
Buxton, Maine: 63, 65, 108
Burnett, Frances Hodgson ("Fanny Hodgson"): 104
Burton, Richard (editor): 197–98
Byrne, Donn (writer): 265

Cain, James M. (writer): 176, 176n., 303
Camden, Maine: Patten moves to, 121; visits, 164; buys summer house at, 169; builds home, "Overocks," at 227–29, 231
Carrigan, Bill: 164–65
Carter, Mrs. Leslie (actress): 170
Cartland, Maine: 108
Castlemon, Harry (writer): 162
Century, The: 158
Childhood games: 59–61
Cleveland, Grover: 148
Cody, William F. (Buffalo Bill): 83, 168
Cohan, George (entertainer): 185
Collier's Weekly: 251
Commercial (Bangor, Maine): 112
Cook, William Wallace (writer): 281
Coomes, Oll: Patten's favorite dime novelist, 32–33; retires comfortably, 168

Index

Coreyell, John R. (writer): 157–58
Corinna, Maine: Sunday activities in, 26–27; baseball team, 71–72; awaits doomsday, 106–108; Patten leaves, 118; visits, 146; revisits, 224
Corinna Union Academy: 92, 103; Patten admitted to, 70
Costello, Maurice (actor): 254
Cottsfield, Maine: 100, 102
Courier-Gazette (Camden, Maine): 298
Crane, Dr. Frank (writer): 277
Creel, George: 173
Croker, Richard: 132
Cutler, John Levi: 177

Daley, Dan (entertainer): 185
Daly, Augustin (theatrical manager): 141
Dana, Charles A. (editor): 130
Davenport, Fanny (actress): 149
David McKay (publishers): 164, 196; publishes Cliff Stirling Series, 251
Davidson, Dore (actor): 189ff.
Davis, Mildred (actress): 298
Day, Bert (boyhood acquaintance): 51
Day, Frederick (writer): 203–204
Day, Holman (writer): speaks at Camden, Maine, 247; entertains Pattens with stories, 247
Deadwood Dick (fictional hero of Patten's boyhood): 70–71
De Morgan, John (writer): 156–57, 160
Denver, Colorado, Patten visits: 204–20 *passim*
Detective Story, Patten writes for: 298
Dexter, Hugh: 92, 101
Dexter, S. Alma: 92–93, 101
Dickens, Charles, Patten inspired by: 93–94, 158, 300
Dime novels: xiv, xix, 50, 70, 93, 145, 198, 243; decline discussed, 290–91; importance of, 321
Dispatch (New York): 154
Dixmont Hills: 27, 88
Dodd, Mead and Company (publishers): 251
Donlon, Annie (boyhood acquaintance): 82ff.; takes Patten to Irish wake, 88
Dorsey, Dr. George: 268–70
Draper, Clarence (boyhood acquaintance): 55

Drew, Sidney (actor): 125
Duffy, Richard (editor): 252
Dunn, William C. (editor): 155–56, 158–60
Durgin, Frank (boyhood acquaintance): 77, 84

Eagin, Eddie: 307
Eastern Gazette (Dexter, Maine): 308
Eastern Herald (Buxton, Maine), Patten works for: 96–100
Eastman, Max: 267
Edwards, Bobby (entertainer): 272
Elder, George (boyhood acquaintance): 70
Elverson, James (publisher): 106, 155, 161
Evening Journal (New York): 308
Eyster, William R. (dime novelist): 168

Family Story Paper (Norman Munro publication): 157
Farjeon, B. L. (writer): 103
Faversham, William (actor): 142
Ferber, Edna, Patten rooms next to: 275
Fernandina, Florida: 169; Patten vacations at, 171–72
Fiction war: 161
Film Daily: 309
Fisher, Herbert (boyhood acquaintance): 73; Patten visits, 224
Floto, Otto (editor): 211–12
Ford, Henry: 300
Frohman, Daniel (theatrical manager): 141

"Gaines, Albert Cecil" (pen name of Arthur Grissom): 147; *see also* Arthur Grissom
Gardiner, Maine: 259
Gardner, Alice (Patten's first wife): 93, 102, 292; sets type for Patten, 112; marries Patten, 117; divorces Patten, 185–86
Gilder, Richard Watson (editor): 158
Godey's Magazine: 104
Golden Argosy (Frank Munsey publication): 155, 244
Golden Days (James Elverson publication): 106, 155
Golden Hours (Norman Munro publication): 155–62 *passim*

327

Goldfield, Nevada: 208
Goldman, Emma: 267
Good News (Street and Smith publication): 162; decline of, 186
Greenwich Village, New York, Patten lives in: 265-73
"Greg, Harvan W." (Patten pen name): 105; *see also* pen names of Patten
Grey, Zane (writer): 203
Grissom, Arthur: 139, 142-43; a fancy dresser, 146; pen name of, 147; looses bet with Patten, 147-48; founds *Smart Set Magazine*, 187; death of, 198-99
Grissom, Herbert (artist): 148, attends party with Patten, 186
Gunter, Archibald Clavering (writer): 248

Hall, Arthur Dudley (editor): 164, 186
Hall, Bill (guide): 260-63
Hall, Gilman (editor): 252
Hall, Sam S. ("Buckskin Sam"): 168; gets robbed, 138-39
Hall, "Tinker" (boyhood acquaintance): 55-56
Hamilton, Jeanie (boyhood acquaintance): 59
Hammerstein, Elaine (actress): 262, 262n.
Hammerstein, Oscar (theatrical manager): 262, 262n.
Hancock, Harry Irving (writer): 156-57
Hanshew, T. W. (writer): 157
Harlan, Kenneth (actor): 298
Harmel Village, Maine: 67
Harmon, Bessie (boyhood acquaintance): 69
Harmon, Horace (boyhood acquaintance): 68
Harvell, Hippolite: 267
Haskell, Al (boyhood acquaintance): 54, 56
Hastings, Charlie (editor): 100-102; Patten sells Corinna *Owl* to, 114
Hayden, Bob (boyhood acquaintance): 56-57
Hazen, Wendell (columnist), quoted: 320-21
Henty, George (writer): 100
Herald (Corinna, Maine): 111
Hickok, James B. (Wild Bill): 83, 168

Hill, David: 135
Hill, James M. (theatrical manager): 143-44
Hills, William H. (editor): 154
Hopkins, Hallie: 112
Hughes, Charles Evans: 271
Hutchings, Addie (boyhood acquaintance): 50, 59, 69-70, 79; marries Charles Maynard, 127; is hostess to Pattens, 128; death of, 224
Hurst and Company (publishers), publish Rex Kingdom and Ben Stone series: 251

Ingersoll, Robert: 168
Ingraham, Colonel Prentiss: 83; description of, 129; Patten visits, 150-52; visits Patten, 193; tells Patten of impending death, 199-200

Jefferson, Joseph (actor): 141
Johnson, Charles Howard (artist): 146, 148; death of, 188
Journal (Lewiston, Maine): 113, 247
Judson, E. Z. C. ("Ned Buntline"): 168

Kemp, Harry (poet): 265-66
King, Captain Charles (writer): 177
Knowles, Joe (stunt man): 260-63
Kramer, Carol (Patten's third wife): meets Patten, 273; marries Patten, 284; death of, 288, 315; poem to, 289

Lee, Eugene (theatrical producer): 144
Lengel, William C. (editor), quoted: 307
Lewis, C. B. ("M. Quad"): 154-55
Lewis, Charlie (boyhood acquaintance): 79; at Biddeford, 77ff.; admirer of Annie Donlon, 82ff.
Lewis, Sinclair, attends party with Patten: 268-70
Lewiston, Maine: 164
Libbey, Laura Jean (writer): 157
Lillie, Major Gordon (Pawnee Bill): 224; host to Pattens, 225-26, 231-32
Lindsey, Judge Ben B.: 206, 211
Literary Digest: 306
Little, Brown and Company (publishers): 171
Lomer, Carrie (boyhood acquaintance): 68-69

Index

London, Jack: 158, 195, 203
Lothrop, Lee and Shepherd (publishers): 197–98

McClellan, C. M. S. (writer and editor): 150
McCullough, John (actor): 142
McIntyre, O. O. (writer): 275; description of, 276–77; quoted, 300
MacKenzie, Cameron (correspondent): 266, 268
McKinley, William: 181, 183
MacLean, Charles Agnew (editor): 203, 280–81
Maine, University of: 177; Barr Patten enters, 246
Manchester, New Hampshire: 123; Patten lives in, 125–26
Mann, William (publisher): 147
Manning, William H. ("Major E. L. St. Vrain" and "Ben D. Halliday"): 165–68
Mansfield, Richard (actor): 142
Mantell, Robert (actor): 125
Maranacook, Lake, Maine: 75–76
Marlowe, Julia (actress): 142, 170
Marr, Curtis J. (theatrical producer): 144–45
Marshall, Tully (actor): 298
Masterson, Kate (writer): 187
Mathewson, Christy, endorses Big League Series: 282
May, Edna (singer and actress): 150
Maynard, Charles, marries Addie Hutchings: 127
Megunticook Mountain, Maine: 124
Merriwell, Dick: inception of, 238–39; character of, 240–41
Merriwell, Frank: xii–xiii, 163; birth date of, xiv, 180; series proposed, 175–76; origin of name, 177; character of, 178, 303; circulation of stories, 180–81; stories win praise, 182; radio program started, 308–309
Metropole Café, popular with Patten and friends: 146–47, 173
Metropolitan Magazine: 267
Metropolitan Museum of Art, New York City: 141
Millay, Edna St. Vincent: 121; writes "Renascence," 174
Morgan, John De: *see* John De Morgan

Morgan, Wallace (artist): 268
Morse, Sam (Corrina, Maine, storekeeper): 39
Munro, George (publisher): 155
Munro, Norman L. (publisher): 155, 157, 160
Munsey, Frank (publisher): 155, 244

Nathan, George Jean, quoted: xii, 300
New Haven, Connecticut: 237–38
New London, Connecticut: 316
Newport, Maine: 224
New York City, New York, description of: 131–37
New Yorker: 299
Nichols, Anne (playwright): 256n.
Nickerson, John (Adventist preacher): 106–109
Niper, Wyman B.: 92
Norman, Marie: 92
Norton, Augustus: 70
Noyes, Fred (editor): 268
Nunn, Mary (Patten's second wife): meets Patten, 188–89; marries Patten, 193; separates from Patten, 264–65; divorces Patten, 283
Nutter, Frank (boyhood friend): 31, 70; encourages Patten to write, 34; cautions Patten about fighting, 57; goes to Biddeford to work, 73; gets Patten a job, 79–80; advises Patten to continue writing, 87–88
Nye, Bill (humorist): 154–55

O'Higgins, Harvey J. (writer): 206
Omohundro, John (Texas Jack): 83, 168
Orrington, Maine: 108
Otis, Elita Proctor (actress): 188
Outlook, Patten writes for: 298
"Overocks" (Patten's home): built at Camden, Maine, 227–29, 231; description of, 235–36; Patten entertains at, 237, 247
Owl (Corinna, Maine): 112–14

Patten, Betsey Simpson (Patten's grandmother): xvi–xvii, 17; description of, 20
Patten, Cordelia (Patten's mother): xvii; temperament of, 10; character

329

of, 20; psychic powers of, 24; worries about Patten's debts, 113–14; death of, 231

Patten, Gilbert: literary production of, xiii, 180–81, 304–305; birth date of, xiv; age of at death, xxi; full name of, 10; ancestry of, 18–19; early reading matter of, 28–30, 32; writes first story, 33–34; writes first poetry, 50; shows first interest in girls, 50–52; has first fight, 52–53; nicknames of, 52, 55, 58, 187; religious views of, 62, 310; first business venture of, 65–67; works for father, 74–75; works at Biddeford, Maine, 80–90 *passim*; sells first story, 104–105; sells first dime novel, 109; founds and edits Corinna *Owl*, 112–14; writing habits of, 115, 179–81, 184, 195, 242, 305; marries Alice Gardner, 117; leaves Corinna, 118; leaves Beadle and Adams, 153; writes for *Golden Hours*, 155–62; sells first story to Street and Smith, 162–63; contracts for Merriwell stories, 179; divorced from Alice Gardner, 185–86; starts Rockspur Series, 192; marries Mary Nunn, 193; conceives Merriwell's "double-shoot," 197; buys first automobile, 223; builds, "Overocks," 227–29, 231; creates Dick Merriwell, 238–39; organizes Camden Board of Trade, 246; starts *Top Notch Magazine*, 248–50; starts Cliff Stirling Series, 249; starts Rex Kingdom and Ben Stone series, 251; ceases writing Merriwell stories, 256–57; writes Big League Series, 281; divorced from Mary Nunn, 283; marries Carol Kramer, 284; description of, 310–11; death of, 319–20; tribute to, 320–21

Patten, Harvan Barr (Patten's son): 149, 154, 160, 293; enters University of Maine, 246; letter to, 311–14; description of, 318

Patten, Mrs. Harvan Barr: ix, 317

Patten, William Clark (Patten's father): xvi; a carpenter, xviii, 3; warns Patten against fighting, 13; character of, 15–16; has encounter with Abraham Lincoln, 16–17; shows family a comet, 25–26; takes Patten to see Edison's inventions, 49–50; injures himself skating, 72–73; wants Patten to be a carpenter, 95; death of, 231

Patten, Zelma (Patten's sister), death of: xvii

Pen names of Patten: 105, 112, 160, 249, 251, 254, 325

Penobscot Bay, Maine: 121, 124, 199

Popular Magazine (Street and Smith publication): 186, 202

Popular songs: 81, 94, 140, 170, 185, 272

Porter, William Sidney ("O. Henry"): 252

Post (Denver): 205–20 *passim*

"Pulps": 110, 253, 291, 297

Radio Art: 310

Ralston, H. W. (Street and Smith circulation manager): 248, 255

Reed, John (writer): 266–67

Reed, O. P. (writer): 244–45

Reid, Captain Mayne (writer): 110

Republican (Denver): 206

Rexford, Eben E. (writer): 106

Richardson, Leander (writer): 198

Richmond, Gilberta Patten (Patten's granddaughter): ix, 317; letter of, 319–20

Ripley, Robert (artist): 277

Robertson, Morgan (writer): 195

Robinson, R. O. (editor): 96–99

Roche, Arthur Somers (writer): 251–52, 268, 275

Rockland, Maine: 228

Rockspur Series, Patten starts: 192

Rohn, Ray (artist): 268, 270

Royle, Edwin Milton (playwright): 195

Rusie, Amos (baseball pitcher): 149

Russell, Lillian (singer and actress): 170; Patten meets, 275

St. Augustine, Florida, Patten visits: 172

St. Louis, Missouri, Patten visits: 204

Salvini, Alexander (actor): 149

Saturday Evening Post: 176, 176n., 251, 281–82; Patten writes articles for, 302

Screen Writers Guild, formation of: 255

Scribner's Magazine: 158

Senarens, Lu (editor): 200

Shaw, Tim (boyhood acquaintance): 53–54

Shea, Cornelius (writer): 156–57

Index

Shea, Thomas E. (actor): 125, 141
Sinclair, Upton, rumored to have written some Merriwell stories: 182
Skinner, Otis (actor): 253
Smart Set Magazine (Arthur Grissom publication): 139
Smith, G. C. (publisher): 162, 196
Smith, O. G. (publisher): 157, 162, 173; proposes Merriwell series, 175–76; offers Patten trip to West Coast, 202; has Patten create Dick Merriwell, 238
Sobol, Louis (columnist): 237, 306
Sport Story, Patten writes for: 298
Spratt, Nora (boyhood acquaintance): 95
"Standish, Burt L.," Patten invents name: 179; *see also* pen names of Patten
Star (Kansas City): 206
Star Weekly (Beadle and Adams publication): 104, 106, 109
Stearns, Albert (writer): 156–57; shares office with Patten, 161, 170
Stedman, Myrtle (actress): 298
Stevens, Hatch (Corinna storekeeper): 72
Stevens, Will (boyhood acquaintance): 48–49
Stevenson, Robert Louis, Patten inspired by: 93, 158, 300
Stratemeyer, Edward (editor): 162–64, 196–97
Street and Smith (publishers): vii, 157, 161; buys first Patten story, 162–63; moves location, 173, 186; Patten signs Merriwell contract with, 179; advances Patten money for building home, 227; gives Patten an automobile, 228–29
Sun (New York): 108, 130
Sunday Post (Boston): 320

Taft, William Howard: 234–35
Talmadge, Norma (actress): 254
Taurog, Norman (motion picture producer): 298
Taylor, Bert Leston (columnist): 126
Telling Tales, Patten writes for: 298
Thieman, Paulos (editor): 205–20 *passim*; life threatened, 217–19
Thomas, Augustus (playwright): 142
Thomas, H. W. (editor): 250–52, 280
Tilney, Frederick (editor): 243
Time: 299, 301
Tip Top Weekly (Street and Smith publication), carries Merriwell stories: 182
Top Notch Magazine (Street and Smith publication), started and edited by Patten: 248–50
Tousey, Frank (publisher): 196; Patten considers working for, 200–14 *passim*
Towne, Charles Hanson (writer): 187, 195
Town Topics (William Mann publication): 147; Patten writes for, 148
Transcript (Portland, Maine): 106
Trowbridge, John Townsend (writer): 100

Vance, Louis Joseph (writer): 203
Van Loan, Charles E. (writer): 203, 281
Variety: 301, 302
Victor, O. J. (editor): 104; Patten meets, 129–30; encourages Patten to leave Beadle and Adams, 153
Vista, California: vii, 317; Patten spends last days at, 318–20

Wakefield, Rhode Island: 144
Warren, Joseph (attorney): 265, 278
Wheeler, Edward L. (dime novelist): 71, 165–67
White, Stewart Edward (writer), rumored to have collaborated on Merriwell stories: 182
Whitson, John H. ("Lieutenant A. K. Sims"): 168; finds Patten a cottage in Florida, 169–71; goes to Maine with Patten, 173; writes part of Merriwell stories, 190–94
Whittaker, Captain Frederick (dime novelist): 168
Wilkens, Mary E. (writer): 158
Wilson, Woodrow: 271
Wilmington, Delaware: 138
Winter, William (drama critic): 142
Witwer, H. C. (writer): 203
World-Telegram (New York): 305

Yankee Blade (Boston): 143
Young, Art: 267
Young, Earnest A. (writer): 304
Youth's Companion: 125

Frank Merriwell's "Father" has been printed on a paper intended to have an effective life of three hundred years, bearing the watermark of the University of Oklahoma Press. The text for this edition has been composed in a machine-set version of the eighteenth-century English Baskerville type face. The title page and part-title drawings are adapted from illustrations which appeared originally on the covers of four *Tip Top Weekly* issues.

UNIVERSITY OF OKLAHOMA PRESS

NORMAN

www.ingramcontent.com/pod-product-compliance
Lightning Source LLC
Chambersburg PA
CBHW020731160426
43192CB00006B/188